Longman Scienceworld

GENERAL EDITOR: BRENDA PRESTT

JUNIOR TEACHERS' BOOK 4

ANDY BAILEY AND HUGH WILCOCK

Longman

General Editor:
Dr Brenda Prestt MBE
who was a member of the APU Science Steering Group and editor of ASE Language in Science. She is a contributor to the Open University Primary Science course, and is Director of the Centre for Industry, Science, Technology, Education Liaison based at Manchester Polytechnic.

Authors of the junior material in *Longman Scienceworld* :
Hugh Wilcock
Head Teacher, Paganel Junior School, Selly Oak, Birmingham and a member of the APU Science Steering Group
and
Andy Bailey
Head Teacher, Elmore Green Primary School, Walsall

Illustrator: Chris Williamson
Cover photograph: David Jamieson
Sub-editor: Stephen Attmore
Series designer: Randell Harris
Junior Books 3 and 4 designer: Liz Knox

LONGMAN GROUP UK LIMITED
Longman House, Burnt Mill, Harlow, Essex CM20 2JE, England and Associated Companies throughout the world

First published 1987
Second impression 1989
ISBN 0 582 00468 3
Typeset in 'Monophoto' Univers 689
Produced by Longman Group (FE) Ltd
Printed in Hong Kong

Acknowledgements

We are grateful to the following for permission to reproduce material: Her Majesty's Stationery Office for an adapted table from McCance & Widdowson: *The Composition of Goods* (4th revised and extended edition of *MRC Special Report No 297*) by A A Paul & D Southgate, 1978; Times Newspapers Limited for an adapted table from 'The Fittest People Hang Around Bars' by Dr Craig Sharp which appeared in *The Times*, May 30 1986; National Academy Press, Washington DC, for table adapted from *Report of Food & Nutrition Board, National Academy of Sciences*, 'Recommended Dietary Allowances', ninth edition 1980.

CONTENTS

LONGMAN SCIENCEWORLD

This scheme covers the years from five to eleven.

Science through Infant topics – the infant years
Junior Books 1–4 – the junior years

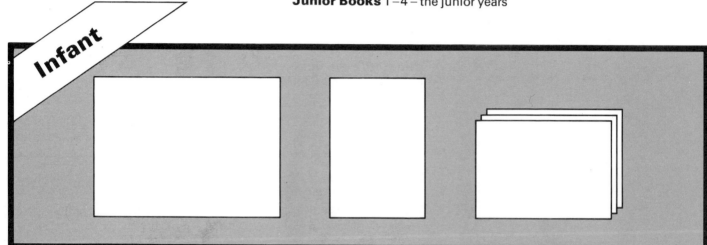

Year 1 *Starter Book A* accompanied by *Science through Infant Topics Teachers' Book A* and *Record Sheets*

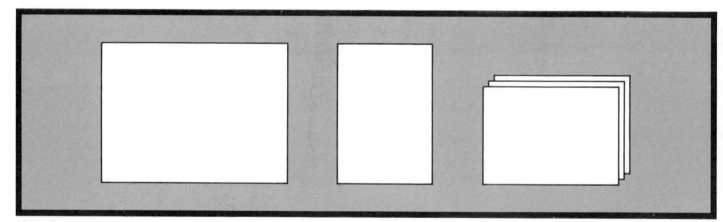

Year 2 *Starter Book B* accompanied by *Science through Infant Topics Teachers' Book B* and *Record Sheets*

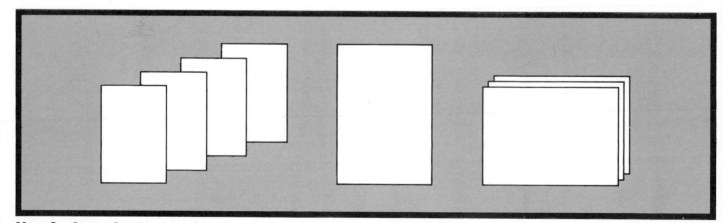

Year 3 *Starter Readers* (set of four) accompanied by *Science through Infant Topics Teachers' Book C* and *Record Sheets*

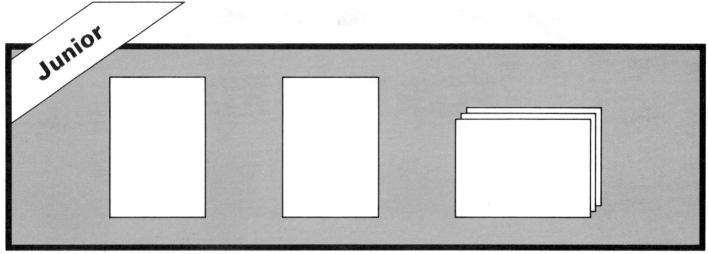

Year 1 *Junior Pupils' Book 1* accompanied by *Teachers' Book 1* (including *Record Sheets* for photocopying)

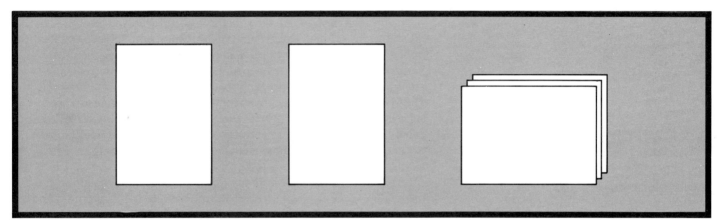

Year 2 *Junior Pupils' Book 2* accompanied by *Teachers' Book 2* (including *Record Sheets* for photocopying)

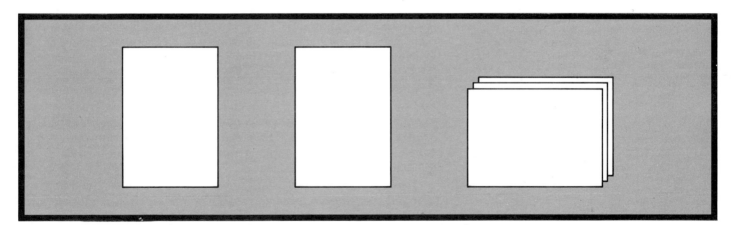

Year 3 *Junior Pupils' Book 3* accompanied by *Teachers' Book 3* (including *Record Sheets* for photocopying)

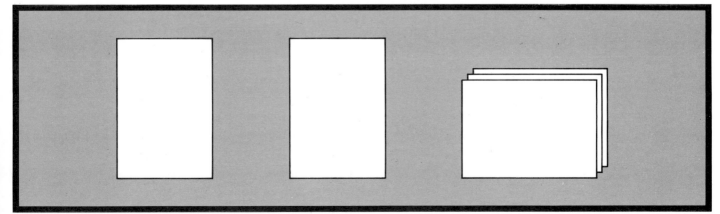

Year 4 *Junior Pupils' Book 4* accompanied by *Teachers' Book 4* (including *Record Sheets* for photocopying)

FOREWORD

Longman Scienceworld is presented as a complete, progressive science scheme covering the primary years. The materials consist of a series of books.

The principles on which the scheme is based correspond closely to the ideas described in the Department of Education and Science statement of policy, 'Science 5–16' (HMSO, London 1985) and the Scottish Education Department HMI paper, 'Learning and Teaching: the environment and the primary school curriculum' (HMSO, Edinburgh 1984). Topics have been chosen for their potential for developing scientific ideas and skills and for their interest to the children. The topics can be used in a specific timetable slot to form a science curriculum, expanded to form more general environmental studies or form 'patch' studies within more general topics.

For children who start *Longman Scienceworld* in the reception class, there will be steady progress even though the rate of this progress and the ultimate achievement of individual children will be different. Children progress erratically and groups of children will show a spread of ability and achievement.

For children who start *Longman Scienceworld* at various entry points, careful consideration should be given to the possibility of starting with material at a lower stage than is indicated in the complete scheme. For example, for children entering junior classes who have done little science and have not used *Longman Scienceworld* materials, it might be appropriate to start with some activities from 'Science through Infant Topics' (*Teachers' Book C*). The topics used are completely appropriate for children in the middle years of primary education. *Junior Teachers' Books 1* and *2* and *Junior Pupils' Books 1* and *2* might form a very suitable introduction for pupils starting to use the scheme in the later primary years.

As is emphasised later (Extension A, page 109), children who start *Longman Scienceworld* at intermediate points will need careful support in the early stages of their work. The Teachers' Books are written to provide teachers with the support they need to foster and encourage every child's development from the first tentative steps to confident competence.

It may help teachers who wish to start using the scheme at intermediate entry points to consider the scheme as a whole, as set out in the following chart.

The books	stages	primary years	
'Science through Infant Topics'			
Starter Book A with Teachers' Book A	I	1	early primary
Starter Book B with Teachers' Book B	II	2	early primary
Starter Readers with Teachers' Book C	III	3	
Junior Book 1 with Teachers' Book 1	IV	4	middle primary
Junior Book 2 with Teachers' Book 2	V	5	
Junior Book 3 with Teachers' Book 3	VI	6	later primary
Junior Book 4 with Teachers' Book 4	VII	7	

INTRODUCTION

Science should be a familiar and comfortable part of the curriculum. Children should be as much at home using science as they are using mathematics or language. In *Longman Scienceworld* this idea is emphasised by introducing the science activities in the context of Newton Street where a group of children live with their families. The children were introduced in the infant stages and now feature in the stories and science activities in the *Junior Pupils' Books.* Many of the activities are designed to answer questions asked in the stories. Other activities repeat investigations carried out by the Newton Street children and enable the pupils to share new discoveries and experiences.

The involvement of the Newton Street children in the stories and descriptions of the activities make it clear that girls and boys are involved equally in all aspects of the work. Other ideas such as cooperation, helping each other and working in groups are all developed by showing the Newton Street children working together in various ways.

Undoubtedly, many pupils who use the books will feel able to identify with individual Newton Street children and for that reason will enjoy their science more. Pupils meet the children in Topic 1.1 'Happy families' in *Junior Pupils' Book 1.*

In *Longman Scienceworld* science is presented as an activity which uses and develops a range of scientific skills – skills such as observing, classifying, controlling variables. Children entering the first year of the Junior scheme will vary greatly in the development of their scientific skills. Those who have followed *Longman Scienceworld* 'Science through Infant Topics' will have developed a range of skills which will enable them to proceed with the work of the Junior scheme with a considerable measure of independence and confidence. Children with less experience will need more help and it will take some time for them to acquire the same degree of independence.

Nevertheless, for all children scientific skills are developed by using them and progress is made by building constructively on past experiences. The manner in which children's skills are developed in this scheme is described in Extension A (page 109), which also includes a description of the skills which it is anticipated children will be able to achieve as they go through the progressive levels of the course.

Although the scheme has its main focus on the development of children's scientific skills, it is also concerned with the development of children's understanding of some of the major concepts of science. The two approaches are complementary. If children are to explore their own environment actively and scientifically they will in the course of their investigations and explorations 'discover' and come to understand a range of scientific ideas. Equally, if a course is to be systematically devised to develop their scientific skills some context for such development must be selected. There is no doubt that the most suitable context is the children's own real, everyday environment and those ideas which are already close to the children even though they have not been recognised or explored. The content of the children's science can be identified therefore in these terms. It is those ideas, experiences and pieces of acquired information which form part of the children's investigations of their own environment. This imposes a limit on what children may be expected to explore and understand but it should be remembered that most children in this 'electronic age' have a wide range of experience and their environment is varied. The concepts and ideas of which children will gain experience are listed in Extension B (page 119).

The teaching of science in primary schools has been the subject of discussion for many years and much effort has gone into trying to find ways and means of introducing science into the primary school curriculum. Almost everyone agrees that the science which is appropriate for primary schools should be investigatory and open-ended. This has imposed a dual burden on the teacher: one of organisation and one of knowing more about investigatory science than the children. The latter problem arises from the fact that most teachers' experience of science has been in secondary school where science has been more concerned with learning facts than with investigation.

In *Longman Scienceworld* we have tried to tackle both of these problem areas. We have provided a combination of Teachers' Books and Pupils' Books to produce a course which in many respects is open-ended but at the same time is structured enough to help the non-specialist teacher guide the children in their investigations. In the sections which follow, 'Using the Pupils' Book' and 'Using the Teachers' Book', the functions of these books and the way in which they interlock are explained.

One aspect of teaching science which is emphasised in exploring the interlocking nature of the books is the important role of language. Using language effectively is crucial in moving from scientific activity to scientific understanding. Results of investigations may mean little without the opportunity to explore in words what has been observed and how it links with past experiences of all kinds (not just scientific experiences). At the same time science provides a wealth of opportunities to develop language usage, both spoken and written. The use and development of language in science is discussed in greater detail in Extension D (page 138).

Recent discussions and statements have confirmed our belief that science provides splendid opportunities to develop not only language work but also work in mathematics. Many children are able to understand and manipulate numbers and mathematical ideas but are unable to apply their understanding. Throughout the pupils' activities, demands for the use of mathematics will be found. The demands could have been extended in many instances but in the interests of brevity it is left to teachers to be aware that there are further opportunities which they may wish to exploit. Further discussion of the use of mathematics in the scheme is the subject of Extension E (page 139).

Two other aspects of the primary curriculum which are currently under discussion are the relationship of the curriculum to the real, everyday world and the place in the curriculum of technology. Both these concerns had occupied the thoughts of the writers of *Longman Scienceworld* long before the present interest became manifest.

The decision that *Longman Scienceworld* should be skill-based and that it should focus on exploration of the children's environment quickly lead to a realisation that the children's environment is full of people who are using science and acting scientifically without being aware of it. Other people have jobs which are much more recognisably science-based. All of these people make science part of their lives. In some of the stories and activities in the Pupils' Books the place of science in the lives of people who live in Newton Street is explored. Some of them use science in their jobs, some in their hobbies and occupations.

For the younger pupils, discussion focuses on people, what they do and the role of science; for older children, further insights and understandings are provided by looking at how goods emerge from being raw materials and a plan on a designer's table to articles in the shop (thanks in most cases to the efforts of scientists and engineers who are able to turn plans into real objects). In Extension G (page 143), 'People and their jobs and occupations', there is further discussion of this aspect of the course.

The possibility of introducing technology into the primary school has been discussed at length and there is a widening understanding of the importance and value of technology as a curricular component. One of the most pertinent features of technology for children is that it provides a focus which brings together skills, ideas and understandings derived from a variety of curriculum areas. Many of the ideas which are needed are scientific, but ideas from other disciplines are needed as well. Technological activity requires pupils to use their newly-acquired scientific ideas and skills. In *Longman Scienceworld* technology appears as 'Making and doing activities' and the activities suggested provide a valuable opportunity to reinforce the pupils' grasp of ideas which have been developed in the science activities. Of equal importance is the opportunity to develop pupils' ability to tackle problems in a structured and systematic manner. Further discussion of 'Making and doing activities' will be found in Extension F (page 140).

In Extension H (page 144) the record-keeping system for the course is described. It provides for recording the children's progress in developing their scientific skills and for detailing the science activities which the children have completed. In this way an informative and useful record can accompany the child in moving from class to class or from one school to another.

Finally, we have tried to assist teachers by providing guidance in classroom organisation (Extension I, page 145) and advice about equipment and techniques (Extension J, page 148).

The next two sections – 'Using the Pupils' Book' and 'Using the Teachers' Book' – are complementary. You should read both of them before the children start work.

USING THE PUPILS' BOOK

There are four Pupils' Books – one for each year of the course. Each of the Pupils' Books contains ten topics. In each book, Topics 1–5 are at Level 1 and it is envisaged that they will be used during the first half of the year. The topics are of approximately equal demand. Topics 6–10 are pitched at a more demanding level and are likely to be used during the second half of the year. They are designated Level 2 Topics.

The topics

Each of the topics, apart from Topic 1 in *Pupils' Book 1*, has the same form:

- the story;
- three or four science activities.

The story

The story is written so that most of the children will be able to understand it. Children with weaker reading skills will be aided by the illustrations which, in most cases, convey the essence of the story. You may arrange your class so that the children read the story individually or you may decide to let them read their books as a group and discuss the story amongst themselves.

Science – Activities

Introduction
In each activity there is an introductory sentence or question which picks up from the story the aspect which is being investigated in the activity.

You need
In this section the materials and equipment required for the activity are described in outline.

The requirements for one individual or for one group are listed so that a group of children working together may only require one set of equipment. Where necessary further details about the material and equipment required for each activity are given in the *Teachers' Book*.

Description of the activity
Instructions for the activities are provided in the Pupils' Book in two ways – by words and illustrations. The text and the words in the speech balloons in the illustrations are both important in conveying information and many illustrations provide information which would be difficult to convey in words. The vocabulary is as simple as possible but you may find it useful to check that particular activities do not hold reading problems for individual children.

The  symbol

Most pupils should be able to understand the instructions but we stress that it is not intended that pupils should work without teacher support and intervention. As a teacher you will be supervising in general the work of the children, but it is not possible to describe every aspect of every activity in the Pupils' Book. There are two major reasons for this. One is that too many words would be needed and the children would become frustrated. More importantly, scientific investigation must involve thinking about what might happen and then proceeding from there. In these circumstances, it is rarely possible to describe what to do next without referring to what has happened as the result of a previous step – thus telling the pupil what ought to happen before he/she has carried out the instructions. We have tackled this problem by including at appropriate points in the pupils' instructions a symbol 🏃 which means 'Go and talk to your teacher about this'.

At corresponding points in the 'Teaching notes' in this Teachers' Book you will find advice about how to answer the questions which the children will raise when they come to consult you, discussion points to explore and any instructions which are required for the next stages of the work. The 🏃 symbol is placed wherever consultation with you is essential but, of course, there will be many points which will merit discussion which will arise as the children are working.

You will need to explain to the children that they must talk to you when they come to the 🏃 symbol.

Recording – reporting – communicating

Most of the activities ask the children to make some report about their work. Sometimes a written account is suggested; in other activities the children are asked to report verbally or to prepare tables or graphs.

USING THE TEACHERS' BOOK

There are four Teachers' Books: *Teachers' Books 1, 2, 3* and *4*.
Each accompanies the respective Pupils' Book.
The four Teachers' Books have the same format:
Contents
Introduction
Using the Pupils' Book
Using the Teachers' Book
The topics at Level 1 and Level 2
Appendix – Extensions

Introduction

The introduction focuses attention on some of the aspects of teaching science to children of primary school age which the authors consider to be of particular importance. It also serves as a guide to the Extensions in which a number of issues are discussed in greater depth and in more detail. The introduction is essential reading.

Using the Pupils' Book

This description shows how the Pupils' Book and the Teachers' Book are interlinked, as well as describing the format of the Pupils' Books. It is necessary to be familiar with the layout of the Pupils' Books before reading the following sections which explain how the teachers' material for each Topic is arranged and how it is intended it should be used.

The Topics

The Levels

There are ten Topics for each year of the course. In each year Topics 1–5 are at Level 1 and it is intended that they should be used during the first half of the year. These topics are of approximately equal difficulty and they can be used in any order. Topics 6–10 are Level 2 topics and these are more demanding so that it is expected that they will be used in the second half of the year. The Level 2 topics are of approximately equal difficulty and can also be used in any order.

Each level of the course is introduced by a statement describing the skill levels which it is intended that children should achieve. These descriptions are extracted from the complete table of skill descriptions for the course which will be found in Extension A (page 109). They are also the descriptions which form the basis for the pupils' record sheets (inside back cover of this book).

Each topic has the same format:

Topic guide
The story
People and their jobs and occupations
Science – Background notes
     – Activities
Making and doing activity

Topic guide

This gives a brief summary of the work covered in the Topic; in particular, there is a statement of the concepts which pupils will explore. These are extracted from the list of concepts in Extension B (page 119). The topic guide also provides brief descriptions of the investigations which pupils will carry out and thereby develop their scientific skills.

    The teaching notes provide detailed guidance for helping children with their work. (In the section 'Using the Pupils' Book' it was emphasised that the Pupils' Book and the Teachers' Book are complementary so it is important to refer frequently to the Pupils' Book as you read the next sections.)

The story

The story sets the scene for the work of the Topic. In the story the text and the illustrations work together to provide the context. The children of Newton Street are usually in evidence and provide a continuity for the episodes. The stories try to put the science in a familiar context and to introduce situations and circumstances with which the children can identify. In addition, the story provides an introduction to discussion about people and their jobs and occupations.

People and their jobs and occupations

In the Introduction there is a brief résumé of our reasons for giving attention in *Longman Scienceworld* to this aspect of children's experience. There is a more detailed discussion in Extension G (page 143). In this Extension there is also a list of key ideas for teachers to use in structuring classroom discussion about what people do and how they spend their time.

    In the 'People and their jobs and occupations' section in each Topic a number of statements are selected from this list as being appropriate for attention in the context of the particular Topic. We want to make clear how much science is used in jobs, occupations and in hobbies and leisure occupations. It is obvious that a telephone engineer will need to know and use science, but it is less obvious that the amateur gardener or pigeon fancier can be helped in understanding what they are about if they know and use some science. Additionally, it is likely to become clear that in many jobs and occupations we could do better if we did adopt a more scientific way of tackling the problems we meet and the decisions which have to be made.

Further activities

These are suggestions which you might like to use. Often it is suggested that you might invite someone into the school to talk to the children. We emphasise that the intention is to help to establish the idea that science and people's use of it is a part of real life and not just a classroom activity. Visitors coming into school need to be briefed. You should explain that the children are learning at this stage to investigate 'like scientists' rather than learning a collection of scientific 'facts'. No doubt the best people to explain this, once the course is established, will be the children.

    If you are seeking visitors to come in to school, organisations such as the local Careers Service, Rotary Club, Soroptomists Club, Chamber of Commerce and, last but most important, parents, will be able to help.

Personal contacts with shops and small companies are all helpful and approaches to the Personnel or Training departments of larger companies may be fruitful. Many people are willing to help if you can tell them just what you want them to do.

Science – Background notes

In the Topic guide the major scientific concepts which the children will be exploring are listed. These background notes are to help (if necessary) clarify your own understanding of the concept and possibly to make clear the limits of children's understanding which is expected. It is not intended that the notes will be taught to the children as an assemblage of facts. The information is for your use, so that you can feel confident in your approach and will be able to answer the questions which the children may ask as a result of their investigations and attempts to explain their findings. Some children may show by their comments and questions that they are ready for fuller explanations and you may feel that it is appropriate to give these children more information. Beware of pushing explanation and elaboration unless the children themselves make clear that they are ready for this. There is nothing more confusing for children than receiving answers to questions they have not asked and do not understand.

Science – Activities

Each science activity is set out as follows:

- Title (as in the Pupils' Book)
- Skill objectives for the activity
- You need – requirements for the activity
- Teaching points – general points
  specific points
- Further activities

Skill objectives

Generally three or four skill objectives are identified. In picking out these objectives it is intended that attention should be focused on them rather than that other skill objectives should be neglected. In any scientific investigation a range of scientific skills will be used but in some it will be appropriate to concentrate on certain skills rather than others. The broad skill objectives for the level are identified in the statement introducing the level and the activity skill objectives will contribute to the achievement of these.

Do not disregard completely those skills which are not mentioned specifically. By this stage, we anticipate that many children will, for example, be competent observers so this skill is often not singled out for particular attention; nevertheless, it is of key importance. Other more sophisticated skills – controlling variables, recognising patterns, making suggestions, investigating – are singled out where the activity is clearly focusing on their development. These are skills which children will need to use in an increasingly demanding way. Every opportunity should be used, by comment, discussion and question, to encourage children to practise these skills even though they are not identified as the most significant skills in a particular activity. For example, children should be encouraged to make suggestions about what might happen in an investigation. Discussion of their suggestions and reasons for making those suggestions sets them thinking firmly along the path of scientific development and should become as much part of their way of working as observing carefully.

You need

In this section there is a more detailed description of the requirements for the activity than is given in the Pupils' Book. (The pupil's list is a checklist for them.) The requirements listed are for one individual or group to carry out the investigation. In Extension I (page 145), 'Classroom organisation', there are comments on the advantages and disadvantages of working in groups of different sizes varying from the individual working alone to groups of five or six children working together. You will find it useful to read this section before you decide how to group the children for a particular activity and your decision will, of course, affect the requirements for the activity.

Teaching points

General points

Under this heading attention is focused on particular aspects to which attention should be directed throughout the activity and an indication is given of the depth of understanding that most children are likely to be able to achieve. The understanding which is suggested as being appropriate for the children is encompassed by the 'Science background notes' provided for the teacher. Using these notes you should be able to help the children towards understanding at the level described.

Specific points

On the left-hand side of the pages in the Teachers' Book there is a reproduction of the page from the Pupils' Book which describes the activity. On the right-hand side, at appropriate points, specific comments are made to assist you in helping the children with their work. These comments include suggestions about how to respond to children who approach you when they reach a 🚶 symbol. You will also find here any further instructions which you will need to give the children when they have completed a section of their work and discussed their results with you as suggested in the Pupils' Book.

It should be emphasised that scientific activity entails planning the next step in light of information derived from a previous step. Both obtaining the information by investigation and planning the next step are vital in developing scientific skills. If we had described in the Pupils' Books the results which pupils will obtain and the steps to take based on these results, the experience provided for the children would be scientifically false and they would have missed many opportunities to develop their scientific skills. For this reason many of these 'next steps' have been described in the Teachers' Book rather than in the Pupils' Book. We are sure that these notes will enable you confidently to help the children and enhance the development of their scientific skills.

Further activities

For most of the science activities there are a number of suggestions for further activities. Some of these extend the activities already carried out. Some of the activities are quite different and some are suggestions which might be handled as 'Making and doing activities', should you so wish.

Making and doing activities

There is a full discussion of the nature of 'Making and doing' in Extension F (page 140) and you should read this before you embark on this aspect of the course with a class for the first time. It is essential to have sufficient materials available for the children not to be frustrated by lack of such items as yoghurt cartons, squeezy bottles and pieces of string. The organisation of a magnificent collection of junk is one of the pre-requisites for 'Making and doing'.

Most of the 'Making and doing' problems are open-ended and give plenty of scope for the children to be creative and imaginative, but we have provided specific suggestions to help if imagination and creativity are proving elusive. As emphasised in the **Introduction**, the 'Making and doing activities' also provide opportunities for pupils to apply the new ideas which have been developed in the science activities. Using a new idea is an important step in assimilating that idea and discussion with the children should encourage them to draw on these ideas and enhance their understanding of them.

Record Sheets

The Record Sheets for *Longman Scienceworld* and their use are
described in Extension H (page 144). It should be noted that there is no
reason why you should not keep some record in note form on a regular
basis to help you complete the Record Sheets at the end of the Level. The
skill objectives specified for each activity will help you if you decide to do
this. A master record sheet is printed on the inside back cover of this
Teachers' Book. This may be freely copied.

Duplicating

Primary school children can spend a considerable amount of time
drawing results tables or charts. This can eat into the time they have for
their scientific investigations. You may wish to copy this simple results
table for the children. Permission is given for this table to be photocopied.

YEAR 4
LEVEL 1: TOPICS

INTRODUCTION TO YEAR 4: LEVEL 1

Scientific skills

These are the general skills for Year 4 Level 1 Topics. It is important that you read through these descriptions carefully before the children start work and familiarise yourself with them.

Specific skill objectives are given for each activity at the start of each topic. Their purpose is to focus attention on these rather than to suggest that in an activity these are the only skills which will be used. There are few activities which do not have the potential for developing a range of skills but which skills will depend on the pupils themselves and in some cases on the comments you make and the questions you ask.

Observing

They are able independently to select which observations are likely to be significant and make these in appropriate detail. They look for similarities and differences in form and behaviour. They look for, and are increasingly able to discern, patterns in their observations of form, behaviour and change.

Communicating

Without prompting, the children attempt to match their communications to the audience. They are able to describe and discuss their observations and the observational patterns they discern. They are increasingly able to convey clear statements about these observational patterns. With help, they can make suggestions connected with these recognised patterns.

Measuring

The children can measure, using their own judgement about what should be measured. With guidance, they can decide how accurate the measurements should be.

Recording

The children plan their recording method(s) in advance, including the recording of a series of events over time. They can keep an observational diary and write an orderly sequenced account from this. They can consider critically the record which they have produced and suggest how it might be improved.

Classifying

They make decisions about which sorting criteria to use with increasing independence and the methods suggested are increasingly appropriate. In retrospect, the children are able to comment on the appropriateness of their choice. They use simple keys with confidence, and more complex keys with help. They are able to construct simple keys with little help and can attempt more complex keys.

Recognising patterns

The children are able more readily to recognise patterns in simple data and with help to recognise patterns in mathematical data presented in both graphical and tabular form. They are increasingly able to describe the patterns clearly, both orally and in writing. They are able to identify other instances which fit the pattern and to discuss their reasons.

Predicting
Increasingly, the children are able, with help, to make suggestions based on derived data. Their suggestions are more precise and take in all the evidence. They attempt to assess the likely reliability of their suggestions.

Controlling variables
The children are increasingly able to identify variables and use their accumulating experience in eliminating non-relevant ones. They can find means of controlling simple variables and with help tackle more complex situations. In retrospect, the children are increasingly concerned with whether relevant variables have been completely identified and whether they have been effectively controlled.

Investigating
The children can investigate simple suggestions and questions with minimal help. They design and carry out simple investigations, paying regard to obvious variables and their control. They consider the level of accuracy required and can use ideas about estimating and approximation.

The story

Fair tests

(*Junior Pupils' Book 4* page 2)
Paul, Camilla, Winston and Camilla's father visit a
fairground and try the Big Dipper and the dodgem cars.
They experience a variety of aspects of force, energy
and movement.

Science

People and their jobs and occupations

Some of the problems
of road designers and
car designers are
discussed.
(*Teachers' Book*
page 5)

Concepts

Pupils will explore some aspects of these concepts:

8.2 Force is needed to move a stationary object or to
     alter the direction of travel of a moving object.
8.5 Energy can be supplied in many ways: . . . by doing
     work and storing the energy, e.g. in an elastic band.
8.6 The faster an object moves, the more energy it has.
8.7 A moving object is stopped or slowed down by
     energy being removed from it.
8.8 An object moving on a surface must overcome
     friction.

Making and doing activity

The problem for the
children is:
'Can you make a "Big
Dipper" along which a
marble can travel so
that it goes as far as
possible on the track
you make and goes
over two humps on the
way?'
(*Teachers' Book*
page 12)

Skills

Pupils will develop their scientific skills by:

Activity 1—Going up   *TB* p7
Investigating how energy can be stored in a   *PB4* p3
stretched rubber band; investigating the
effect of altering the friction of the surface
on which a cotton reeler is travelling

Activity 2—Going down   *TB* p8
Investigating the motion of balls   *PB4* p4
on a U-shaped track

Activity 3—Boing!   *TB* p10
Investigating what happens when balls   *PB4* p5
moving on a U-shaped track collide

Activity 4—Bump!   *TB* p11
Investigating what happens when a model   *PB4* p6
car and driver in motion hit a stationary barrier

The story

Fairs are always popular with children and they provide much excitement. The ideas raised by the story will give rise to lively discussion and exchange of experiences. Some of the children will be able to describe how they felt when they were riding on a Big Dipper or what it feels like to be bumped in a dodgem car. Other children will have experienced the forces exerted when a car or bus has to brake suddenly or when an aeroplane is pelting down the runway for take-off. There are a wide range of ideas which can be discussed in an introductory session and these ideas can be kept in mind and reworked as the children carry out their investigations and explore the effects in a controlled manner.

People and their jobs and occupations

Road designers and the engineers who build the roads have to have a wide variety of skills and knowledge of many aspects of science. They must determine the route which a road should take so they need knowledge of the shape of the country and of its underlying structure (geology). They need to know how steep a slope cars and lorries can negotiate – both going up and coming down. They must work out how tight bends can be at the speed traffic is likely to be travelling. Bends on a motorway must be very gentle and slopes must be of minimum steepness, so road engineers may have to make decisions about whether to cut through the land or to build embankments or to go round hills. Deciding where and how to build a road is a large scale 'making and doing activity' where some of the factors which influence a final decision will be scientific but others will be economic and social. A simulation of a public enquiry into the route to be followed by a new road could give rise to a lively debate.

Some aspects of vehicle design and road design go hand in hand. Cars and lorries must be able to travel safely and easily on the roads and road designers must work to produce roads which enable vehicles to use all the up-to-date engineering refinement which is built into them so that people can travel quickly and safely. Car designers, particularly, must make sure that cars use frictional forces to advantage so that the cars have good road-holding characteristics and the braking systems are able to keep a vehicle travelling at speed out of trouble.

Particular points which could be developed include:

10 People may need special knowledge, expertise and skills in their work and hobbies.
11 People have to acquire the special knowledge, expertise and skills which they need.
16 People use scientific information in their jobs, occupations and hobbies.
17 People need to use a scientific viewpoint in their jobs, occupations and hobbies.

Further activities

1 Contact either a civil engineering contractor or the Institute of Civil Engineers (1–7 Great George Street, London SW1) and ask an engineer to come and talk about designing and building roads.
2 Look at some local roads and suggest why they take the particular directions you observe, e.g. going round hills, through cuttings, across embankments to avoid sharp dips or wet ground etc.
3 Take a ride on a Big Dipper and observe how it is constructed.
4 Look at car advertisements and notice which points they emphasise. Which features are particularly important in getting up and down hills safely?

Science

Background notes

This topic introduces some important ideas about energy. The essential ideas are simple.

We cannot create energy. We can only change it from one form to another.

Human beings and other animals get their energy from the food they eat. Animal eats animal but ultimately animal eats plant and plants acquire their energy from the sun. The sun gives plants the energy they need to convert very simple chemical substances into more complex ones. Human beings and animals can convert these complex substances into simple substances; and in doing so release the energy which the plants used in making these substances. Whenever we do anything, we get the energy from the breakdown of our food.

In this topic, human energy is the starting point. In Activity 1 a rubber band is twisted – human energy is used. Twisting the rubber gives it a form which is unstable. As soon as the twisting stops, the rubber band releases energy so that it can return to its normal stable state. The energy which is released drives the reeler. The reeler pushes against the surface of the slope and the slope counteracts the push so that the reeler is able to move forward. If the slope or the reeler is very smooth, the reeler is not able to push against the surface and cannot move forward properly. The force between the reeler and the surface is a frictional force. In the case of the reeler climbing the slope, cars moving on roads and people walking, frictional force is useful (essential); because of this, roads are given a roughened surface, floors should not be slippery and the reeler slope can advantageously be given a surface which offers the reeler better grip. (In moving machinery, friction is a nuisance and interferes with efficient working; so every effort is made to reduce friction by making surfaces as smooth as possible and by using lubricants.)

In Activities 2 and 3 the ball is placed at a point on the track which is higher than the lowest point. Human energy is used to put it there. The ball stores the energy which has been given to it by being in a position where potentially it can release this energy. This it does when it starts to roll downhill. As it travels, it goes faster. When it reaches the bottom of the dip it is going fastest. Then it is holding no energy because of its position; all its energy has become associated with its motion. Position energy is called **potential energy**. Motion energy is called **kinetic energy**. For a ball on a slope the energy changes can be represented like this.

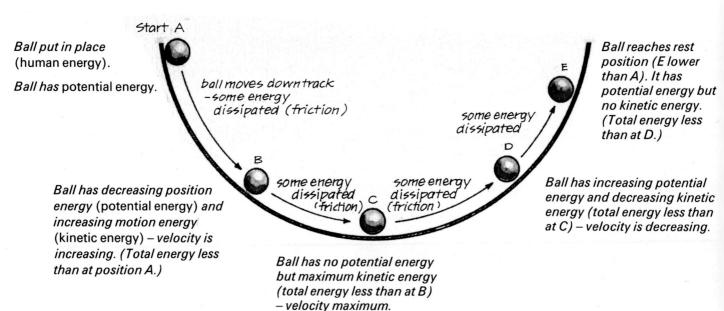

Start A

Ball put in place (human energy).

Ball has potential energy.

ball moves down track – some energy dissipated (friction)

B

Ball has decreasing position energy (potential energy) and increasing motion energy (kinetic energy) – velocity is increasing. (Total energy less than at position A.)

some energy dissipated (friction)

C

some energy dissipated (friction)

Ball has no potential energy but maximum kinetic energy (total energy less than at B) – velocity maximum.

D

some energy dissipated

E

Ball reaches rest position (E lower than A). It has potential energy but no kinetic energy. (Total energy less than at D.)

Ball has increasing potential energy and decreasing kinetic energy (total energy less than at C) – velocity is decreasing.

Potential energy (position energy) depends on the height at which the ball is placed. Motion energy (kinetic energy) depends on how fast the ball is moving. The total energy which the ball has at the lowest point is all in the form of motion energy and this is less than the potential energy with which it started since some energy is dissipated (in overcoming friction) as the ball rolls over the surface of the track.

When the ball starts to go up the other side of the dip it slows down and loses kinetic energy but its height above the low point increases and it gains position energy. Again some energy is dissipated as it moves over the track. Eventually the ball will reach a stopping point slightly lower than the height from which it started, i.e. the potential energy will be less than it was when the ball started its travels. If the slope of the track is made greater or less, it makes little difference to the final position of the ball since this is dependent on its starting point on the track.

Potential energy is also related to the weight of the ball. If a heavy ball and a light ball are at the same height, the heavy ball will have greater potential energy. (More human effort was required to put it in that position.) The more important point to remember is that under no conditions can a ball released on one side of a dip reach a higher position on the other side. Some energy will always be dissipated in the movement of the ball over the track.

If balls are released simultaneously on both sides of the dip from the same height they will collide at the bottom of the track. If one ball is heavier, it will have greater energy (at this point, kinetic energy) and both balls will move a little way in the direction in which the heavier ball was moving.

In Activity 4 the car and the table tennis ball both acquire kinetic energy as the car runs down the slope. When the car collides with the barrier, its energy is dissipated in various ways but the table tennis ball will continue until gravity brings it down to earth.

Activity 1—Going up

Objectives
At the end of this activity the children should be better able to:
1 keep notes throughout the activity and use these to write an orderly report of their investigations;
2 look for and recognise patterns in their observations;
3 identify variables, recognise ones which are not relevant and find means of controlling simple relevant variables;
4 investigate simple suggestions and questions with minimal help.

Preparation
The children will need to make a cotton reeler. The material required for this is listed on page 3 of *Junior Pupils' Book 4*. More detailed instructions for making a reeler are given in *Teachers' Book 1* page 75. The board and blocks should enable the pupils to make a steep slope.

You will also need to have to hand materials which the children can use to alter the surface texture of the slope e.g. carpet, rough wallpaper, sandpaper, corrugated cardboard, felt etc. The children will possibly ask for materials to modify the reeler e.g. sandpaper, corrugated cardboard, rubber bands etc. Wind-up toy cars will also add an extra dimension to the activity if you have them or the children can bring them from home.

Teaching points

General points
The children are finding out what can be done to help a car climb a steep slope and, in particular, they are investigating the effect of increasing the frictional force by altering the surface of the slope. The children are asked to write a report of their investigation. They will need to keep notes during the investigation so that they can do this. You should check that they do not forget.

By comment and discussion make sure that the children have firmly grasped the idea that the energy which they used in twisting the rubber band is stored in the band and is being released as it untwists. This provides the energy to drive the reeler. In understanding how energy can be put into something and then got out again, the crucial principle to remember is that you never get 'owt for nowt'!

Specific points
If the children have forgotten how to make a reeler, they may need help. (See note in the 'Preparation' section.)

To make the rest of the work valid the children need to establish that their reelers perform consistently. The children will find that the distance becomes progressively less for the same number of turns as the slope gets steeper. The time taken also increases.

They will probably decide to increase the number of turns. Does the reeler go further/go faster or both? (Having the stop clock amongst the items supplied may give them a hint that time is something they could measure.)

Although increasing the number of turns will help, the children will become aware that the slipperiness of the slope is a major retarding factor and they may decide to make modifications to their reelers or to the slope or to both. If they decide they want to make the slope less slippery, you can ask them what they could use to do this and hopefully they will mention some of the materials which you have in readiness! Possible ways of modifying the reeler include:
fitting it with wide rubber band 'tyres';
making notches in the rims;
encasing the reel in some rough material e.g. sandpaper.

In section 4 you will need to check that the children remember to control the variables – to make it a fair test.

For section 5, the children may need guidance in using their notes to write a report of their work and in deciding how best to present their findings (using neat tables and graphs where appropriate).

Further activities
1 Different surfaces could be compared when the surface is flat and on a slope when the reeler is moving downhill.
2 A slope could be set up and treated with various substances which might reduce friction and the effect on the progress of the reeler could be investigated. Convenient materials include water, cooking oil and washing-up liquid. Why are roads slippery after rain? Why is an oil spill on a road dangerous?

Activity 2—Going down

Objectives
At the end of this activity the children should be better able to:
1 look for and recognise patterns in their observations;
2 identify and control simple variables;
3 investigate simple suggestions with minimal help.

Preparation
The children will need a number of balls of various sizes and made of a variety of materials giving balls which are approximately equal in size but different in weight, e.g. marbles, ball bearings, polystyrene spheres, plastic balls etc. The track should be flexible so that it can be bent to make a dip. It should also be wide enough to allow all the balls to run along it freely; if it is too wide the balls may zigzag as they roll down the slope and produce inconsistent results. Plastic curtain track is usually suitable or plastic edging used for trimming the rough edges of decorative veneered board may be available. The balance scales should be able to measure differences of one gram. The Lego blocks are to enable the children to build supporting towers for the track.

Activity 1 Going up

What can be done to help a car climb a steep slope?

You need: a cotton reel; a piece of candle; a rubber band; a matchstick; a lollipop stick; Blu-Tack; a smooth board about 1 m long – or longer; some blocks; a stop clock

1 Make a cotton reeler. Ask your teacher how to do it.

2 Wind it up well. Put it at one end of the board. Measure how far it will go. Wind it up the same amount and measure how far again.

Write down the number of turns.

You measure how far it goes.

3 Lift your board up at one end with a block. Wind up your reeler the same amount. Measure how far along the board it will go now. Check your results.

We'll use the same number of turns.

This is a one block slope.

4 Make steeper slopes and measure how far your reeler will go each time for the same winding. What happens as the slope gets steeper?

This is a four block slope.

We must check the distance.

Can you think of ways to help your reeler climb the slope? Try out your ideas. Remember to make it a fair test.

5 Write about what you did and what happened.

— 3 —

Teaching points

General points
The children are trying to find answers and evidence to help them decide whether weight helps to make a Big Dipper car travel higher on the up-slope of a dip or whether the weight retards it.

Specific points
The children will need to arrange the balls physically in weight order before producing the written record.

The track should be arranged symmetrically with the towers of equal height and the centre of the track at the lowest point. Make sure that the children hold the metre rule exactly vertical when they make their measurements and that they read the metre rule at eye level.

When the children check their results, do they do it honestly? Do they seek reasons for discrepancies? Do they take an average if the results are not exactly the same?

Encourage the children, as a matter of course, to think about what the result is likely to be when they have evidence which shows a pattern which they can discern, even if their appreciation of the pattern is in the broadest terms.

The length of the track remains the same in section 4 but the supporting towers are made higher.

Further activities

1 Find out what happens when a collection of balls of approximately the same weight but different sizes are tested on the track.
2 Find out what happens when the track is made asymmetric.

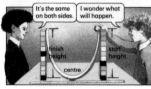

Activity 2   Going down

David thought that the Big Dipper car would not get to the top. Winston thought that all the people in it were making it too heavy. Camilla thought they were going to fly over the top. Make a pretend 'Big Dipper' slope and see what happens. You will have to use balls instead of Big Dipper cars.

You need: a length of track; collection of small balls; Lego blocks; Blu-Tack; balance scales; a metre rule

1 Weigh all your balls. Put them in weight order in your record.

2 Arrange your track like this. Put the heaviest ball at the top of the track and let it go. Mark the point it reaches on the other side. Measure the start height and the finish height. Try different start heights. Record your results. Check your results.

The track is the same on both sides.

Mark where it gets to on your side.

finish height   start height

3 Do the same thing with your next two balls. Before you try the next one, decide what you think its finish height will be. Test your idea. Try with all the other balls.

Further? Not as far?

4 Change the slope of your track. Try your three heaviest balls again. Measure the start height and the finish heights. Can you suggest what the finish heights will be for the other balls?

It's the same on both sides.

I wonder what will happen.

finish height   start height

centre

5 Were David's, Camilla's and Winston's ideas right? Write a letter to them explaining what you have done and what you have found out.

4

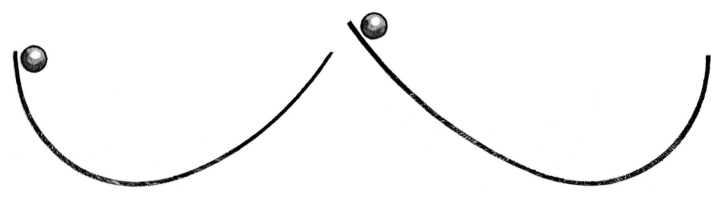

3 Investigate the conditions which will result in a ball shooting over the end of a track arranged like this. Where do the balls land when they overshoot? Investigate size, weight and release height.

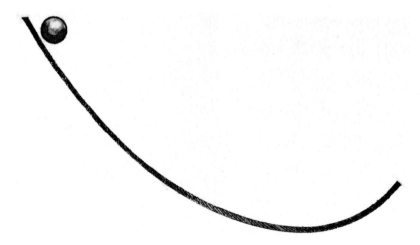

4 Arrange a symmetrical track. Release a marble and mark the release height and the height reached on the other side of the dip. Now release a marble from this point but before doing so suggest the height that the marble will reach on the other slope. The results can be presented graphically and the shape of the graph can be discussed.

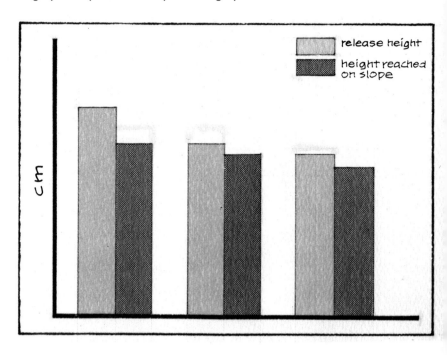

Activity 3—Boing!

Objectives
At the end of this activity the children should be better able to:
1 plan an investigation;
2 recognise variables which are relevant and find means of controlling these;
3 decide which observations will be of significance;
4 decide in advance how to record their observations.

Preparation
The children will need the collection of balls which they used in Activity 2. In addition, they will need a collection of balls of different sizes but approximately the same weight. They will also need the other items which are listed on page 5 of *Junior Pupils' Book 4*.

Teaching points

General points
The children are trying to find out what happens when things collide, particularly in terms of the effect produced when the things which collide are of differing weight or size. The extent to which the children will be able to decide precisely whether a particular result is due to size or weight will depend to a large extent on the range of balls which are available.

Specific points
The children will need to observe very carefully if they are to see exactly what happens to both balls in sections 2 and 3.

Again, in sections 4 and 5, the collision has to be watched very carefully to see what happens to each ball.

Further activities
1 Find out what happens when varying numbers of identical balls are either placed stationary in the dip or are released to collide.
   For example, see top of page opposite.
2 Try the above activity with a set of balls of different weight or different size. Does the same thing happen?

Activity 3 Boing!

David hoped they would not bump into another car. What happens when things collide?

You need: collection of small balls; callipers; balance scales; Blu-Tack; a ruler; a metre rule

1 Weigh all your balls. Put them in weight order in your record.

2 Fix your track like this. Get a friend to let a ball roll down one side. At exactly the same time, you let your ball go. What happens? Where do they collide? Do they go up one side or the other? What happens if both balls weigh the same? What happens if one is heavier? Find out as much as you can about the effect of weight.

3 Find out what happens if the sizes of the balls are changed.

4 Put one ball at the bottom of the dip. Let another ball run down and hit it. What happens to the balls? What happens if one ball is very heavy and the other is very light?

Now try putting two balls in the dip. What happens when one ball hits them?

5 Write an account of what you find out. Draw lots of pictures if that makes it clearer.

Are you ready?

One ... two ... three, go.

Let's put them in size order.

I'll measure them.

This is heavy. This is light.

5

Activity 4—Bump!

Objectives

At the end of this activity the children should be better able to:

1 plan recording methods in advance;
2 carry out an investigation recognising and controlling relevant variables;
3 recognise patterns in results and make suggestions based on these patterns;
4 find means of testing their suggestions.

Preparation

The children will need the items listed on page 6 of *Junior Pupils' Book 4*. It would be possible to use a toy car rather than a Lego car.

Teaching points

General points

The children are investigating what happens when a moving object is halted by a barrier. If the object is a car, what happens to its driver? The children should be encouraged to keep careful notes so that they can write the account required in section 4.

Specific points

As the car runs down the slope, the car and the table tennis ball go faster until the barrier is reached. The car stops and the energy of the car is changed from being energy of motion (kinetic energy) to other forms, including heat and sound. The table tennis ball is not affected in the same way and continues to travel forward until the force of gravity brings it to the ground.

A piece of carpet or similar will stop the ball rolling. A sand tray is another alternative.

The steeper the slope the greater the kinetic energy the car and table tennis ball will have at the bottom and the further the ball will fly when the car hits the barrier. The children should be able to recognise the pattern of increasing distance as the slope gets progressively steeper.

In section 4, you may want to discuss the written account with the children before they start.

Further activities

1 What happens to the distance which the table tennis ball is thrown at the barrier if the slope is made longer?
2 What happens if the car is made heavier or a heavier ball is used?
3 Set up the slope and let the car run down the slope. How far from the end of the slope does it go before it stops? What happens if it is put at different points on the slope? What happens if the slope is made steeper?
4 Make a second Lego car and give it a table tennis ball driver. Arrange the slope and let the first car run down the slope so that it hits the second car squarely at the back. What happens to the cars and the drivers? Continue the investigation varying the angle of the slope, weights of cars and drivers.

Activity 4 Bump!

Why do people think dodgem cars are fun? What happens when cars hit each other or hit a wall?

You need: Lego blocks and wheels to make a car; a smooth board about 1 m long – or longer; some blocks; table tennis balls; Blu-Tack; a ruler; a metre rule

1 Make a Lego car. Give it a table tennis ball driver.

That looks fine.

The ball makes a good driver.

2 Put blocks under one end of the board. Put the ruler across the end. Let the car run from the top of the slope and hit the ruler. What happens to the driver? Measure the distance of the driver from the car.

Remember that's a one block slope.

Watch out, driver!

Put another block under the board. Let the car run down again. What happens this time? Measure where the driver is. Why is there a difference?

3 Make the slope steeper block by block. Try to suggest where the driver will end up each time before you do the test.

4 What would have happened if the driver had been a real person in a real car? Why should people wear seatbelts? Why should motor cyclists wear crash helmets? Write about what you find out and how your results help you to answer these questions.

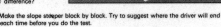
6

Making and doing activity

The problem for the children is:
  'Can you make a "Big Dipper" along which a marble can travel so that it goes as far as possible on the track you make and goes over two humps on the way?'

You need:
20 sheets of newspaper; a sheet of card; strong adhesive; a marble; 30 pins. (**Note**   This should give the children scope to solve the problem satisfactorily but you may decide to vary the materials provided as the work gets underway and the skills of the children become apparent. The more material the children have, the longer the tracks they will try to build. This could produce organisational problems!)

1	The problem	To make a track along which a marble can travel as far as possible and go over two humps on the way.
2	Exploring the problem	What do the children know about balls rolling on tracks? What do they know about building structures to support a track? What must be the height relation between the starting height of the marble and the heights of the two humps? How wide must the track be? Does the track need sides?
3	Ideas for solving the problem	Build a tower or a series of towers to support a track. Make tubes by rolling newspaper. Use the card to make folded girders. Could the marble run through newspaper tubes? Could the card track be suspended by newspaper strips from a series of newspaper tubes?

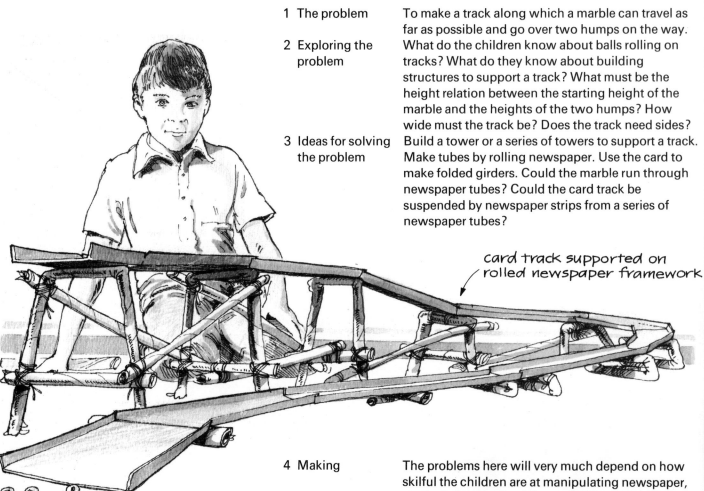

card track supported on rolled newspaper framework

4	Making	The problems here will very much depend on how skilful the children are at manipulating newspaper, particularly at rolling it into stiff tubes. They should be able to manage this reasonably well. Rolling round a thin stick to act as a former to start off may be useful – but make sure that they remove the stick before they use the tube. If they try to use the card for building the supporting structure they will probably run out of materials – but that is part of the problem. The children must produce a structure so that the starting height is as great as possible, the two humps are progressively smaller and the track is long enough to take the final run of the marble.
5	Evaluating	Who has managed to use skill, materials and knowledge to the best advantage? What can be learned from the various attempts? Does anyone want to have another try or to make adjustments to their efforts?

The story

(*Junior Pupils' Book 4* page 7)
Anna and her family take Bimla to visit an air show and watch various events.

Science

People and their jobs and occupations

Some of the events taking place at the air display are discussed and in particular attention is focused on risk-taking hobbies e.g. parachuting, hot-air ballooning. Why do people choose hobbies such as these? (*Teachers' Book* pages 14–15)

Concepts

Pupils will explore some aspects of these concepts:
7.1 There is air round the earth.
8.2 Force is needed to move a stationary object . . . .
8.5 Energy can be supplied in many ways: . . . by doing work and storing the energy e.g. in a rubber band.
8.7 A moving object is stopped or slowed down by energy being removed from it.

Making and doing activity

The problem for the children is:
'Can you make a hovercraft?'
(*Teachers' Book* pages 21–2)

Skills

Pupils will develop their scientific skills by:

Activity 1—Earth bound   *TB* p16
Investigating parachutes   *PB4* p8

Activity 2—A bit of a drag   *TB* p17
Investigating the effect of drag   *PB4* p9

Activity 3—Jetting along   *TB* p18
Investigating propulsion by air escaping   *PB4* p10
from a balloon

Activity 4—A lot of hot air   *TB* p20
Investigating the behaviour of a hot-air   *PB4* p11
balloon

The story

Many children will not have visited an air display but they will probably have seen such an event on television. Sky diving, with its free fall routines in formation, has become an established event and the children will have experienced in some degree the nail-biting wait for the parachutes to open. Parachuting to land on a target is also seen quite often on the television screen and children will have watched the parachutist manipulating the parachute lines to guide the landing towards the target.

Jet propulsion is used for all modern aircraft. More and more effective jet engines have made possible longer, cheaper and faster flights and opened up prospects of holidays abroad for vast numbers of people and made world travel routine for a few. At an air show it is the spectacular which people come to see: a flight of small planes diving through the sky with streams of coloured vapour coming from them is breathtaking. The pilots must fly with split-second accuracy, relying totally on their own skills and the technical perfection of their aircraft (as also do pilots of passenger-carrying planes).

Hot-air ballooning has a history going back many years and has become increasingly popular as a spectacle. It has also come within the reach of enthusiasts.

The story provides many starting points for discussion about the children's experiences or dreams and a focus for a range of topic work concerned with flight and the history and development of different modes of flight.

People and their jobs and occupations

Which of the people taking part in an air display are being paid for what they are doing and which are doing it for fun – as a hobby? Parachuting has become a hobby sport for a growing number of people. Why would someone choose such a hobby? Would the children like to parachute? Why? Do all people in aeroplanes have parachutes? Why? Why not?

Anyone using a parachute depends utterly on the skills of the people who prepare the parachute. Can the children think of what would be involved in making sure that the parachutist has a safe and effective parachute? (*Designing a prototype based on existing scientific information and understanding; selecting materials which have been scientifically tested and whose performance characteristics are known; making the prototype; testing the prototype scientifically in the laboratory and with dummies; proving the prototype in use etc. The parachute packer is crucially important in the use of the parachute. If the parachute fails to open properly the result is inevitably fatal.*)

You might like to centre the main discussion around the idea of risk-taking hobbies. Why do people choose hobbies like parachuting? Hobbies such as this and hang gliding and motor racing expose participants to very considerable hazards. What is the attraction? Do the children have any ideas about this? The special knowledge and skills of hot-air ballooning might be explored. What would a hot-air balloonist need to know or be able to do to make flights as safe as possible? (*Weather knowledge and understanding; navigational skills; knowledge and understanding of how the balloon works.*)

You could introduce children to the idea that whatever we do there are some risks. We usually plan our lives to avoid risks as far as we are able but some people take deliberate risks in their chosen hobbies. They respond to these risks by taking every precaution possible and ensuring that they know exactly what they are doing and understand exactly what is happening. Specific points which are applicable might be singled out.

10 People may need special knowledge, expertise and skills in their work and hobbies.

11 People have to acquire the special knowledge, expertise and skills which they need.

16 People use scientific information in their jobs, occupations and hobbies.

17 People need to use a scientific viewpoint in their jobs, occupations and hobbies.

Further activities

1 If you can find someone who has made a parachute jump ask him/her to describe to the children what it felt like. (There are a number of amateur parachuting clubs which might provide a contact.)

2 Find out about the history of hot-air ballooning and perhaps about the development of the airship.

3 Read parts of stories about spies and secret agents who parachuted into Europe during the Second World War.

4 Visit an air show if you have the chance.

Science

Background notes

Air resistance

Any object travelling through the air has to overcome the resistance of the air. The effect is similar to the resistance which has to be overcome by an object travelling through water. We tend to think that still air lets things pass through it without hindrance but this is not the case. Everything is made up of very tiny particles. In a solid, these are very close together –

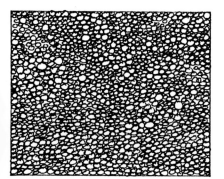

solid

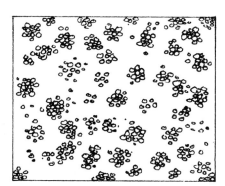

liquid

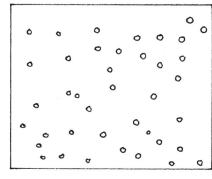

gas

close enough to stop anything going through without a lot of effort e.g. using a hammer to knock a nail into wood. In a liquid, the particles are further apart but close enough to require some effort to pass through; for example, a swimmer is very conscious of the effort needed; anyone who has done a 'belly-flop' dive knows that water offers considerable (and painful) resistance. Air is very much like water except that the particles in the air are further apart than those in water but the effect of air on something trying to get through it is very much the same as that of water on an object. In air, this opposition to an object moving through it produces 'drag'.

In flight, drag is a nuisance. It slows down flight; increases power requirements; decreases efficiency; increases costs. Aircraft fly as high as they can – where the air is thinner and the air particles are further apart. The parachute exploits drag and uses it to slow down the rate of fall. There is a compromise between making the parachute as large as possible to get maximum drag and making it small enough to be controllable.

Jet propulsion

If you blow up a balloon you push air into it so that the air in the balloon is under pressure held by the stretched skin of the balloon. If air is allowed to escape through a small hole, the air escapes rapidly producing a jet of air with high velocity. The air has momentum because of this and the balloon acquires an equal and opposite momentum which sends it in the opposite direction.

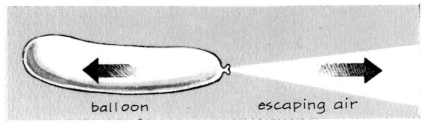

balloon   escaping air

This is the effect which causes the balloon to move along the fishing line in Activity 3. It is the principle which is used in jet engines and rockets.

Hot-air balloons

If you have a litre of air at 0°C and a litre at 100°C (the pressure being the same), there will be more particles in the litre of air at 0°C than in that at 100°C. The sample of warmer air will weigh less than the sample of colder air. If you could enclose the sample of air at 100°C and release it in air at 0°C it would float and rise because it would be less dense than the surrounding air. It would rise until the particles in the enclosed sample and those in the surrounding air were equally distributed.

The hot-air balloon works on this principle. Since the balloon has to have a skin, the balloon will only rise if the weight of the skin plus the air it contains is less than the volume of air which it is displacing.

The greater the difference between the temperature of the air inside the balloon and the air outside, the greater the difference in density and the better the balloon will fly.

Activity 1 — Earth bound

Objectives

At the end of this activity the children should be better able to:
1 plan and carry out an investigation;
2 identify and control the relevant variables;
3 recognise patterns in their results and use ideas arising from these recognised patterns in their investigations;
4 communicate their findings to a specified audience.

Preparation

The children will need the items listed on page 8 of *Junior Pupils' Book 4*. Provide a good variety of materials for parachute making, including very thin, light materials; some heavier, coarse fabric as well as different grades of plastic and types of paper. The minimum size for a parachute is about 20 cm square – anything smaller is unlikely to work.

The small weights can take the form of washers. If these are all of the same size it will help the children to control this variable when they start to test their parachutes – although this does not need to be pointed out to them.

Teaching points

General points

The children are investigating the effectiveness of different parachutes and what happens when various variables are manipulated. There may be some problems about how to launch the parachutes. If the school has upper storeys the parachutes can, with supervision, be thrown out of a window or dropped down a stairwell. If this is not possible, some other 'dropping' method should be looked for. If all else is impossible, the parachute can be thrown into the air. This makes the launch variable more difficult to control.

Timing the fall of the parachutes will be difficult unless the fall distance is considerable. The children will probably find it more satisfactory to compare the parachutes directly.

Activity 1 Earth bound

Parachutes let people fall slowly and safely to earth. See what you can find out about parachutes.

You need: different materials from which to make parachutes; thin string; thread; scissors; plasticine; a stop clock; small weights

1　Make a parachute like Bimla and Anna are doing. Test it. If you make it from different material, can you make it fall more slowly? Make other parachutes and test them. Which material makes the best parachute? Was your test fair?

I've got a square piece of cloth.

You must make sure that all the strings are the same length.

2　Can you improve the design of your best parachute? Make a list of the things you can alter. Make changes to your parachute. Make your tests fair. Now answer these questions. Does a bigger parachute fall more slowly than a smaller one? Does a parachute with longer strings fall more quickly than one with shorter strings?

3　What happens if you make a hole in the parachute? What happens if you make holes of different sizes? What happens if you use different shapes?

4　Write an article for your school magazine about making parachutes.

8

Specific points

In the first section, the children are asked to find out which material is best. They will have to identify which are the other variables and control them. They could draw up a variables table to help them. The children may think of other variables.

variable	to be investigated	to be changed	to be controlled
material			
size			
shape			
length of string			
weight			
dropping height			
time of fall			
air conditions			
temperature			

In section 2, the children will be using the same set of variables but putting their 'to be investigated' and 'to be changed' ticks in different places. They should remember that only one variable at a time can be investigated, only one changed and the rest have to be kept the same.

There are a very wide range of variables which can be investigated and you might like to suggest to the children that they work in groups and share the investigations between them. They will have to plan the investigations carefully in advance and agree on a common method if their results are to be brought together at the end.

Further activities

1　What happens if you use more strings on your parachute?
2　Look at natural 'parachutes' e.g. dandelion seeds, sycamore and ash keys etc.
3　Compare the fall of different types and makes of badminton shuttle.

Activity 2—A bit of a drag

Objectives

At the end of this activity the children should be better able to:
1　plan and carry out an investigation;
2　identify and control variables;
3　recognise patterns in their findings;
4　use mathematical means of communication.

Preparation

The children will need the items listed on page 9 of *Junior Pupils' Book 4*. The nail should be long enough to go through the cotton reel and have enough to spare to enable it to be held either in a clamp or hammered into a wooden block to be held by a clamp. The groove cut in the cotton reel should be deep enough to hold the piece of card (a bit of sellotape will help, if necessary). The thread should be stuck to the cotton reel with sellotape and should be a little longer than the fall distance which must not be less than 1.5 metres.

Teaching points

General points

The children are investigating the drag effect by increasing the size and shape of a card which is resisting the air as it spins. The children will have to adjust the size of the plasticine ball so that the fall with a small card attached to the cotton reel can be timed.

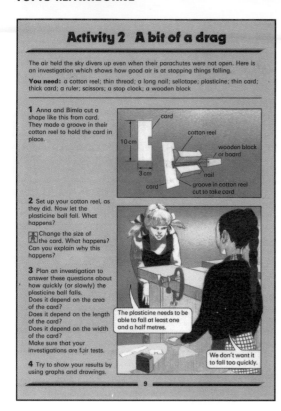

Activity 2 A bit of a drag

The air held the sky divers up even when their parachutes were not open. Here is an investigation which shows how good air is at stopping things falling.

You need: a cotton reel; thin thread; a long nail; sellotape; plasticine; thin card; thick card; a ruler; scissors; a stop clock; a wooden block

1 Anna and Bimla cut a shape like this from card. They made a groove in their cotton reel to hold the card in place.

2 Set up your cotton reel, as they did. Now let the plasticine ball fall. What happens?

Change the size of the card. What happens? Can you explain why this happens?

3 Plan an investigation to answer these questions about how quickly (or slowly) the plasticine ball falls.
Does it depend on the area of the card?
Does it depend on the length of the card?
Does it depend on the width of the card?
Make sure that your investigations are fair tests.

4 Try to show your results by using graphs and drawings.

The plasticine needs to be able to fall at least one and a half metres.

We don't want it to fall too quickly.

Specific points

The larger the area of the card the more resistance there is, but the effect is most marked when the length of the card is increased. The children should be encouraged to draw up a variables table and use this to plan their investigations.

variable	to be investigated	to be changed	to be controlled
drop height			
weight			
thread			
area of card			
length of card			
width of card			
time of drop			

In section 4, the children may be able to draw a graph of time against one of the card dimensions and explore relationships and look for patterns.

Further activities

1 The children could fix cards of different sizes and dimensions to a truck running down an incline and investigate the effect on the time taken for the truck to travel a marked distance or on the distance travelled.
2 In a similar way, the effect of drogues of varying sizes could be tested.

drogue – cone made from paper and attached to the truck with thread

Activity 3—Jetting along

Objectives

At the end of this activity the children should be better able to:
1 plan and carry out an investigation;
2 identify and control variables;
3 recognise patterns in their findings;
4 communicate their findings to a specified audience.

Preparation

The children will need the items specified on page 10 of *Junior Pupils' Book 4*. Nylon fishing line can be bought from a fishing tackle shop. Smooth nylon is needed and a breaking strain of between 5 lb and 15 lb (2.5–7.5 kg) is suitable. You will need a run of line across the classroom so you must site this with great care and put it at a height where nobody can walk into it. Near a wall at above head height is desirable and the height and placing should be such that the balloon moving along at speed cannot hit anyone in the eye. Alternatively, site the line near the floor where nobody can trip over it.

Nylon is not easy to tie and it is worth fastening the knots with sellotape. The line can be tied directly to pot hooks; but if you are going to take it down and put it up a number of times it is worth fixing one end of the line to a small curtain ring. Since the children will be testing different balloons it would be useful to tie a loop at the other end of the line so that it can be threaded easily through the straw attached to the balloon.

The line needs to be fixed so that it is absolutely taut.

Teaching points

General points

The children are investigating the movement of the balloon when the compressed air inside it is released. They should discover that the size of the hole through which the air escapes affects the speed and distance travelled by the balloon.

Note Make quite sure that the line is fixed so that it cannot injure anyone and that the balloons travelling along it cannot hit anyone.

Specific points

The children will need to identify the variables and make sure that they are under control.

If it is difficult to remove the balloon from the line each time a new arrangement is to be tested, you may find it satisfactory to attach the balloon to the straw with Blu-Tack.

The children will need a good run of line to measure the distance. If the run is too short to enable the balloon to come to a stop, the children will have to rely on timing the balloon over a specified distance – but this is difficult to do with any accuracy. Throughout this work the children should be aware that one measurement is not sufficient and that they will need to take a mean of a number of runs. They will have to keep an orderly record of their results to help in the production of their final reports (section 4).

In section 3, card or polystyrene wings can be added by fixing them with glue or Blu-Tack. The children will have to decide where is the best place to fix wings and what shape and size they should be. Are long wings better than short ones? Are wide better than narrow? What shape is best?

Further activities

Make and test a squeezy bottle rocket. The rocket can be fired dry or one third filled with water. It is quite safe as long as it is fired away from people. If the pressure build-up is too great, the washing-up liquid bottle splits. If the rocket is fired 'wet', the launcher gets wet! It can reach up to 30 metres – so give it plenty of room. (See below and on page 20.)

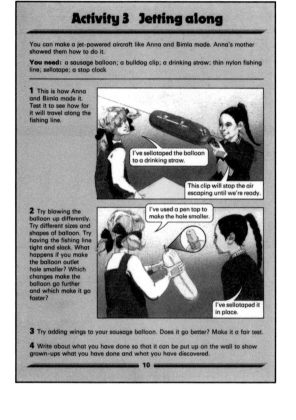

Activity 3   Jetting along

You can make a jet-powered aircraft like Anna and Bimla made. Anna's mother showed them how to do it.

You need: a sausage balloon; a bulldog clip; a drinking straw; thin nylon fishing line; sellotape; a stop clock

1 This is how Anna and Bimla made it. Test it to see how far it will travel along the fishing line.

I've sellotaped the balloon to a drinking straw.

This clip will stop the air escaping until we're ready.

2 Try blowing the balloon up differently. Try different sizes and shapes of balloon. Try having the fishing line tight and slack. What happens if you make the balloon outlet hole smaller? Which changes make the balloon go further and which make it go faster?

I've used a pen top to make the hole smaller.

I've sellotaped it in place.

3 Try adding wings to your sausage balloon. Does it go better? Make it a fair test.

4 Write about what you have done so that it can be put up on the wall to show grown-ups what you have done and what you have discovered.

— 10 —

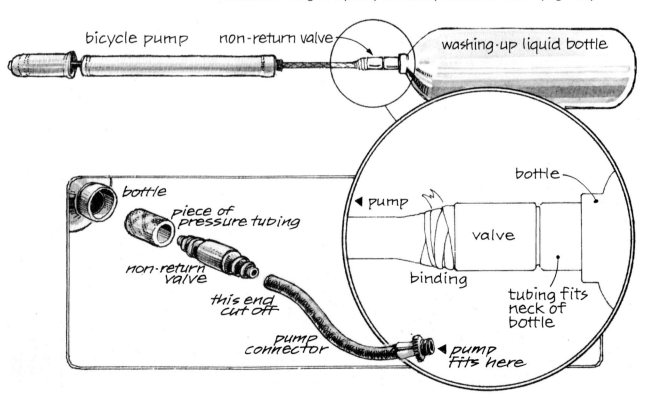

Make sure that the launcher points the rocket away from his/her face.

launcher

pumper

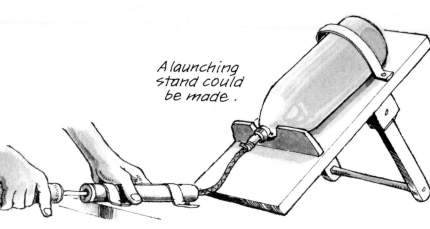

A launching stand could be made.

Activity 4—A lot of hot air

Objectives

At the end of this activity the children should be better able to:
1 carry out an investigation;
2 observe appropriately and accurately;
3 make appropriate measurements.

Preparation

The children will need the items listed on page 11 of *Junior Pupils' Book 4*. Dry-cleaning covers can be saved from clothes that have been cleaned. They usually get holes in them so if you can scrounge a few new covers from a local dry cleaners it will be better. It is essential that all holes are repaired but take care to use the minimum of glue or sellotape since these will increase the weight of the balloon.

Teaching points

General points

The children will discover that a bag full of hot air will rise and take off in dramatic fashion. Let the children talk about why this happens without imposing a 'correct' explanation (see page 16). It is quite likely that the children will explain the rise by postulating that there is heat mixed up with the air in the bag and heat rises. If they hold this view, you can suggest that there may be other explanations and if you feel it is appropriate you can discuss ideas with them; the principal outcome should be the realisation that a bag full of hot air does rise.

Specific points

The effect is not very great – hence the suggestion that giant balloons should be used so that the change in size of the balloon with change in temperature should be observed and measured easily. The children are left to decide how to measure the balloon. They will probably decide to measure round it with a piece of string or to measure its diameter. They should be able to detect that the balloon becomes bigger when it is warmed up and smaller when it is cooled down.

In section 2, the warm balloon should respond more easily to being patted upwards than the cold one.

For section 3 it is important to make sure:
a) there are no holes in the bag,
b) the balloon is as light as possible,
c) launch conditions are calm and cool.
The hoop can be made of very fine but stiff wire or very thin basket cane. The minimum of sellotape or glue should be used in attaching the hoop to the cover.

Test flights can be done in the school hall if the ceiling is high enough. **Remember** that the hall will be warm and it may be difficult to get the temperature difference between the air in the balloon and the surrounding air which is necessary for lift-off.

Activity 4   A lot of hot air

Why do hot-air balloons go up whilst parachutes come down? See if you can find out.

You need: three giant round balloons; a dry cleaning cover with no holes in it; some thin wire or basket cane; sellotape; scissors; a hairdryer

1 Blow up a balloon and measure it. Leave it in a freezer for an hour or so. Measure it again. Put in on a radiator and let it get hot. Measure it. Is it the same or is it not? Why?

Tell your teacher what you think.

How shall we measure it?

We had better decide before we get it out.

2 Take two round balloons and blow them up to the same size. Put one on a radiator and one in the freezer. After a time, take them out and pat them into the air. Do they behave in the same way or not? Why?

3 Make a hot-air balloon, as Anna and Bimla have done. Use the hairdryer on 'hot' to put hot air into it. Let it go when it begins to pull. What happens? Why?

The sellotape is holding the hoop to the bottom of the bag.

I must not touch the plastic. It might melt.

11

It is suggested that a hairdryer is used to heat the air which is put into the balloon. This is a safe arrangement. However, some hairdryers do not blow very hot – you may need to do a little experimenting. Two hairdryers work better than one. Care has to be taken not to melt the plastic cover!

Two or three children need to work together to hold the balloon and fill it with hot air. It is essential to be patient and not to let go of the bag until it is well rounded and tugging to get away. The eventual flight never fails to delight.

If you decide to fly your balloon outdoors you must remember that
a) you must be at least 3 miles from the nearest airport,
b) your balloon must not go higher than 60 metres,
c) you must never fly near power lines.

Note A paint stripper will provide much hotter air but its use requires the most stringent safety precautions. It should only be used by an adult.

Further activity

A more sophisticated (and decorative) balloon can be made from tissue paper. You first need to cut a template from card. The size depends on how big you want your balloon to be. Up to 3 metres long is quite possible but to make large balloons you need to piece sheets of tissue paper together.

You need 12 sheets of tissue paper at least as long as your template and a little more than twice as wide. The sheets are folded lengthways and the straight edge of the template placed on the fold. Cut round the curved edge.

Keep the folded sheets in a pile and glue the curved edges together. Start with the second edge and glue this to the third, then the fourth to the fifth, the sixth to the seventh, and so on. Finally, the top piece of tissue paper and the bottom piece are opened out and the last edge is glued to the first edge.

A hoop of fine wire or cane is then glued to the bottom edge to form the neck of the balloon.

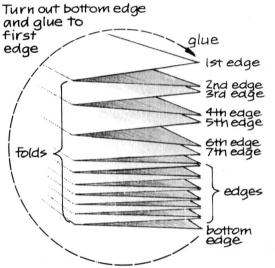

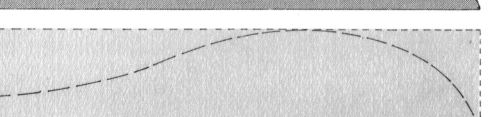

Making and doing activity

The problem for the children is:
'Can you make a hovercraft?'

You need:
junk; polystyrene tiles; larger pieces of polystyrene; straws; wire; balloons; rubber bands; pieces of wood; electric motors; propellers; hairdryer; glue; sellotape; thin plastic sheet; fine cloth; card; tools.

1 The problem	To make a hovercraft.
2 Exploring the problem	What is a hovercraft? What does a hovercraft do? What ways are there of lifting something up with a cushion of air? How can the supply of air be

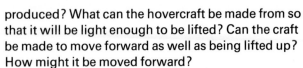

produced? What can the hovercraft be made from so that it will be light enough to be lifted? Can the craft be made to move forward as well as being lifted up? How might it be moved forward?

3 Ideas for solving the problem

Polystyrene is a very light material – or card might be used. What can be used for a skirt? (For example: thin plastic, paper, cloth, card) What about the air? Do you blow through a hole in the top of the craft, blow through a straw, use a hairdryer to do the blowing, or use a balloon full of air? Could air be sucked under the craft by using a propeller driven by a rubber band or an electric motor?

How can the craft be driven forward? Can it be driven like a plane? The children have tackled this problem (see Topic 3.6 'Flying high').

4 Making

Here are some ideas which might be similar to the ones produced by the children. The problems they are likely to enounter depend on their ambitions and the sophistication of what they are attempting to do.

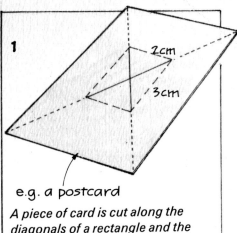

1

2cm

3cm

e.g. a postcard

A piece of card is cut along the diagonals of a rectangle and the quarters are folded up.

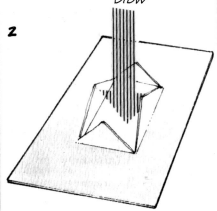

2

blow

If you blow into the space created, the card will hover.

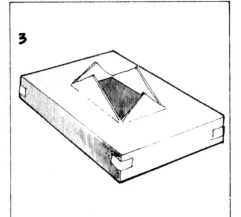

3

The card can be folded to form a skirt – or the skirt can be made of plastic sheet.

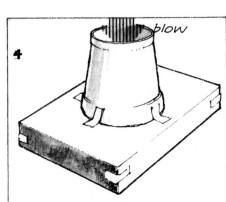

4

blow

The hole can be refined by using a yoghurt carton to form an inlet. Or you may find a moulded piece of polystyrene that fits over the hole.

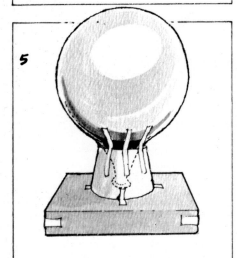

5

You can use a hairdryer to blow the air – or you can use a balloon.

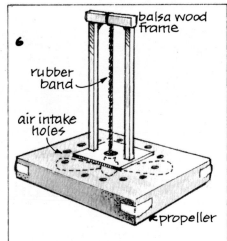

6

balsa wood frame

rubber band

air intake holes

propeller

You can drive the propeller by rubber-band power.

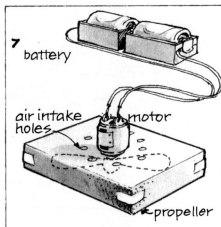

7

battery

air intake holes

motor

propeller

You can use an electric motor to drive a propeller which will suck in air.

5 Evaluating

Does the craft hover? Can it be driven forward? What happens to forward motion when the air cushion stops working? What would happen if it were a real hovercraft? Have any of the children travelled in a hovercraft? What was it like? Was it a smooth journey? Did it feel as if they were riding on an air cushion?

Paul's party

The story

(*Junior Pupils' Book 4* page 12)
Paul is having a party. He and his mother and Afzal are
preparing the food.

Science

People and their jobs and occupations

The work of a food
scientist is discussed.
(*Teachers' Book*
page 24)

Concepts

Pupils will explore some aspects of these concepts:
12.1 Change may be reversible or irreversible.
13.4 Some substances are soluble in water and some
are not.

Making and doing activity

The problem for the
children is:
'Can you design a set
of disposable cups,
dishes and plates for
Paul's party? Design
and make a box to hold
something for the
children to take home
from the party. Can you
make the box from a
single piece of folded
card?'

Skills

Pupils will develop their scientific skills by:

Activity 1—Jelly wobble   *TB* p26
Investigating the ratio of gelatine to liquid   *PB4* p13
which is required to make a 'good' jelly

Activity 2—Hunt the label   *TB* p27
Using a key to identify a number of white   *PB4* p14
powders

Activity 3—Salad dressing   *TB* p28
Investigating what happens when oil and   *PB4* p15
vinegar and other ingredients are shaken together

The story

Paul is having a party. He and his mother and Afzal are preparing the food. The two boys are engaged in all the tasks that are involved. This could give rise to a useful discussion about what the children (and boys, in particular) do to help in the house and in the kitchen. Are the children able to cook a meal? (Are they allowed to cook?) Many children of this age are quite capable of cooking a simple meal. The idea of the boys doing the cooking in the story might help to dispel the idea that it is the girls who help with the cooking and the boys who help in the garden or with the car. Both boys and girls are usually enthusiastic cooks if they are given the opportunity.

You could also discuss what the children like to eat at parties. Do they like sweet things or savoury food? What are the party favourites? When do people have parties? You could encourage the children to explore the variety of occasions on which different ethnic and cultural groups have parties. Do they eat traditional dishes on some of these occasions or do they just eat special 'party' food?

A wider discussion can encompass the extent to which processed and manufactured foods form part of the children's diets. This discussion will form a useful backcloth to consideration of the work of the food scientist.

People and their jobs and occupations

Prepared, processed and manufactured food forms a large proportion of the food which is sold. People are willing to pay for their food to be available in an easy-to-cook form. They welcome invented foods which add to the variety of what is available and they look to modern methods of preserving food to give them a wide variety of vegetables and fruits all the year round rather than only at the time of year when the fruits and vegetables are harvested.

The food industry employs many food scientists whose role it is to monitor scientifically the processing of foods, the preservation of it and to develop new products. The children will be able to think of many examples of food which owe much to the food scientist e.g. potato crisps and related products, 'instant' foods of all sorts, breakfast cereals etc. Preservation by dehydrating, canning or freezing must be carefully controlled so that the food is selected when it is in prime condition and then treated so that it reaches the eater in equally good condition. Not only must it taste good, it must look good and it must be free from any harmful contamination, particularly bacteria which will make the food deteriorate and cause illness (and even death).

Food scientists have produced many chemicals (additives) which are used to flavour, colour and preserve foods. Although many of these are not really necessary, the consumer is likely to react unfavourably to such things as pale greeny-yellow peas and dirty pink strawberries emerging from a tin. Yet these are the natural colour of such items when they are canned. Addition of a small amount of colouring produces the appetising green or strawberry colour which is expected. There is, however, general agreement that the use of food additives and colourings should be monitored carefully and the possibility of dispensing with all those that are not essential to the safe-keeping of food should be considered.

In talking about the work of the food scientist you might like to emphasise these points:

5 The work of some people helps us indirectly – they work behind the scenes.
10 People may need special knowledge, expertise and skills in their work and hobbies.
11 People have to acquire the special knowledge, expertise and skills which they need.

16 People use scientific information in their jobs, occupations and hobbies.
17 People need to use a scientific viewpoint in their jobs, occupations and hobbies.

Further activities

1 The children could look at the labels on cans and packets of food and see what is listed. What sort of colourings, flavourings and other additives are listed? For further information see page 159.
2 You could make a collection of labels from 'invented' foods. What is in them?
3 What would be available in the shops to eat in the winter if there were no preserved foodstuffs?
4 A wider study could let the children find out where our food comes from, how it reaches us, how far it has to travel.
5 You could have a party in the style of a particular culture. Mothers and fathers could be involved to provide the cooking expertise. The party could be the centre piece of a wider study of some aspects of the culture.

Science

Background notes

Gelatine

This is made by cooking animal bones and treating the gelatine which is extracted. It is commonly used in cooking for making jellies – both sweet and savoury. It has the property of being able to dissolve in hot water to form a solution which, on cooling, will set to a jelly. The stiffness of the jelly depends on the ratio of gelatine to water and on the temperature. If a jelly is left to stand it will gradually lose water and become increasingly stiff.

Oil–water emulsions

Oil is lighter than water i.e. a given volume of oil will weigh less than the same volume of water. Oil and other fats float on top of water or vinegar or similar solutions. If the oil and water are shaken together a thick mixture – an emulsion – is formed. In an oil–water emulsion either the oil or the water forms very tiny droplets which are suspended in the other component. The emulsion is either oil in water or water in oil. Emulsions tend to separate out into the component parts and agents called emulsifiers are added to keep the emulsion stable. Natural emulsions contain stabilisers which are a natural component. The best known oil/fat–water emulsions are milk, cream, butter, margarine, mayonnaise, salad dressings and salad cream.

Milk, cream, butter and margarine are stabilised by a substance called caseinogen which is found in milk, although an artificial stabiliser (additive) may be used in margarine. Mayonnaise and salad cream are stabilised by a substance called lecithin which is found in egg yolk. Mustard is also a stabiliser.

Whether the emulsion is oil in water or water in oil depends to some extent on the proportions of oil and water which are present. The one which is present in the smallest proportion tends to form the drops. Milk, cream, mayonnaise and salad cream are oil in water (or vinegar) emulsions. Butter and margarine are water in fat/oil emulsions. In Activity 3, by careful observation, the children should be able to decide whether they have an emulsion which is drops of oil in water or drops of water in oil since the cookery colouring will colour the vinegar but not the oil. In the 'Further activities' it is suggested that the children make butter – a process which involves the change from an oil in water emulsion to a water in oil emulsion. The children will be able to observe how a large amount of water is eliminated in the process.

If butter or margarine is heated to melting point, the water and oil separate and on cooling remain separated. Cooking fat and lard are not emulsions. They are almost completely fat with no water component.

Activity 1—Jelly wobble

Objectives
At the end of this activity the children should be better able to:
1 choose in advance what will be appropriate observations;
2 plan an investigation paying due regard to controlling variables which are identified as relevant;
3 present an agreed oral account of their findings.

Preparation
The pupils will need the items listed on page 13 of *Junior Pupils' Book 4.* It is suggested that mugs are used to contain the jelly mixtures since these are more stable than the possible alternative of yoghurt cartons. A liquid measure is required to measure 10 ml and 90 ml. The plastic box should hold the four mugs so that they will not fall over and any spillage will be contained within the box. You will need an electric kettle to supply hot water for dissolving the gelatine.

You will probably find that gelatine is sold in a carton containing packets of granulated gelatine each of which is sufficient for one pint of jelly (about 500 ml). You will need to work out how much gelatine will be needed for 100 ml – for normal strength jelly. Then work out how much will be needed for half strength, double strength and quadruple strength. These are the quantities which the children should be provided with for their investigation.

In addition to the items in the *Pupils' Book* you will need to have to hand materials which the children may require to make a jelly stiffness tester e.g. needles, skewers, weights, Blu-Tack, plasticine, balance scales and weights, test tubes (if you have them).

Teaching points

General points
The children are investigating how much gelatine is needed to produce a jelly of the 'right' degree of stiffness. This is very much a food science problem requiring a scientific approach to a problem which has not an explicit 'right' answer.

The children will have to find a way of measuring jelly stiffness which can be repeated accurately and to agree on what degree of stiffness is generally acceptable to a group of people.

Specific points
In section 1 the children will need four portions of gelatine as calculated. (See 'Preparation'.)

Obviously if you are using very hot water you will need to take great care to make the working conditions safe. Instruct the children to put the blackcurrant cordial in the mugs and to put the mugs in the plastic box. The box should then be put well on to a table and the children should work standing up. (This means that hot liquid cannot fall on to knees and it is easy to get out of the way!) You should measure out the required quantity of hot water (90 ml for each mug) – it does not need to be boiling – and pour it into the mugs for the children. They can sprinkle the gelatine carefully into the mugs and stir the mixtures gently. They should be told not to lean on the tables – again so that spillage can do no harm. As you insist on the safety precautions being taken, you should discuss with the children the purpose of each safety point.

The children will have to consider the variables if they are to make a fair comparison of 'setting time' and they will also have to devise a means of deciding what state constitutes 'set'. The jelly stiffness tester may be unique to each group. The children will have to find a means of standardising their results. One group of children used a device like this.

Activity 1 Jelly wobble

Paul could not read what it said on the gelatine packet. He had to find out how much gelatine was needed to make the special blackcurrant jelly. See if you can find out how to make a good jelly.

You need: a packet of gelatine; four mugs; a measure; a thermometer; blackcurrant cordial; a 5 ml measuring spoon; a plastic box

1 Put 10 ml of blackcurrant cordial into each of your four mugs. Measure out four portions of gelatine. Ask your teacher how much to use.

"I'll measure out the blackcurrant."
"I'll measure the gelatine."

2 Ask your teacher to add 90 ml of hot water to each of your mugs when they are standing in the plastic box. Sprinkle a portion of gelatine into each mug. Stir in the gelatine very carefully until it all dissolves.

"The box will stop us spilling the jelly."
"You have to stir it well."

3 Put your box of jellies to set. Find out how long it takes them to set. Can you find a way to measure how stiff the jellies are? Which mixture gives a jelly of the right stiffness?

Do you and your friends agree about this?

4 Can you think of a way to make a jelly set more quickly? How? Test your ideas.

13

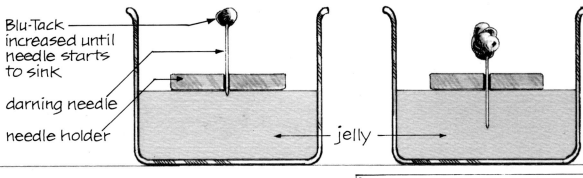

Blu-Tack increased until needle starts to sink

darning needle

needle holder

jelly

The children found what weight of Blu-Tack caused the needle to start sinking into the jelly.

For section 4, a jelly will set more quickly at lower temperatures and with a larger proportion of gelatine.

Further activities

1 Make other kinds of jellies e.g. using orange juice or apple juice. Do they need the same amount of gelatine? Do they set to the same stiffness (under the same conditions) as the blackcurrant jelly?
2 The children can try making different makes of jellies and assess their qualities. Is there a best buy?
3 Fresh pineapple will stop a jelly from setting. It contains a substance which interferes with the action of the gelatine. The children could discover this for themselves and try to decide why.

Activity 2—Hunt the label

Objectives

At the end of this activity the children should be better able to:
1 observe in detail and appropriately;
2 follow a key and use it to identify a number of substances;
3 make an accurate record of their findings.

Preparation

The children will need a box containing packets or jars of the following: baking powder; washing powder (without blue bits); cornflour; bicarbonate of soda; salt; citric acid; icing sugar. These items should be labelled A–F so that you know what is in them. Also in the box should be labels bearing the names of the items. The children will also need small screw-topped jars for testing the powders, some vinegar and a teaspoon.

Teaching points

General points
The children are using a key to identify a set of white powders. They will need to work methodically.

Specific points
There should be no particular problems other than those involved in methodical working.

Further activities

1 Children can be introduced to the computer program SEEK. See page 158.
2 The children could try to devise a key for a collection of powders: e.g. plaster of Paris; talcum powder; scourer; instant coffee; custard powder; instant whipped dessert etc.
3 The children could use other simple keys to identify plants, trees, birds etc.

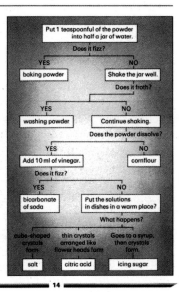

Activity 2   Hunt the label

Paul found a box of things which had lost their labels. His mother showed him how to find out what the things were so that they could put the labels back. She gave him a key to use. You can use the key as well.

You need: a box of things like Paul found in the cupboard; some jars with screw tops; vinegar

1 This is the key.

2 Use the key to test each of the powders and put the labels back. Show your teacher what you have done.

Put 1 teaspoonful of the powder into half a jar of water.

Does it fizz?

YES — baking powder

NO — Shake the jar well.

Does it froth?

YES — washing powder

NO — Continue shaking.

Does the powder dissolve?

YES — Add 10 ml of vinegar.

NO — cornflour

Does it fizz?

YES — bicarbonate of soda

NO — Put the solutions in dishes in a warm place?

What happens?

cube-shaped crystals form — salt

thin crystals arranged like flower heads form — citric acid

Goes to a syrup, then crystals form. — icing sugar

14

Activity 3 — Salad dressing

Objectives
At the end of this activity the children should be better able to:
1 observe accurately and in detail;
2 plan and carry out an investigation;
3 produce an agreed written report of their findings.

Preparation
The children will need the items listed on page 15 of *Junior Pupils' Book 4.*

Teaching points

General points
The children are finding out what happens when oil and vinegar or oil and water are mixed together. They will discover that oil floats on top of the water layer and that when the mixture is shaken an emulsion is formed which is more or less stable.

By careful observation, using magnifying glasses or a microscope, the children should be able to decide whether the emulsion formed is oil in water or water in oil.

Specific points
You will have to discuss with the children what they see happening. Ask them if they can tell whether the oil is forming tiny droplets in the vinegar or whether the vinegar is forming tiny droplets in the oil. You must make sure that the children observe that the cookery colouring only colours the vinegar.

Does it make any difference to the final result if you start by adding vinegar to oil or oil to vinegar?

In section 3, the children should be able to discover that both egg yolk and mustard make the emulsion more stable.

You could continue with making mayonnaise (see 'Further activities').

Further activities
1 Make mayonnaise or salad cream. Most general cookery books will contain a recipe. What is the significance of the various steps in producing a stable emulsion? *(Proportions of oil and vinegar are important at all stages as is the proportion of egg yolk which is acting as an emulsifier and stabilising the emulsion.)*
2 Make butter. Collect the cream off two or three bottles of milk and put it into a screw-topped jar. Shake the jar and watch very carefully what happens. *(Cream is an oil-in-water emulsion, butter is a water-in-oil emulsion. During butter making the emulsion is 'inverted' and much of the water is excluded from the butter.)* The butter pat produced will need to be worked to get rid of the last of the superfluous liquid and then salted to taste if it is to be eaten.
3 What happens if washing-up liquid is added to an oil and water emulsion and shaken? Start with one teaspoonful of oil in half a jar of water and add the washing-up liquid a drop at a time. Washing-up liquid is an emulsifier and makes the oil form a stable emulsion in the water. Washing-up liquid with hot water will make the grease or fat leave dirty plates and form a stable emulsion in the water, leaving the plates clean.
4 What happens if the water/vinegar and oil are warm when they are shaken together?
5 Weigh equal volumes of water and oil. Is oil lighter than water? Weigh equal volumes of water and vinegar. Can any difference be detected?
6 Try dissolving substances in oil. What dissolves? *(In fact, very few things dissolve in oil – try butter and margarine; try cooking bacon and tomatoes and looking at the colour of the fat in the pan; look at the colour of the fat when curry is cooked; look at the colour of the fat when green peppers are gently cooked in it.)*

Activity 3 Salad dressing

Afzal wondered why the oil floated on the vinegar when he was making salad dressing. Paul said it doesn't if you shake it. See what you can find out about oil and vinegar.

You need: cooking oil; vinegar; salt; mustard; egg yolk; kitchen towel; cookery colouring; small screw-topped jars; teaspoons; tablespoons; a magnifying glass

1 Put one tablespoonful of vinegar into one of the jars, with a touch of cookery colouring. Add half a teaspoonful of cooking oil. What happens? Shake the jar. What happens now? Leave it to stand. What happens?
Add oil half a teaspoonful at a time until the volumes of oil and vinegar are the same. Shake and watch after each addition.

I wonder if vinegar is heavier than oil.

How can we find out?

2 Now start with one tablespoon of cooking oil and add vinegar half a teaspoonful at a time. Put in a little cookery colouring.
Shake and watch after each addition.

3 Into each of three jars put one tablespoonful of oil and one tablespoonful of vinegar. To one jar add a pinch of salt, to another add a pinch of mustard and to the other a little egg yolk. Shake each jar and leave to stand. What happens?
Talk to your teacher about what you have observed.

15

Making and doing activity

The problem for the children is:
    'Can you design a set of disposable cups, dishes and plates for Paul's party? Design and make a box to hold something for the children to take home from the party. Can you make the box from a single piece of folded card?'

You need:
paper; newspaper; paints; brushes; crayons; felt tip pens; thin and thick card; ruler; compasses; glue; scissors.

1 The problem	To design a set of disposable cups, dishes and plates; to design and make a box from a single piece of folded card.
2 Exploring the problem	Can the children draw up a 'specification' for the cup, dish and plate e.g. rigid? waterproof? lightweight? resistant to hot food? size? The children will have to make a number of decisions about the qualities they think the items should have. What material should be used? plastic? paper? waxed paper? pottery? metal foil? How can the material be decorated? Given that the children decide that a colourful design on paper or plastic is indicated, you could encourage them to decide where the design should be. If they choose to make a border round the plates or dishes, you could help them to solve the geometrical problems which arise. The major problem is to produce the box. The box could be a simple cuboid shape or you could encourage the children to explore their experience of more decorative and interesting packages (often seen in sweet shops and at festive seasons).
3 Ideas for solving the problem	The children may produce a range of ideas. Perhaps some of them would like to work on things for a 'theme' party e.g. a space party or a pirates' party or a pop stars' party. They could design the tableware to fit the theme and make an appropriate box. They might be able to make a space capsule or a pirate ship or treasure chest. Making the item from a single piece of folded card is quite a difficult challenge and you might like to collect examples to show the children. You could also show them examples of picnicware which is available and very attractive. (If the children are interested and you have examples, they could also look at disposable cutlery and consider the 'specifications' for this.)

4 Making	Designing the decoration for cups, dishes and plates will require drawing and measuring skills. If you want the children to have experience of using compasses and measuring you might stipulate that they produce a border pattern. How do they cope with the difference in scale between plate and cup?
	    Making the box will require precise measuring skills and probably the making of a rough prototype before the finished version can be produced. Taking bought examples to pieces will greatly help the children to understand how different effects can be produced. The children may need to be reminded that they must make flaps so that the box can be glued together.
	    Some ideas are shown on page 30.

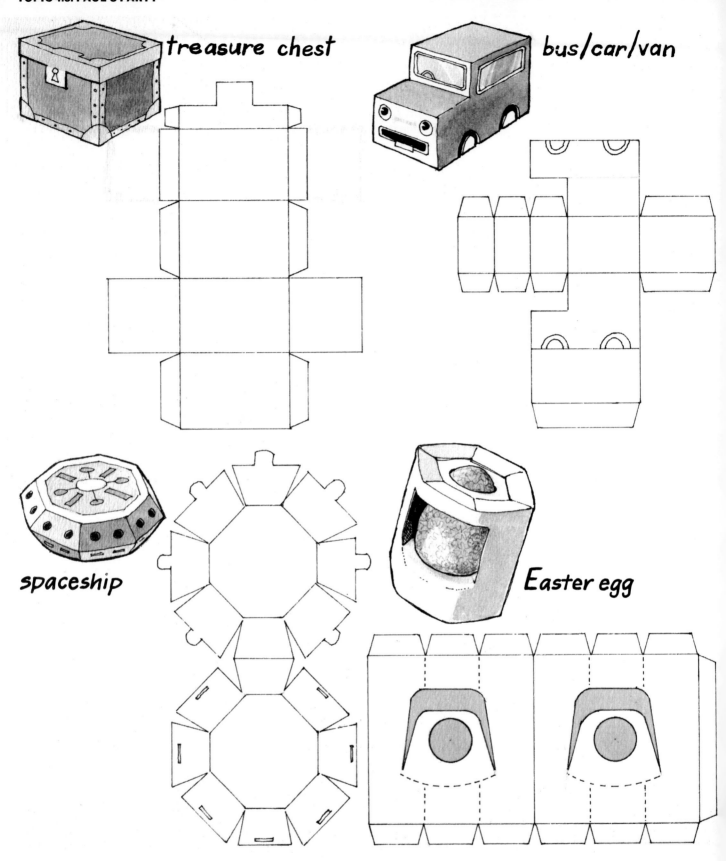

treasure chest

bus/car/van

spaceship

Easter egg

5 Evaluating

You could hold an exhibition of tableware. Let the children vote for their favourite.

If you have collected a range of commercially produced boxes, you could have a display of these alongside those of the children. (If you inspect the commercial versions carefully, you may find that they are marked with a patent number. What does this mean? Why is it there?)

Do the children's boxes look good? Are they carefully made? Is the decoration imaginative? Do the children have more ideas they would like to try?

Built to last

The story

(*Junior Pupils' Book 4* page 16)
Rosa and Tan Hing pay a visit to a nearby building site and talk to a bricklayer and his mate. On the way home they look at a brick railway arch and the concrete piers which are being constructed for a new building.

Science

People and their jobs and occupations

The trades involved in building a house are considered.
(*Teachers' Book* page 32)

Concepts

Pupils will explore some aspects of these concepts:
9.1 Forces are needed to change the shape of an object.
9.2 The strength of an object or structure depends on its shape and on the material from which it is made.
12.1 Change may be reversible or irreversible.
13.1 Different materials have different properties.
13.2 Materials are used for purposes for which their properties make them appropriate (paper, wood, metals, plastics, wool, cotton, synthetic fibres, glass, brick, stone, rubber).

Making and doing activity

The problem for the children is:
'Build the tallest tower you can from newspaper.'
(*Teachers' Book* page 41)

Skills

Pupils will develop their scientific skills by:

Activity 1—Stick 'em up   *TB* p34
Investigating the strength of mortar when the *PB4* p17 proportions of sand and cement are varied

Activity 2—Damp course   *TB* p36
Investigating the water absorbency of some *PB4* p18 building materials; investigating ways of preventing water being absorbed

Activity 3—Arches   *TB* p37
Investigating how the strength of an arch *PB4* p19 depends on its shape

Activity 4—One or a bunch?   *TB* p39
Investigating how the strength of a material *PB4* p20 depends on its shape

The story

Tan Hing and Rosa visit a building site and their questions open up a variety of discussions about traditional and modern methods of building. What determines which materials are used for building? Why is brick used so widely? How are bricks made? Discussion should help children to realise that for domestic building availability of materials is all important. Although brick may be used in some areas, there will also be places where stone is (or was) the usual building material. What is different about brick and stone? *(Stone is a natural material and the building blocks have to be cut to size and shape; whereas brick, although of natural origin, can be moulded to the desired shape and size – a much cheaper procedure.)*

The brick railway arch will be familiar to many children. It shows how in the past brick was used for very strong, large scale construction; whereas nowadays concrete is more usual for large structures. The round arch is the commonest kind of arch but many children will have visited cathedrals and churches where arches of different shapes are used. In all these cases, the arch is used not only because it looks pleasant but also because it is immensely strong and can support a great weight.

Many modern buildings are supported by an internal structure. The exterior is largely a cosmetic cladding providing the possibility of large windows and a light and airy interior as opposed to the rather dark and heavy interiors of older buildings which rely on their outside walls for strength. Of course, the availability of large sheets of glass has also played an important role in transforming the appearance of buildings. There is wide scope for discussion and development.

People and their jobs and occupations

Rosa and Tan Hing talk to the bricklayer and his mate. What does each of them do? What skills does the bricklayer need to have? It would be most informative to take the children to a building site and let them see for themselves how a bricklayer works quickly and carefully. How does the bricklayer make sure that the walls are vertical? How does the bricklayer make sure that the layers of brick are horizontal? How does the mate know how to mix the cement and sand in the correct proportions?

How does the bricklayer learn the job? You could talk to the children about the apprenticeship system and explain how, as they learn the job, apprentices also have to study so that they understand about the materials they are using and about the strength of the structures they are building.

Can the children think of all the other trades which are involved in house building – carpenters, joiners, plasterers, tilers, plumbers, electricians and so on? All of them need to know about the materials they are using and how to work those materials safely and effectively. They all use science in their jobs.

Particular points you might like to emphasise include:

3 Different people do different jobs and follow different occupations.
10 People may need special knowledge, expertise and skills in their work and hobbies.
11 People have to acquire the special knowledge, expertise and skills which they need.
16 People use scientific information in their jobs, occupations and hobbies.

Further activities

1 It is likely that there will be a parent involved in the building industry. Perhaps you could persuade the parent to come into school to talk to

the children. Alternatively, two or three children could interview the parent and produce a tape recording.

2 Visit a building site to find answers to some of the questions which arise from the story and which will arise from the activities.

3 Try to build a wall and experience the problems first hand.

Science

Background notes

Cement

This is made by heating lime and clay strongly and grinding then produces the fine powder. Cement forms a rock-like material when it is mixed with water and allowed to set. This is a chemical change and it is an irreversible change. You can't get the cement powder and water back.

cement powder $\xrightarrow{\text{water}}$ **hard cement**

Bricks

These are made by firing clay at a very high temperature. Again a chemical change takes place. You cannot get the clay back once it has been fired.

clay $\xrightarrow{\text{heat}}$ **brick**

Bricks are strong and cheap but they are porous – water soaks into them and ground water can rise through them by capillary action (see page 37). Water is prevented from rising from the ground through a brick wall by introducing a damp course – a layer of material which will not allow moisture to pass e.g. bitumen or some form of plastic. Water penetration from outside is prevented by building houses with a double cavity wall so that the inside wall is not in contact with the weather or the ground.

Structures

In earlier Topics some consideration has been given to structures. (See Topic 2.5 'Circus time'.) Particular attention has been focused on frame-type structures in which frame members are subjected to stress either as a tension or a compression. In this Topic we are looking at arches and columns.

Early building projects did not feature arches. If the Greeks or Egyptians wanted to create an opening on a vast scale they used pillars and enormously heavy stone slabs across the top of the pillars. It was only later that the various forms of arch were introduced.

Arches are strong because the forces which press down on them cause the arch to be compressed. This compression makes the arch stay more firmly together. Provided the materials from which it is made will withstand compression, as will stone and brick, the arch is a very strong structure.

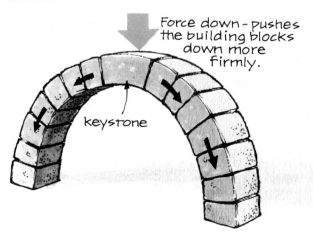

Force down – pushes the building blocks down more firmly.

keystone

The slab placed across the supporting columns is weak because the forces pressing down on it produce a tension in the material. They are, in effect, trying to stretch the material. Under this sort of force most building materials are weak.

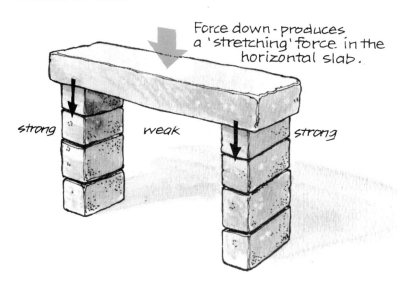

Force down - produces a 'stretching' force in the horizontal slab.

strong   weak   strong

Activity 1—Stick 'em up

Objectives
At the end of this activity the children should be better able to:
1 look for patterns in their results;
2 plan and carry out an investigation paying particular regard to safe working;
3 communicate for a specific purpose.

Preparation
The children will need the items listed on page 17 of *Junior Pupils' Book 4*. Cement powder should be stored in sealed containers as it absorbs moisture and sets if left open to the air. The sand can be low-grade building sand. It is envisaged that the children will test the blocks by dropping a weight on them under controlled conditions. The cardboard tube and cardboard box are to keep the weight safely away from feet etc. It is possible that the children will think of other ways of testing the blocks so that you may wish to bear this in mind. The blocks are best made in small margarine tubs but the 'drop' tube must be wide enough to enclose the block – make one from card, if necessary.

Teaching points

General points
The children are trying to find out how to mix mortar 'right'. They should realise quickly that mortar needs to be of a stiffish consistency if it is to be slapped from trowel to bricks and that it should set to a strong, rock-like state if the bricks are to stay together and the building is to stay up and last. They should appreciate that the setting of cement powder when it is mixed with water is a chemical change – a new substance is produced – and the change is irreversible. Sand is not involved in the chemical change. Can the children suggest what its function is?

Specific points
The children will have to decide what a 'spoonful' is. They should manage without making too much mess but cement powder does fly about and care is needed in handling it. The children should avoid getting it on their hands as it soon makes hands rough. Finally, the mixtures will need to be firmed down to expel air.

There are a number of variables which the children will need to consider and decide whether they are relevant e.g. amount of stirring, amount of time spent firming down the mixture etc.

Drying time will depend on how much water has been used. Under normal classroom conditions three to four days should be enough.

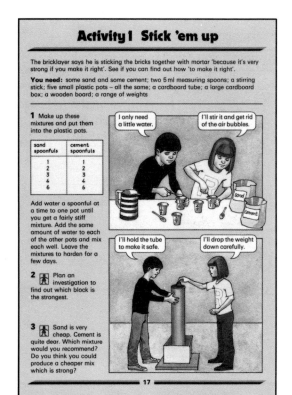

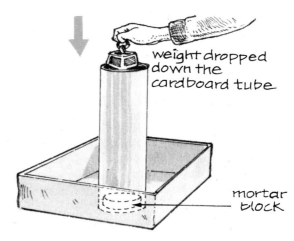

In section 2, the cardboard tube and the cardboard box are required if the children test the mortar blocks by dropping a weight on them. The cardboard box should be put on the floor and the weight dropped down the cardboard tube which is placed above the block. There are a number of ways of testing a block. A variables table for the investigation shows this.

variable	to be investigated	to be changed	to be controlled
mortar block			
strength			
weight			
drop height			
number of hits			

A block can be tested by either altering the weight and keeping the drop height the same or by keeping the weight the same and altering the drop height. A decision has to be made as to how 'strength' is defined. The children will probably decide that they will test until the block breaks. Once the children have decided on a method they must test each block in the same way.

If they decide to alter the weight, do they start with a smallish weight and gradually increase the weight? Another variation is to keep both height and weight the same and count how many times the block has to be hit before it breaks.

Keep a close eye on the children as they are working – to maintain safe practice and make sure that they are positively planning for safety.

If sand is mixed with water it simply becomes wet sand and when it is dry it will be dry sand. There is no chemical change. The change from dry sand to wet sand is reversible. What does sand do in mortar? What do the children think? Encourage them to test their ideas, if it is possible.

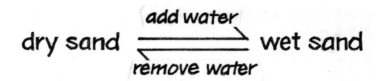

Mortar is usually made by mixing three or four parts of sand to one of cement. This takes advantage of the cheapness of sand and gives a mix of satisfactory strength. None of the mixes which the children use is of these proportions. From their results they may recognise that there are a range of mixtures which they have not tested. Can they recognise a pattern in their results and use it to suggest which mixes might be worthy of investigation, bearing in mind both strength and cost? They could investigate the mixes which they suggest.

Further activities

1 Investigate the strengths of mixtures of sand and cement in other proportions.
2 What is the effect of altering the amount of water used in mixing?
3 Some of the mortar mixes could be tested out with bricks. This is a possible method. It needs very careful supervision since a swinging weight is used.

4 The children could find out how cement is made and used. (See page 33).
5 What is concrete? The children could make samples of concrete using different proportions and cast small beams using a simple mould. The beams can be tested for strength by hanging a weight from the centre.

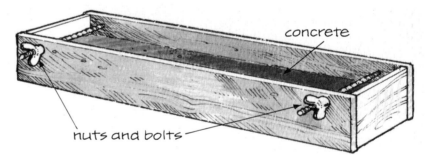

Activity 2—Damp course

Objectives

At the end of this activity the children should be better able to:
1 plan and carry out an investigation;
2 use known concepts in making suggestions;
3 prepare a communication for a specific audience.

Preparation

The children will need the items listed on page 18 of *Junior Pupils' Book 4*. They will also need a range of materials which they may suggest could be used as a damp course e.g. plastic sheet, roofing felt, aluminium foil, glazed tiles, slate etc.

Teaching points

General points

The children are investigating what happens when various building materials are left standing in water. Some of the materials – stone, slate, roofing tiles – only get wet up to the level of the water. Bricks become wet for a considerable distance above the water level. The children, from their previous experience, may be able to suggest that the water rises by capillary action. (See Topic 3.3 Activity 2.) Equally, they should be able to suggest from their previous experience materials which might stop water rising through the brick.

Specific points
The samples need only stand in a small depth of water. The rate at which water rises will vary from one brick to another. Do the children realise that if a brick wall was built on the ground, the moisture from the ground would rise up into the bricks? What would it be like living in a home with damp walls?

The story should show them where a damp course is placed and the children should be able to list the properties which material that is to be used for a damp course should have. They should be able to suggest suitable materials and test the effectiveness of these. They may decide to test them by placing them under bricks so that the bricks are not in the water. Is this a fair test? Are the materials strong enough to stand up to rough handling on a building site or to last the life of the building? Can the children carry out further tests or suggest how they would attempt to set up long term tests? (See 'Further activities'.)

Can the children 'invent' the cavity wall (if they do not know about it already)? Can they work out how two walls can be constructed so that there is no possibility of water passing from the outer to the inner wall and no way in which ground water can rise in either wall?

Further activities

1 The children could investigate how robust various possible damp course materials are.
   a) Bending, folding, creasing – how many times before wear or stress shows?
   b) How does the material stand up to pulling or stretching?
   c) Weight bearing – suspend a sheet by its four corners. How much weight can be put on the sheet?
   d) Abrasion – how many rubs with a sandpaper block before a hole appears?
   e) Resistance to sharp or pointed objects – drop a dart down tubes of different lengths.
2 The children can find out how bricks are manufactured.
3 They could research the history of brick making.
4 Small bricks can be made from clay if you have local deposits. They can be dried and used for building. Why are 'raw' bricks not useful in this country? *(The clay in 'raw' bricks is chemically the same as wet clay. As soon as the dried 'raw' bricks have water poured on them the clay absorbs the water and reverts to its pliable, sticky state.)* What sort of countries can make use of unfired bricks?

Activity 3—Arches

Objectives
At the end of this activity the children should be better able to:
1 make appropriate observations;
2 select in advance an appropriate method of recording;
3 look for patterns in their results;
4 make suggestions based on recognised patterns.

Preparation
The children will need the items listed on page 19 of *Junior Pupils' Book 4*. The strips of card should be about 20 cm × 8 cm. (230–280 gsm card is ideal since it is pliable.) The Lego blocks or wooden blocks are for building the supports for the bridge. A variety of weights will be needed to test the strength of the arches.

Activity 2   Damp course

Why are the builders putting a damp course in the wall? What is a damp course? Why did the bricklayers mate say 'You'd know if we forgot it'?

You need: four or five building bricks of different types; a breeze block; a piece of stone; roof tiles; a roof slate; a washing-up bowl

1 Stand your bricks and other building materials in water, like this. Have a look at them every day and watch what happens. Why do you think this happens?

We only need a little water.
We'll have to leave them to stand for a bit.

2 What do you think a damp course will do? What do you think would make a damp course?

Try out your ideas with your bricks.

We must make sure our damp course is above the water.
We must make it a fair test.

3 What happens on a rainy day to a brick wall which has a damp course?

The wall's getting very wet.
Where will the water go?

4 Write a letter to tell someone in a very dry country how house walls are built here and why they are built like that.

18

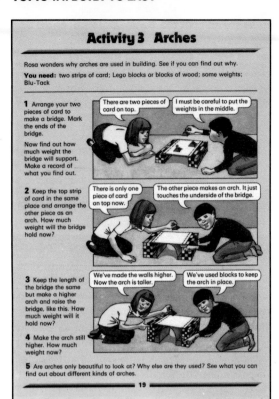

Teaching points

General points

The children should be able to appreciate from this activity how altering the shape of a piece of card can alter its strength greatly. They should be able to understand that the arch shape distributes the weight which is pressing on the top of it.

Specific points

The flat pieces of card will support very little weight. The children will have to decide at which point the bridge is no longer supporting a weight. They will probably choose the point of collapse, but they may choose a certain degree of sag. Whatever they decide, they must work consistently.

The arch will bear considerably more weight, although the children will have to take care not to overbalance the structure when they are putting weights at the centre point. (Blu-Tack may help here.)

Since the two pieces of card are the same length, the arch will need holding at its sides as it gets more curved. This is shown in the illustration in the *Pupils' Book.* The straight piece of card should always be in the same position relative to the supports so that the length is always the same. The height of the blocks at the sides of the arch would be kept the same although the width will be altered.

 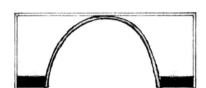 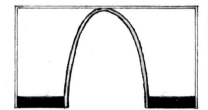

Do the children detect a pattern in their results? Can they suggest in advance what the effect will be of making the arch taller once they have tried two or three positions?

Further activities

1 What is the relative strength of a series of bridges like the ones below? From their experience what do the children suggest? Let them test their suggestions.

 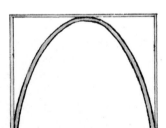  

The bridges have equal spans.

2 What is the relative strength of a series of bridges with equal heights? From their experience what do the children suggest? Let them test their suggestions.

The bridges are of equal height.

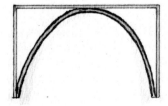 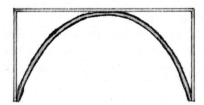 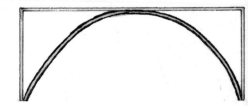

3 The children could make arches from clay, cut them into blocks, dry the blocks and then build the arches from the blocks. They can arrange a frame to hold the arches and test their strength. Can they plan the investigation so that the only variable is the shape of the arch? Which shape is the strongest?

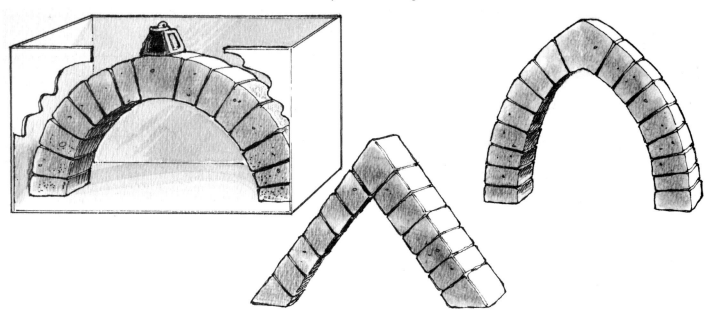

4 The children could look for arches in local buildings. What shape are they? What sort of forces will be acting on them?

Activity 4—One or a bunch?

Objectives
At the end of this activity the children should be better able to:
1 look for and recognise patterns in their findings;
2 make suggestions based on recognised patterns;
3 plan and carry out an investigation.

Preparation
The children will need the items listed on page 20 of *Junior Pupils' Book 4*. The rubber bands will help them to hold the tubes they are making in place whilst the glue is drying.

Teaching points

General points
The children are investigating how shape affects the strength of material. They make paper tubes of varying dimensions from a standard piece of paper and compare the strengths of the different forms produced from identical single sheets of paper. Rolling paper into cylinders of smaller diameter does increase its strength as a column.

The cylinders which the children make need to be glued in place carefully, otherwise it will be difficult to test them fairly.

Specific points
The children will need to think about how they are going to record their results before they start. Do they appreciate that using a single sheet of paper each time is controlling the variable 'amount of material'?

Do they begin to look for a pattern in their results? Can they describe the pattern? Can they use the pattern to suggest in advance what will happen?

Can they suggest what they think will be the strength of the different shapes of column in advance? Can they suggest what they think the pattern of their results will be? Do they make the columns carefully and test them all under the same conditions?

Activity 4 One or a bunch?

Is it better to have one large support or a number of smaller ones?

You need: some sheets of sugar paper; glue; scissors; weights; a board

1 Take two pieces of paper exactly the same size. Make a tube as fat as possible from one sheet. Use the other sheet to make two tubes of the same height as the fat one. Find out how much weight the fat one will hold up and how much the two smaller ones together will support.

I've put the weights on my big fat tube.

I've used the same amount of paper.

2 Using the same size sheets of paper, make three tubes – and then four tubes. How much weight do you think they will hold up? Test your suggestions. Do your results follow a pattern? What is it?

We'll try your two tubes now.

3 Try making tubes of different shapes. Are they as good as the round shapes? Do your results follow a pattern? Is the pattern the same for all the shapes?

I'm making different shapes.

So am I. I'll put these closer together.

4 Write a report of your investigation.

20

Further activities

1 Is the pattern of results the same if different kinds of paper are used?
2 Does it make any difference if the columns are made from the paper rolled or folded longways rather than across?

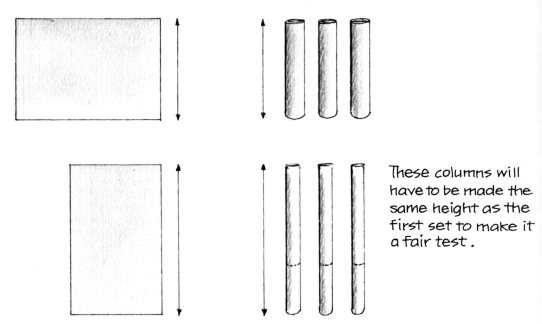

These columns will have to be made the same height as the first set to make it a fair test.

3 In the main activity the children have tested their columns under compression. What happens if they are placed horizontally and tested under tension?

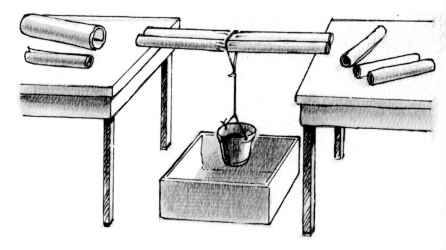

4 Make a series of tubes by rolling identical sheets of paper into tubes of varying diameters. Test the resulting single tubes by hanging weights at the centre point to find the strength. Is there a pattern? What is it? (This is a particularly interesting investigation.)

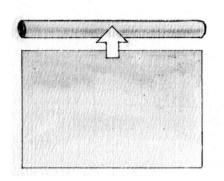
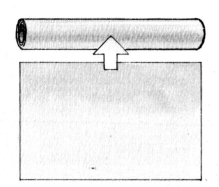
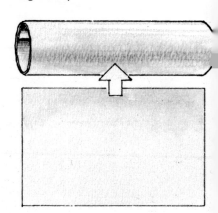

5 The children could look at local buildings and find where and how columns and beams are used to support buildings.

Making and doing activity

The problem for the children is:
'Build the tallest tower you can from newspaper.'

You need:
newspaper; glue; scissors.

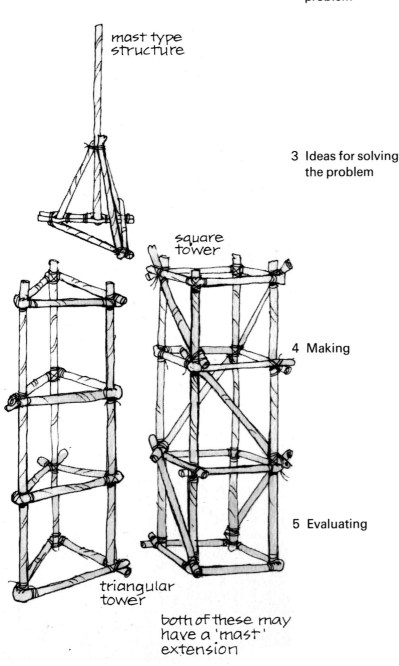

mast type structure

square tower

triangular tower

both of these may have a 'mast' extension

1 The problem	Build the tallest newspaper tower.
2 Exploring the problem	In this problem there is no restriction on the amount of newspaper which the children can use. By not allowing them to stand on chairs, tables or step ladders you can transform the problem into one requiring considerable ingenuity. The children will either have to build along the ground and then erect their towers or they will have to find means of 'jacking up' their towers and inserting new portions at the bottom of the tower. They will also have to find the means to stick their sections of newspaper using only glue.
3 Ideas for solving the problem	The children should be now be familiar with the properties of newspaper and what can be done with it. They will have to decide how to give it strength by altering its shape, e.g. by rolling or folding. Do they remember their previous experiences with strong triangles? Do they remember that the heavier the top of the tower becomes, the greater the pressure on the bottom of the tower? Do they remember that the tower will be more stable if its main weight is kept low i.e. its centre of gravity is low? Do they attempt to sketch out ideas on paper? Here are some ideas that they may produce.
4 Making	The children should be able to roll or fold the newspaper tightly and neatly – which they must do if they are to give it strength. They may want to find the means to make long tubes by overlapping sheets of paper. They may discover the possibility of using strips and other shapes of pieces of paper to secure and strengthen corners and joins, using a judicious amount of glue.

Undoubtedly the main problem will be to get the tower upright. You will have to decide whether it is permissible to wedge it up against the ceiling! Who has built the tallest tower? Is it the design which is particularly successful or is it careful construction which has been the most important factor? Would the children use a different design if they were trying again? Can they explain why some ideas worked better than others in terms of kind of structure, position of most of the weight etc.?

5 Evaluating	

The children could collect information about tall towers and how they have been constructed. They might be able to see one on a visit e.g. radio masts/towers, tower cranes, tower lighting round football grounds and railway sidings, electricity pylons etc.

The story

(Junior Pupils' Book 4 page 21)
Mark's and Julie's mother is in hospital having had a very tiny baby. The children and their father go to visit her and meet Winston and his mother. Winston has broken his arm and is going to have it set.

Hospital

Science

People and their jobs and occupations

The work of a dietitian is considered.
(*Teachers' Book* page 43)

Concepts

Pupils will explore some aspects of these concepts:
12.1 Change may be reversible or irreversible.
13.1 Different materials have different properties.
15.1 Living things have common properties: . . . nutrition . . .
16.1 Living things must eat: . . .
18.1 All living things have a fixed life cycle.
18.3 Parents produce offspring of the same kind as themselves.
19.1 People are living things. They exhibit variability.
19.5 Children must spend many years learning to care for themselves; this contrasts with other animals.

Making and doing activity

The problem for the children is:
'Can you make a model human skeleton with joints that move in the right directions?'
(*Teachers' Book* pages 52–3)

Skills

Pupils will develop their scientific skills by:

Activity 1—You're warm   *TB* p45
Investigating the body temperature of   *PB4* p22
human beings

Activity 2—Well wrapped up   *TB* p46
Investigating heat loss from a small object *PB4* p23
compared with a larger one

Activity 3—Feed them right   *TB* p47
Investigating some aspects of a healthy diet *PB4* p24

Activity 4—All set   *TB* p50
Investigating plaster of Paris   *PB4* p25

The story

This story provides the opportunity for children to contribute from their own experience. Many will have had the experience of mother being taken off to hospital to have a baby; many of them will have broken limbs or know someone who has. Hospitals can be either alarming or cheerful places depending on why the contact with the hospital has been made. Maternity wards are usually friendly, cheerful places but there can be worries when babies are born very small or premature and need special care. It is amazing how tiny scraps of humanity can survive and be cared for in a modern special care unit. No doubt there will be children in the class who started that way themselves or have brothers and sisters who were tiny or premature.

You could encourage the children, in discussion, to consider how helpless human babies are when they are born compared with some other creatures which they know. Some children will be familiar with newborn lambs or calves and will have seen them struggle to their feet immediately and go in search of food. The children will also be aware that even creatures which are born very dependent on their mothers become independent within a very short space of time, whereas human offspring need to be looked after for many years.

In the story on page 21 of *Junior Pupils' Book 4* the all important temperature chart can be seen at the foot of the mother's bed and a 'special diet' chart is seen on the baby's incubator. These provide starting points for the pupils' activities.

People and their jobs and occupations

A hospital dietitian is responsible for making sure that all the patients in the hospital eat the kind of food and amounts of it which will be best for them. Many people can eat a normal diet but some patients will have special requirements because of the nature of their condition. They may require diets which are low/high in fat or protein. There may be some substances which they must not eat. Mothers who are feeding babies need a very ample diet and they need a lot of food.

Babies whose mothers are not feeding them have to have a very carefully controlled diet. Children must have all the things which are needed to make sure that they have energy to run about and keep them warm and all the things which are needed to make strong bones and adequate flesh. A dietitian must know a great deal about what is in different kinds of food and what the special requirements are for people of different ages, different occupations etc. The dietitian must work scientifically and know a lot of science to understand what everybody needs to eat to be healthy. Particular points about the work of a dietitian which could be emphasised include:

3 Different people do different jobs and follow different occupations.
10 People may need special knowledge, expertise and skills in their work and hobbies.
11 People have to acquire the special knowledge, expertise and skills which they need.
16 People use scientific information in their jobs, occupations and hobbies.
17 People need to use a scientific viewpoint in their jobs, occupations and hobbies.

Further activities

1 Ask someone who is a dietitian to come and talk to the children. He/she could talk about the work of a dietitian and at the same time talk to the children about what is good for them to eat and what they should not eat. You could link this up with Activity 3.

2 You could extend the discussion to consider the great variety of people who will work in a hospital and contribute directly or indirectly to the welfare of patients – porters, ambulance drivers, kitchen workers, doctors, consultants, nurses, pathologists etc. They all need some scientific understanding and many of them are practising scientists. Medicine has become increasingly scientific.

3 A topic about the history of medicine or hospitals could be developed.

Science

Background notes

Body temperature

Body temperature is usually quoted as having a 'normal' value of 37°C. It is measured with a clinical thermometer – a special type of mercury-in-glass thermometer with a constriction which lets the mercury pass to register body temperature but does not allow it to fall back until after the thermometer has been read. (A quick flick of the wrist will cause the mercury to go back into the bulb.)

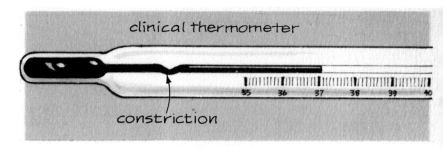

Although everyone has a normal temperature around 37°C, the actual 'normal' temperature for the individual may be a little way off the accepted and quoted normal. The children will discover this when they survey temperatures amongst their friends. It can cause some consternation.

The body is programmed to maintain body temperature at normal value whatever the circumstances – hence sweating to cool the body. In illness the body temperature rises as the system fights invading organisms. If the temperature rises well above normal, the chemistry of the body begins to break down because it is not geared to working at the higher temperature. If the high temperature persists, the victim will die.

It is interesting that all warm-blooded animals have a body temperature around that of human beings – much of the basic chemistry and normal conditions for it are the same from one creature to another.

Heat loss

Heat will always pass from a warmer body to a colder body until the temperature of both is the same. Lagging the warmer body will slow down the process but it will happen eventually. A larger body will lose heat comparatively more slowly than a smaller body: a tiny baby will lose heat very rapidly compared with an adult; a tiny animal will lose heat very rapidly compared with a larger animal. The reason for this can be seen if the ratio of volume to surface area is considered for two cylinders: imagine they represent the bodies of a small animal and a large animal or

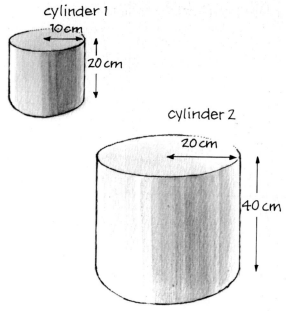

	cylinder 1	cylinder 2	cylinder 2 dimension / cylinder 1 dimension
radius	10 cm	20 cm	$\frac{2}{1}$
height	20 cm	40 cm	$\frac{2}{1}$
surface area $2\pi r\,(r+h)$	$600\,\pi\,cm^2$	$2400\,\pi\,cm^2$	$\frac{4}{1}$
volume $\pi r^2 h$	$2000\,\pi\,cm^3$	$16{,}000\,\pi\,cm^3$	$\frac{8}{1}$

a baby compared with an adult. The dimensions of cylinder 2 are twice as big as those of cylinder 1.

In essence, a larger body has comparatively more body inside its outer skin than a smaller body. A smaller body will require more insulation to compensate since, although its surface area is a quarter of that of the larger body, the amount inside (its volume) is only an eighth.

Diet

Ideas about what constitutes a healthy diet have come under considerable scrutiny and there is much discussion about how much and what kind of fat we should eat and about amounts of sugar and fibre which are desirable. Growing up with sensible attitudes to food and diet is probably the most important thing in determining good eating habits for life. A table showing the amounts of different foods which the children will need is given on page 24 of *Junior Pupils' Book 4.* A table giving the composition of various foods is on pages 48–50 in this book. These pages may be copied freely for the children to use.

Plaster of Paris

Plaster of Paris is probably a substance which the children will have used in making plaster casts in school or possibly in making models at home. It is interesting, as an example of an irreversible change, when it sets after mixing with water and also because as it sets it gets warm – the chemical reaction which is taking place is accompanied by the emission of heat. The strength of the cast is lowered if bubbles of air are included. The plaster will set even if excess water is used. Be very careful if you want to get rid of excess plaster – it will set in the drains without any problem!

Activity 1—You're warm

Objectives

At the end of this activity the children should be better able to:
1 measure temperature;
2 keep an appropriate record planned in advance;
3 recognise patterns in the temperature data obtained and make suggestions based on these patterns;
4 identify relevant variables and control them.

Preparation

The children will need the clinical thermometer. They will also have to decide how to keep an appropriate record – clipboards could be useful. The children will probably need to be shown how to use the thermometer and how to read it and return the mercury to the bulb. It should be emphasised that the thermometer must not be washed by putting it in hot water. It can be sterilised by putting it in a cold, antiseptic solution.

Teaching points

General points

The children must realise that a thermometer registers its own temperature. To measure the temperature of a body the thermometer must have enough time to attain the same temperature as the body. The variation of temperatures from 'normal' may cause surprise and some concern. You can reassure the children if they think they must be ill if their temperatures are not quite 'normal'.

Specific points

The thermometer will take about a minute to reach body temperature. Obviously the children must take great care with the thermometer and it should be placed in the bare armpit. The thermometer is constructed so that there is no rush to read it once it is removed. It is essential to make sure that the mercury is returned to the bulb, or a low point in the stem, before it is used by the next child.

The children should recognise that everyone has a temperature around 'normal' but that individuals do show some variation. They should

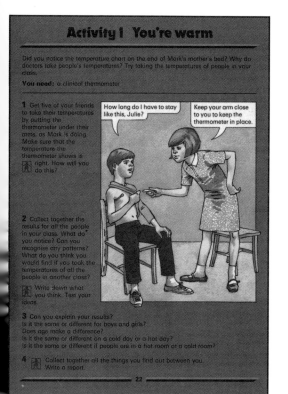

suggest that another class will show a similar pattern of readings.

They will probably want to take more readings to answer some of the questions in section 3. Alternatively, they may realise that they have the data required but will need to look at it again to answer the questions. If they do want to make more measurements, they should be required to plan what they want to do carefully and work together as a group.

Further activities
1 What happens to people's temperatures if they run around and feel very hot?
2 Are people's temperatures the same in the morning as they are in the afternoon?
3 Does a person always have the same temperature – every day, every week?

Activity 2—Well wrapped up

Objectives
At the end of this activity the children should be better able to:
1 plan and carry out an investigation;
2 identify and control relevant variables;
3 keep a record;
4 devise an appropriate means of communicating to a specified audience.

Preparation
The children will need the items listed on page 23 of *Junior Pupils' Book 4*. The hotter the water in the bottles can be the better, but you must ensure that the water is not hot enough to harm the children. You may feel it is useful to put the bottles in identical separate containers so that if there is any spillage it is contained.

The children will have to take care in using the thermometers since it is easy for them to tip up the bottles. The plastic bottles should, if possible, be identical apart from size. The larger the difference in size the better.

Teaching points

General points
The children should be able to grasp the idea that the small bottle does not have much in it compared with its outside surface. The big bottle has more in it. They should realise that it is important for tiny babies to be kept warm and that tiny animals and birds have a great problem keeping warm.

Specific points
The children may decide to draw cooling curves for the two bottles recording the temperature, say, every two minutes or they may choose to find out how long each bottle takes to cool to some chosen temperature. If you wish them to practise graph work, you may decide to tell them to draw cooling curves. An alternative approach is to find out how long it takes each bottle to cool down to room temperature.

It will be a matter of trial and error to make the cooling rate the same (see section 2 in the *Pupils' Book*).

Babies have very large heads compared with their bodies. The surface area of a baby's head is a considerable proportion of its total surface area – proportionately much more than for an adult or older child.

Further activities
1 Investigate the insulating efficiency of other materials e.g. felt, aluminium foil, waddings of various kinds, composite layers – cotton with 'string' vest, anorak materials etc.
2 Investigate how the shape of the container affects the rate of cooling of a given volume of water.

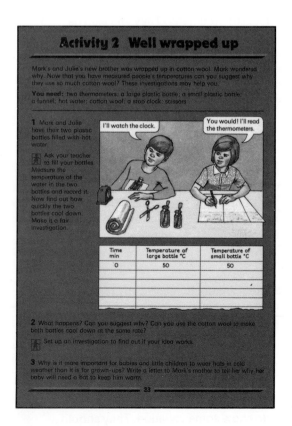

Activity 3—Feed them right

Objectives

At the end of this activity the children should be better able to:

1 use given information selecting that which is pertinent;
2 keep a careful record over a period of time;
3 choose an appropriate method of communicating to a specified audience.

Preparation

The children will need copies of the lists of foods and their composition (pages 48–50). They will need balance scales and samples of some of the main types of food so that they can find out what a helping of various foods weighs.

Teaching points

General points

If you have been able to get someone to talk to the children about diets you will have a good lead into this activity. Section 1 on page 24 of *Junior Pupils' Book 4* gives some basic information about the composition of various main food categories. You will need to expand this a little to make it clear that although foods generally have major constituents, they also contain other components. This is particularly important for children who are vegetarians and therefore have to make sure that they get sufficient protein from vegetables and/or dairy produce.

You could point out that we know the composition of the different foods because food scientists have analysed and measured the amounts of the components. Other scientists are able to make measurements and carry out tests which help to establish how much of the different kinds of food we need.

If you have a class where children are drawn from different cultures you will need to be sensitive to the different dietary patterns that they follow.

You should discuss with the children the examples of meals shown in the *Pupils' Book.* Each of the dishes on its own could have its place in a reasonable diet but it is the balance when some pairs of dishes are put together which is being questioned. Spaghetti and tomato sauce is delicious, but following it with an equally tasty chocolate biscuit does not produce a balanced healthy meal.

Specific points

The children will need to explore what the various requirements look like and to get a feel for amounts. Section 2 provides a useful opportunity for estimating and weighing.

Section 3 may prove quite a time-consuming exercise and will produce an interesting range of ideas. Encourage the children to present their ideas in a form which would attract Mark and Julie.

No reference is made to energy values since the emphasis is on the idea of a balanced diet. However, you could extend the work to include calculations of energy values if you wish.

Section 4 will require careful record keeping and using estimating skills to decide on quantities eaten. The children may detect that their eating habits need amendment and suggestions may be sought from you. You may need to use considerable diplomacy!

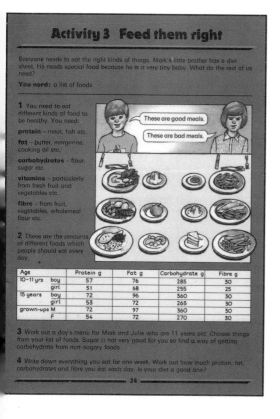

Protein, fat, carbohydrate, fibre content of foodstuffs

Amounts (g) per 100g – to nearest 1g

	Protein	Fat	Carbohydrate	Dietary fibre	Energy kj (to nearest 10)
Meat/fish					
lamb	26	18	0	0	1110
beef (roast)	24	21	0	0	1180
(stewed)	31	11	0	0	930
minced meat	23	15	0	0	960
curried meat	10	10	8	0	670
chicken	27	4	0	0	600
bacon rashers (fried)	24	42	0	0	1980
(grilled)	25	35	0	0	1720
ham (boiled)	25	19	0	0	1120
(grilled)	30	12	0	0	950
luncheon meat	13	27	6	0	1300
liver	25	10	0	0	830
sausage	13	25	12	0	1320
frankfurters	10	25	3	0	1140
faggots	11	19	15	0	1120
haggis	11	22	19	0	1290
salami	19	45	2	0	2030
beefburgers	20	17	7	0	1100
moussaka	9	13	10	0	810
Bolognese sauce	8	11	3	0	580
steak and kidney pie	15	18	16	0	1200
white fish	19	1	0	0	350
fried fish	20	10	8	0	830
fishfingers	14	13	17	0	980
Sweets and snacks					
chocolate (milk)	8	30	60	0	2210
(plain)	5	29	65	0	2200
toffees	1	1	98	0	1810
boiled sweets	0	0	87	0	1400
potato crisps	6	35	47	12	2220
plain biscuit	10	20	64	6	1980
chocolate biscuit					
(one side coated)	7	24	63	6	2070
(both sides coated)	6	28	63	3	2200
Drinks					
coffee (instant)	15	0	11	0	420
drinking chocolate	6	6	77	0	1550
tea	20	0	3	0	460
coca-cola	0	0	11	0	170
lemonade	0	0	6	0	90
Dairy foods					
milk (whole)	3	4	5	0	270
(skimmed)	3	0	5	0	140
yoghurt (fruit)	5	1	18	0	410
cheese (hard)	26	34	0	0	1680
(soft)	23	23	0	0	1250
eggs (boiled/poached)	12	11	0	0	620
(fried)	14	20	0	0	960
(scrambled)	11	23	0	0	1020
Fats					
butter	0	82	0	0	3040
margarine	0	81	0	0	3000

	Protein	Fat	Carbohydrate	Dietary fibre	Energy kj (to nearest 10)
low fat spread	0	41	0	0	1510
cooking oil	0	100	0	0	3700
lard	0	99	0	0	3660
Other foods					
coconut (desiccated)	5	60	6	24	2490
peanuts (fresh shelled)	24	49	9	8	2360
pizza	9	12	25	0	980
french salad dressing	0	73	0	0	2710
mayonnaise	2	79	0	0	2950
salad cream	2	27	15	0	1290
Sugar and preserves					
sugar	0	0	100	0	1680
jam	1	0	70	1	1110
honey	0	0	76	0	1230
[marmite]	41	1	2	0	760
Puddings					
steamed sponge pudding	6	16	46	1	1440
apple pie (pastry top only)	2	8	28	2	760
jam tart	4	15	63	2	1620
rice pudding	4	4	20	0	550
trifle	4	6	24	1	670
custard (from powder)	4	4	17	0	500
ice cream	4	7	25	0	700
cake (sponge)	6	27	53	4	1940
(fruit)	4	11	58	1	1400
Soup					
tomato (canned)	1	3	6	0	230
vegetable (canned)	2	1	7	0	160
Fruit					
apple (raw)	1	0	9	2	150
banana (skinned)	1	0	19	3	340
orange (peeled)	1	0	9	2	150
grapes	1	0	15	0	260
peaches (canned)	0	0	23	1	370
(fresh raw stoned)	1	0	9	1	160
pineapple (canned)	0	0	20	1	330
sultanas (dried)	2	0	65	7	1070
dates (stoned)	2	0	64	9	1060
prunes (stewed with stones)	1	0	19	7	320
plums (raw stoned)	1	0	10	2	160
apricots (canned)	1	0	28	1	450
Cereals					
white bread	8	2	50	3	990
brown bread	9	2	45	5	950
wholemeal bread	9	3	42	9	920
matzo	10	2	84	4	1630
chapatis (with fat)	8	13	50	4	1420
(without fat)	7	1	44	3	860
macaroni (boiled)	4	1	25	0	500
rice (boiled)	2	0	30	0	520
spaghetti (boiled)	4	0	26	0	500
cornflakes	8	2	80	10	1570
porridge	1	1	8	1	190
muesli	13	8	66	7	1560

	Protein	Fat	Carbohydrate	Dietary fibre	Energy kj (to nearest 10)
Vegetables					
baked beans	5	1	10	7	270
mung beans (dal)	6	4	11	6	450
lentils (boiled)	8	1	17	4	420
(masoor dal)	5	3	11	2	380
frozen peas (boiled)	5	0	4	12	180
dried peas (boiled)	7	0	19	5	440
chick peas (dal)	8	3	22	6	610
(chana dal)	5	5	10	5	410
sweetcorn (cooked)	4	2	23	5	520
yam (boiled)	2	0	30	4	510
okra/bhindi (boiled)	2	0	2	3	70
potatoes (boiled)	2	0	20	1	340
(mashed)	2	5	18	1	500
(fried – chips)	4	11	37	0	1070
(baked)	2	0	20	3	360
(roast)	3	5	27	0	660
cabbage	1	0	1	3	40
carrots	1	0	4	3	80
cauliflower	2	0	1	2	40
onions (boiled)	1	0	3	1	50
(fried)	2	33	10	1	1420
spinach	5	1	1	6	130
beansprouts (canned)	2	0	1	3	40
runner beans	2	0	3	3	80
broad beans	4	1	7	4	210
Salad					
tomatoes	1	0	3	2	60
cucumber	1	0	2	2	40
lettuce	1	0	1	2	50
water cress	3	0	1	3	60

Further activities

1 The lists of foods on pages 48–50 include the energy values of the foods. The children could extend their diet planning and checking activities to include energy content. The approximate energy requirements for various groups are shown in the table on page 51.

2 You could let the children research/collect information about the diets of people from different cultures. Are these healthy, balanced diets or do people have to take care to add things to make sure that they get all the nutrients they need?

3 What are the problems of diet in many of the third world countries? Is it simply that they do not have enough to eat?

4 Use the computer program DIET (Microelectronics Education Project).

Activity 4—All set

Objectives

At the end of this activity the children should be better able to:

1 use appropriate standard measures with confidence;

2 plan and carry out an investigation;

3 recognise and control relevant variables;

4 produce a communication for a specific purpose.

Preparation

The children will need the items listed on page 25 of *Junior Pupils' Book 4.* Plaster of Paris tends to fly about so plenty of newspaper and aprons

*Table showing approximate energy
requirements for different groups*

	years	*kj*
men	18–35	12200
	35–55	10900
	55–75	9200
women	18–35	8800
	35–55	8000
	55–75	6700
	during last 6 months of pregnancy	+840
	while nursing infant	+4200
children	1–3	5500
	3–6	6700
	6–9	8800
boys	9–12	10100
	12–15	12600
	15–18	14300
girls	9–12	9200
	12–15	10500
	15–18	9700

for the children are advisable. In section 2 the children will want to test the strength of their plaster of Paris samples. The method is left open but they will probably think of dropping a weight on to a sample or making a beam of the plaster and hanging weights from the beam. You should be prepared for requests for these or similar collections of equipment. (Investigations of the strength of mortar are described in Topic 4.4 'Built to last' Activity 1.)

Teaching points

General points
The children should realise that plaster of Paris undergoes an irreversible change when it sets. They should also notice the heat produced. This is an indicator that a chemical change is taking place. The nature of the plaster is changing. This contrasts, for example, with solid wax being heated to melt it and then allowed to set again. Heat has to be put in to make the wax melt. As it cools, that heat is given out and the wax returns to its original state. There has been a change in the state of the wax but not a change in its nature.

Before they start work the children will need to plan their investigation and to identify the variables which will have to be controlled. You may wish to suggest that they work in groups and divide up the parts of the investigation amongst the group and then bring their results together. If they do this, they will have to agree on a plan before any of them starts work.

Specific points
The variables involved will include:
mixing – amount of plaster of Paris
          amount of water
          kind of container
          amount of stirring
          temperature of water
setting – size of sample
          container
          property to be monitored for 'set'
          place where sample is put – temperature and other conditions.

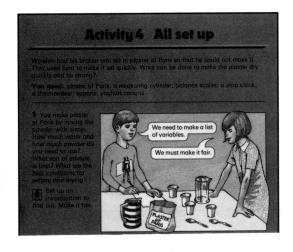

The children will have to decide which are being investigated, which are being changed and which are being controlled. They will need to remember that only one at a time can be investigated, only one changed and the rest must be controlled.

Again, in section 2, the children will need to plan their investigation carefully, controlling the variables as appropriate.

You could discuss with them what particular qualities an instruction sheet needs to have e.g. unambiguous, brief and to the point etc.

Further activities
1 Synthetic resin casts can now be used for setting limbs. They are much lighter than plaster of Paris casts. The children could find out about this material and how it is used.
2 Plaster of Paris-impregnated bandage (Modroc) can be bought. This offers a wide variety of possibilities for model making and creative sculpture. The bandage is soaked in water and can then be wrapped around 'frames' made from wire, twigs, wood or other bits and pieces – producing interesting shapes and forms. The bandage sets quickly so that it can be held in twists whilst it sets – and, of course, only a small length should be soaked at one time.

3 If the children have not already done so, they could make plaster casts of twigs, leaves, footprints etc. For example, a twig print cast can be made by rolling a piece of plasticine to about 1 cm thickness and pressing a twig carefully into the plasticine. A plasticine wall about 1 cm high is then built round the twig impression and the mould produced is filled with plaster of Paris and left to set. When the cast is set and dry it can be painted and varnished.

Making and doing activity

The problem for the children is:
'Can you make a model of a human skeleton so that the limbs bend in the right directions?'

You need:
junk; straws; pipe cleaners; garden canes; wire – stiff and flexible; string; card; glue; brass paper clips; sellotape; plasticine; Blu-Tack; old table tennis balls; other old balls; rubber bands; elastic; round balloons; tools.

1 The problem	To make a model of a human skeleton with limbs that bend in the right directions.
2 Exploring the problem	You may like immediately to suggest to the children that they do not have to tackle every joint in the body but limit their concern to the more major joints. Alternatively, you could suggest that groups of children concentrate on bits of the skeleton and then put it all together. Or you may decide to let things take their course and see what happens.

The children will probably have to do some research in order to find out exactly how the different joints move. Do they go backwards and forwards like a hinge? Do they go from side to side? Can they turn? It can be surprisingly difficult to decide what is happening. Once they have decided what kind of movement takes place at a particular joint they can start to explore the problems of constructing a joint which will do the same thing.

3 Ideas for solving the problem

The children could tackle the joints one at a time and establish some working ideas. For example, the knee is like a hinge and it will fold right up in one direction but will not go beyond being straight in the other direction. It will not move from side to side. A hinge-type construction is possible. The elbow can bend like a hinge but the lower arm can also be twisted. It needs a modified hinge. The hip joint is very flexible and probably requires a ball in a socket (e.g. a table tennis ball in half an old tennis ball?)

4 Making

Sticks for bones, balls for hip joints, card hinges for knees – are all possibilities. Movement restriction can be provided by using pieces of elastic and rubber bands. Washing-up bottles are very useful and can be pinned and fixed with rubber bands or elastic. Card can be cut and shaped and held in place with wire. Here are a variety of ideas.

card finger

brass paper fastener

wire

wire

beads or pieces of candle

part of a hand
(but finger joints bend both ways!)

pin or elastic

joint
straight pin for a 'hinge' joint; elastic if some turning movement is appropriate

part skull

(papier mâché stuck on a balloon; balloon then deflated and removed)

washing-up liquid bottle(s)

balsa wood

hinge joint
stuck on card

socket (half tennis ball)

elastic threaded through socket to give restricted movement

table tennis ball

dowel rod

ball and socket joint

5 Evaluating

Do the joints bend in the right directions? Have the children both identified the movement correctly and constructed a joint that more or less imitates that movement? Obviously, some of the attempts will be very rudimentary but was the intention right?

If the children have worked as a large group, have they managed to make the parts of the skeleton so that they will fit together and are on the same scale?

The children will learn a great deal about the skeleton in the course of solving this problem. You might like to reinforce this understanding and talk to them about the importance of ligaments and tendons and about how our muscles work. You may be able to let the children see a real skeleton and examine the structure of the different joints.

YEAR 4
LEVEL 2: TOPICS

INTRODUCTION TO YEAR 4: LEVEL 2

Scientific skills

These are the general skills for Year 4 Level 2 Topics. It is important that you read through these descriptions carefully before the children start work and familiarise yourself with them.

Specific skill objectives are given for each activity at the start of each topic. Their purpose is to focus attention on these rather than to suggest that in an activity these are the only skills which will be used. There are few activities which do not have the potential for developing a range of skills but which skills will depend on the pupils themselves and in some cases on the comments you make and the questions you ask.

Observing
The children can observe using the senses in combination. They can observe in detail. They can distinguish in advance between more and less significant observations, determine the level of detail which will be appropriate and make their observations accordingly. They look for and observe similarities and differences; with some prompting, they recognise observational patterns of form, behaviour and change, as well as of more obvious qualities such as colour.

Communicating
The children can communicate in detail, using a refined range of methods, and can choose for themselves the most appropriate method of use.

Measuring
The children are able to use appropriate standard measures with confidence: (m, cm, mm, cm², cm³, kg, g, l, ml, min, sec, newton). They can record using decimal notation. They can estimate with a reasonable degree of accuracy. They can select the appropriate measuring instrument to suit a particular purpose and read a variety of scales, e.g. thermometer, kitchen scales (both dial and linear), force meter and spring balance.

Recording
The children can record using a wide range of methods, including mathematical representation. They can choose in advance the most appropriate method for a particular purpose.

Classifying
The children can classify into sets and subsets using simple and complex criteria selected appropriately by themselves. They can use and construct simple keys.

Recognising patterns
When making observations, the children seek patterns in the information obtained. They recognise common factors in the information obtained by observing a number of instances. They are able to recognise other instances which fit the pattern.

Predicting

The children base their suggestions on firm evidence, including recognised patterns. There is increasing recognition of causal, as distinct from casual, relationships. They use known concepts in making their suggestions.

Controlling variables

The children are aware of a wide range of variables and, on most occasions, can identify and control those which are relevant.

Investigating

The children can design and carry out simple investigations with confidence. They can identify and control most relevant variables. They can review their investigations critically and they check their results by repetition.

Seaside

The story

(*Junior Pupils' Book 4* page 26)
Paul's family and Afzal and Parveen are at the seaside.
They find swimming in the sea easier than in fresh water.
They dream of desert islands and decide they would
have to make drinking water from salt water. A boatman
tells them that sea water is nasty stuff.

Science

People and their jobs and occupations

The jobs and occupations of people who work on or near the sea are discussed. (*Teachers' Book* page 58)

Concepts

Pupils will explore some aspects of these concepts:

7.7 Floating and sinking depend on both the kind of material and on the shape.

12.1 Change may be reversible or irreversible.

12.4 During a change of state, the substance itself does not alter, it merely changes its form, e.g.

$$\text{water liquid} \xrightarrow{heat} \text{water vapour} \xrightarrow{cool} \text{water liquid}$$

13.1 Different materials have different properties.

13.2 Materials are used for purposes for which their properties make them appropriate (paper, wood, metals, plastics, wool, cotton, synthetic fibres, glass, brick, stone, rubber).

13.4 Some substances are soluble in water and some are not.

Making and doing activity

The problem for the children is:
'Can you make a boat that will go under its own power?'
(*Teachers' Book* pages 62–3)

Skills

Pupils will develop their scientific skills by:

Activity 1—Light weight *TB* p59
Investigating whether objects weigh less in *PB4* p27
water than in air and whether they weigh less in
salt water than in fresh water

Activity 2—Nasty stuff? *TB* p60
Investigating the action of salt water on a *PB4* p28
number of materials

Activity 3—A drink, a drink . . . *TB* p61
Investigating ways of making sea water into *PB4* p29
drinking water

The story

There must be very few children who do not love to mess about on the beach and splash or swim in the sea. Wet sand is a material of endless fascination. The story provides the setting for a wide range of discussions. You might like to explore with the children where they go for their holidays. Are there any children who have not yet seen the sea? You might like to talk about the different kinds of sea shores which there are. Why is the sea salty? Why are there pebbles or shingle or sand on the shore? Where do they come from?

The children's daydreams about desert islands emphasise the idea that human beings cannot exist by drinking salt water. Like many other creatures they need fresh water.

Finally, the boatman who is repainting his boat can bring the discussion round to consideration of those whose livelihood is derived from the sea.

People and their jobs and occupations

Many people derive a living from the sea by going out in boats of all kinds to fish, carry cargoes or transport people. What do the children think the man who is painting the boat may do? He might go after small catches of fish or he may take holidaymakers for 'trips round the bay'. Is he likely to go far out to sea? Why not? What sort of things does he need to know if he is a fisherman? He will need to know what to paint his boat with so that it is kept waterproof and well-preserved from the effects of salt water. He will need to know about how fish behave so that he knows where to look for them. He will need to be able to watch the weather so that he does not get caught in a storm. He has to know about the sea and how it behaves as it flows over beaches and rocks. He must know where there are rocks lurking below the surface. He must be prepared to tackle any problems which arise – he needs to be a maker and doer.

You might like to discuss the work of the lifeboat crews who turn out in the most appalling conditions as volunteers to assist other seafarers who run into trouble. Particular points which you could make include:

5 The work of some people helps us indirectly – they work behind the scenes.
7 Some work has to be done all the time.
9 People take pride in their work.
15 What is a job for one person may be an occupation or hobby for another.
16 People use scientific information in their jobs, occupations and hobbies.

Further activities

1 The children could find out how much of their food is brought by ship from overseas. Where does it come from? What kind of ship carries it?
2 A visit to a ship would be a great experience for the children if you can arrange it.
3 You might invite someone from the Royal National Lifeboat Institute to come to the school and talk about the task of the lifeboats.

Science

Background notes

Loss of weight in water
When an object is weighed in air and when immersed in water, it apparently weighs less in water. The water is supporting it to some

degree. If some salt is dissolved in the water, the supporting effect is greater and the object appears to weigh even less.

If an object which floats in water is put into the water, the water line can be marked. If salt is dissolved in the water, the object will float higher. Both Parveen and Afzal were right with their comments in the story.

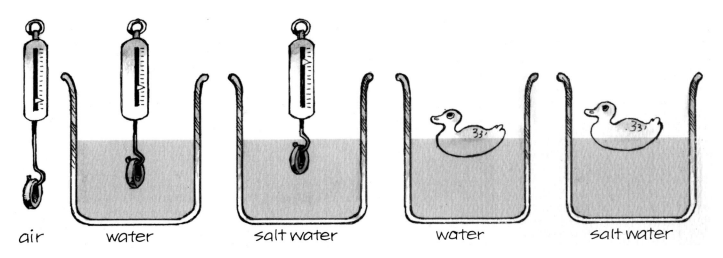

air   water   salt water   water   salt water

Corrosion

Salt water causes iron and steel to corrode rapidly – more quickly than if they are exposed to fresh water. Metals such as aluminium, tin and zinc are not much affected (barely at all in most cases). Brass and copper will eventually be affected on the surface but they will not be corroded away completely, as will iron and steel. Iron and steel undergo a chemical reaction which produces rust. This falls away from the surface which has been attacked exposing new metal which is in turn attacked until the metal is all reduced to rust. Brass and copper are attacked, initially, but the substance formed stays tightly attached to the surface and prevents any further attack. In order to prevent attack, metals have to be varnished or painted or coated with a metal which is not attacked e.g. chromium or nickel.

Activity 1 — Light weight

Objectives

At the end of this activity the children should be better able to:
1 weigh accurately and decide how accurately to weigh;
2 keep a careful, clear record of results;
3 carry out an investigation;
4 look for patterns and use these as a basis for suggestions.

Preparation

The children will need the items listed on page 27 of *Junior Pupils' Book 4*. The objects should be small enough to sink or float completely in the bowl. In section 4, a fairly heavy weight is needed to give a reasonable reading (0.5–1.0 kg is suitable). The spring balance needs to be of appropriate range.

Teaching points

General points
The children are trying to find out if Parveen is right in thinking that she weighs 'less in the sea'. There is a loss of weight in going from fresh water to salt water but it is a fairly small effect and the children will have to weigh carefully to follow the weight loss.

When the children weigh 'floaters', they may be surprised to find that no weight is registered unless they start to pull the object off the surface.

If the weight loss in salt solution is too small to discern in adding one spoonful of salt at a time, you may decide to increase the quantities of salt added each time.

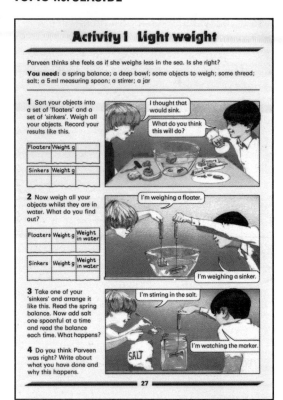

Once the children have weighed some of the objects, talk to them about the pattern which their results are following – i.e. when objects are weighed in air and in water the spring balance shows a loss in weight. Ask them before they weigh their next objects to estimate what the spring balance will show when the object is put into water.

Make sure that they use an object in section 3 which gives a reasonably high reading on the spring balance. Again ask them to identify the pattern and to make suggestions based on this pattern.

The children can explore their ideas about why this happens. Explore their ideas with them and encourage them to develop their ideas. We are concerned to have them express ideas rather than to come to right answers.

Further activities
1 The children (if they are interested) could try weighing objects when they are immersed in liquids other than water e.g. cooking oil, golden syrup (ugh!) They might try golden syrup at different temperatures – does temperature make a difference?
2 Can the children estimate how much less one of their legs would weigh in fresh water and in salt water?

Activity 2—Nasty stuff?
Objectives
At the end of this activity the children should be better able to:
1 plan and carry out an investigation;
2 choose in advance an appropriate method of recording and keep the record accurately over a period of time;
3 identify and control variables.

Preparation
The children will need the items listed on page 28 of *Junior Pupils' Book 4*. The pairs of pieces of materials should be identical. If you can provide an extra piece of material which is not identical, you can see if the children select the identical specimens for their work i.e. that they realise that the form of the material is a variable which ought to be controlled. Screws and nails are very useful as a source of different kinds of metals. The wood should be unpainted and untreated.

Teaching points
General points
The boatman who is painting his boat says that sea water (salt water) is 'nasty stuff'. The children are finding out what he means by investigating the effect of fresh water and salt water on various materials which are used in boat construction. The investigation needs to be set up carefully and then monitored over a period of time to ensure that conditions are carefully controlled to make a fair test. The children will have to be very well disciplined in their record keeping to follow the test through.

Specific points
All the objects should be completely immersed. Make sure that the metal objects do not touch each other or you will introduce an unsuspected, uncontrolled variable. *(Explanation: very complicated – electrolytic action.)*

Make the salt solution very concentrated. (About 360 g of salt will dissolve in 1 litre of water.) The objects placed in the salt solution should be identical to those placed in water.

The bowls will need to be kept in the same place so that conditions are the same for both bowls.

3 At the end of the week fish out all the objects and look at them carefully. Is salt water 'nasty stuff'? Which are good materials for boats? Which materials need painting?

A magnifying glass helps.

We must put them side by side to compare them.

4 Can you plan an investigation to find out whether it would make a difference if the water was warmer? It must be a fair test.

28

You can either let the children talk about their results or write about them.

Let the children try to set up the investigation in section 4. The temperature effect is quite marked – a 10°C rise in temperature will double or treble the rate of corrosion. (A car which has wet, salty material on it will corrode very rapidly if it is kept in a warm garage.)

Further activities

1 Let the children paint or varnish pieces of the materials which they decided needed painting to preserve them. They can then test the painted or varnished materials under the same conditions as before. Is the paint or varnish effective?

2 What other ways of preserving materials are used e.g. putting a thin coat of a metal which resists corrosion on to iron or steel – zinc (galvanising), chromium (plating), tin (plating), plastic coating (as for pot drainers)? Are these methods effective? Can the children find examples of these methods? You could make a display of methods of preserving materials from corrosion.

3 Are other liquids corrosive? What about liquids that we put in pans when we are cooking e.g. cooking oil, fruit juice, vegetable water, sugary mixtures? The children could try a variety of metals in the various liquids and decide which metals seem to be suitable for pans and which do not.

4 What about washing-up materials? Are they suitable for pans? Liquid detergents have no effect on metals, but washing powders which are alkaline (soap-based washing powders) will cause corrosion of aluminium and zinc. A solution of washing soda in water will play havoc with aluminium and zinc – but if you try this it is only for observation of the results by the children – no participation for safety reasons.

Activity 3—A drink, a drink . . .

Objectives

At the end of this activity the children should be better able to:

1 recognise patterns in their results;
2 base suggestions on identified patterns and on known concepts;
3 communicate to an identified audience.

Preparation

The children will need the items listed on page 29 of *Junior Pupils' Book 4*. Funnels and filter paper are readily available for making coffee and these are ideal for the purposes of this activity. Fine gravel of the type used for aquarium tanks is required. It is better if the bottles are transparent so that the water condition can be clearly seen. Blotting paper can be used to make a filter, if necessary, and a yoghurt carton with holes in the bottom will hold it.

Section 4 of the activity will inevitably call for good supplies of junk.

Teaching points

General points

The children are trying to produce fresh drinking water from sea water so that they will be able to survive on their imaginary desert island. You can make some 'sea water' by dissolving salt in water – adding a bit of sand, a few shells and a bit of dried seaweed if you can acquire some.

Filtration depends for its effectiveness on finding a filter material – the holes of which are smaller than the size of the particles to be removed. Particles of silt and clay are often very small and can cause problems; generally, sand can be removed without too much difficulty. Cotton wool or filter paper are easily understandable and immediate in their action; in water purification on a large scale, the filter bed is made of layers of graded sands and grit and other materials.

61

Activity 3   A drink, a drink...

Afzal decided they would have to have water that was not salty to drink on their desert island. They brought some sea water home so that Paul could show them his way of cleaning it.

You need: some sea water; a bottle; a funnel; blotting paper; cotton wool; pieces of cloth; sand; gravel; a sieve; filter paper

1 Paul started like this. You try it on your sea water. What happens? Does the water look fit to drink?

I'll pour this through, like this.

2 Try some other ways of cleaning the water. Which ways could you use on your desert island?

But we wouldn't have those on a desert island.

I'm sure we'd have these.

What can we do with them?

SEA WATER

3 Will the water you have cleaned be good to drink? Tell your teacher what you think.

4 If your island was very hot and sunny can you think of a way to get better water to drink and salt to put on the fish you catch and cook? Tell your teacher your ideas.

29

Specific points

It would be worth checking that your sea water sample produces a clear sample after filtering so that the children will be able to make a reasonably straightforward comparison when they try other methods of filtration.

The children are not likely to have filter paper on their desert island so they will need to use materials which are more likely to be available. The drawing on page 29 of *Pupils' Book 4* shows a possible method.

In section 3, the children should realise that the water will still be salty; but there may be one or two children who will expect the filter to have removed the salt (soluble material), as well as the sand (insoluble material).

Section 4 is a real problem for the children and you will have to discuss it with them in some detail. Do they realise that water can evaporate from the surface of a salt solution leaving the salt behind? Do they appreciate that air always contains water vapour and that water vapour can be turned to water droplets by letting the air touch a cold surface? The condensation of steam from a soapy bath is an example of this. They may be familiar with the idea that the steam from a kettle will condense and produce droplets of water on a cold wall. Explore their understanding with them until you feel that they realise that the problem is to get water vapour to leave the sea water and then come in contact with a cold surface to form water droplets which can be collected.

The children may come up with all sorts of ideas. Do they realise that sea water could provide the means of cooling a surface on which water vapour will condense?

Further activities

1 The children could find out how water is purified before it reaches our taps.
2 Car engines have air and oil filters. Why? You may be able to show the children what such filters remove from the air and oil passing into the engine.
3 Can the children find out how fresh water is produced from salt water in countries surrounded by sea but without adequate fresh water e.g. middle eastern countries?

Making and doing activity

The problem for the children is:
'Can you make a boat that will go under its own power?'

You need:

junk of all kinds; pieces of wood of all kinds; card; pieces of cloth; plastic sheet; string; waterproof glue; nails; aluminium foil; batteries; wire; paint; varnish; brushes; propellers; rubber bands; balloons; candles; night lights; tools.

1 The problem	To make a boat that goes under its own power.
2 Exploring the problem	The boat must float and it must be waterproof. It will have to be a good shape. It must be powered. What materials are available? How might they be used for making a boat? How can a boat be powered? wind? electricity? steam?
3 Ideas for solving the problem	The boat can be made from wood or some other material which floats, but if the shape is right it can also be made from material which does not usually float. It might be made from a plastic bottle or a tin can of some kind. It could be fitted with a sail. It could have a propeller driven by a twisted rubber band or by an

electric motor – or these might be used to drive
paddles. It might be driven by a jet of steam or by
the air coming out of a balloon.

The boat will need to be shaped so that it will
move easily through the water – it will need to be
streamlined. It will need to stay upright in the water
so it may need ballast or a heavy keel to make sure
that its centre of gravity is low.

The possible solutions will include a wide range of
approaches. Here are some examples.

4 Making

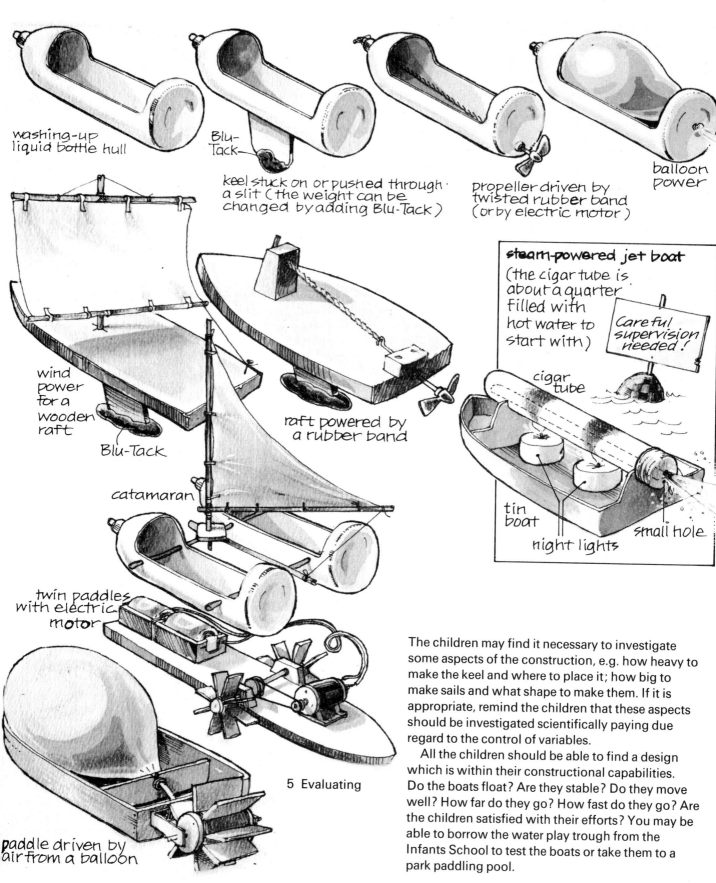

washing-up
liquid bottle hull

Blu-
Tack

keel stuck on or pushed through
a slit (the weight can be
changed by adding Blu-Tack)

propeller driven by
twisted rubber band
(or by electric motor)

balloon
power

wind
power
for a
wooden
raft

Blu-Tack

catamaran

twin paddles
with electric
motor

raft powered by
a rubber band

steam-powered jet boat
(the cigar tube is
about a quarter
filled with
hot water to
start with)

Careful
supervision
needed!

cigar
tube

tin
boat

night lights

small hole

5 Evaluating

paddle driven by
air from a balloon

The children may find it necessary to investigate
some aspects of the construction, e.g. how heavy to
make the keel and where to place it; how big to
make sails and what shape to make them. If it is
appropriate, remind the children that these aspects
should be investigated scientifically paying due
regard to the control of variables.

All the children should be able to find a design
which is within their constructional capabilities.
Do the boats float? Are they stable? Do they move
well? How far do they go? How fast do they go? Are
the children satisfied with their efforts? You may be
able to borrow the water play trough from the
Infants School to test the boats or take them to a
park paddling pool.

Pond life

The story

(*Junior Pupils' Book 4* page 30)
Rosa and Tan Hing see a tank of tropical fish,
discuss their varied shape and colour, wonder whether
they might find similar fish in a local pond and go on
a fishing expedition to find out.

Science

People and their jobs and occupations

The keeping of tropical
fish as a hobby is
discussed.
(*Teachers' Book*
page 65)

Concepts

Pupils will explore some aspects of these concepts:

15.1 Living things have common properties: growth,
respiration, reproduction, nutrition, excretion, and
possibly movement.
16.1 Living things must eat; they need water and air.
17.1 Plants and animals are very diverse in form.
17.2 Their form fits their environment: . . . fish.
17.3 Plants and animals are sensitive to their
environment and respond to it.
17.4 Plants and animals in a particular environment are
dependent on each other.
18.1 All living things have a fixed life cycle.
18.2 The life cycle of all members of the same species is
the same.
18.3 Parents produce offspring of the same kind as
themselves.
18.4 The life cycles of living things are often linked to
seasonal change.
19.5 Children must spend many years learning to care
for themselves; this contrasts with other animals.

Making and doing activity

There are two problems
for the children:
i 'Can you make a
device which will
enable you to find the
temperature of the
water in a pond at
different depths?'
ii 'Can you make a
device that will drop a
measured quantity of
food from a storage
container into a fish
tank? Can you operate
the device by remote
control?'
(*Teachers' Book*
pages 74–6)

Skills

Pupils will develop their scientific skills by:

Activity 1—Creatures great and small   *TB* p67
Investigating and sorting the variety of   *PB4* p31
creatures in a sample of pond water

Activity 2—Eggs without shells   *TB* p71
Investigating the hatching of frog spawn   *PB4* p32
and the behaviour of tadpoles

Activity 3—Fishy goings on!   *TB* p72
Investigating the behaviour of fish   *PB4* p33

The story

Pond life holds a particular fascination for most children. How many can pass a pond or stream without peering into the water to see what is lurking there? Many homes have a tank of tropical fish or goldfish and some of the children will be familiar with their requirements.

The story raises questions which can be used as starting points for a variety of discussions. Does the shape of a fish affect the way it swims? Why are there so many different forms? Are brightly coloured creatures common in ponds and streams? Why not? Where are brightly coloured water creatures found? (Many of the children will have seen programmes on television about life under the sea. They may be more familiar with life around a coral reef than with the contents of a nearby pond!) What sort of things might you expect to find in a bucket of pond water?

People and their jobs and occupations

The story opens with the children looking at a tank of tropical fish in a waiting area. Why are the fish there? Why not plants or a picture? What is it about fish that people find attractive?

Where do the fish come from? Who is involved in supplying the fish? Does somebody catch them in the wild? How are they produced? What is involved in running a shop where they are sold? How is it different from selling other things? Where do aquarium tanks come from? Who makes them? What are they made from? Why?

The customers are people who keep the fish as a hobby. Are the fish any use? Why do people buy them and care for them? What would you need to know if you were going to start keeping tropical fish? *(For example, you would need to know about their habits and life style, about which fish will live together happily, the best water temperature, what they eat, their breeding habits etc.)* How can this knowledge be acquired?

The pond which the children in the story visit has been sadly abused and you might like to consider who is responsible for the care of streams and ponds in a particular local area. It is largely an urban problem and you may not consider it of special interest to your children if you live in a country area. In some areas, both local authorities and voluntary organisations have made great efforts to improve and restore water areas such as canals and canal basins which have become derelict. People who do such work must understand the needs of the many creatures for which the water and its surrounding areas is home. Like the tropical fish keeper, they need particular knowledge and the skills necessary to tackle the task scientifically.

Points you might like to emphasise include:

10 People may need special knowledge, expertise and skills in their work and hobbies.
11 People have to acquire the special knowledge, expertise and skills which they need.
16 People use scientific information in their jobs, occupations and hobbies.
17 People need to use a scientific viewpoint in their jobs, occupations and hobbies.

Further activities

1 Ask someone who keeps tropical fish to come into school to talk about his/her hobby. The children may know someone or you may be able to contact a local club.
2 Visit a place where a display of tropical fish can be seen. (Some local shops have a very wide selection.)
3 The children could find out about keeping tropical fish and about some

of the different varieties and where they come from.
4 Start keeping fish yourself.
5 Someone from the local authority may be able to visit your school to tell the children how ponds, streams and other water areas are looked after in your area. There may be a suitable area for the children to visit.

Science

Background notes

Ponds and pond life

The character of every pond or lake is determined by the relationship between the plants and creatures living in it and the nutrients and minerals available to them. The abundance of living things in any pond will depend on the right balance of dissolved substances in the water (including oxygen) and the amount of light. Oxygen is used in respiration by most living organisms and light is essential for photosynthesis by which green plants make their food.

You need only leave a bowl of water outdoors for a few days to see how quickly living organisms will begin to populate it. In a pollution-free, well-balanced pond there will be an abundance of life but the basic conditions – size, depth, shape and bottom material – generally dictate which species of creatures and plants will be found. In a new pond a large number of only a few species will be the colonists. As more arrive, competition develops confining individual species to the regions of the pond where they can best survive in competition with all-comers. These different 'zones' which are established will support different varieties of plant and animal life – some more abundant than others.

The open water zone supports the algae which float on the surface. There will be many herbivores feeding on the algae – some almost too small to see, like the water flea, and others larger like the midge larvae. These creatures complete their life cycles very rapidly. Other parts of the pond may be filled with floating plants or pondweed. This zone is often very rich in life and there is more likely to be an abundance of more conspicuous creatures, like the pond snail and other herbivores, as well as a wealth of the larger carnivores, like the water boatman or water scorpion, which feed on the herbivores. The most productive zone is the layer of detritus on the bottom which becomes the feeding area for thousands of small creatures 'cleaning up' the remains not consumed by those in the zones above.

So the whole pond becomes a delicate balance of the optimum conditions required for each species to survive – floating and submerged plants providing plenty of food for the herbivores and left-overs for the detritus feeders on the bottom. The herbivores provide food for the carnivores which will therefore be found amongst the plants and detritus where prey is most plentiful. Some of the larger carnivores, like the stickleback, may be found in many areas – searching for a variety of organisms. Herbivores will usually be slow-moving since their food stays still and waits to be eaten whereas carnivores must hunt and depend for survival on being quicker off the mark than their prey. Creatures which can move will do so for a number of reasons as well as seeking food, e.g. to escape predators, to find a mate or to move to other parts of the pond.

Animals which extract oxygen from the surrounding water are denser than the water and therefore can crawl around; other creatures move by flexing their bodies, some can use a jet stream of water to shoot rapidly forward (e.g. *dragonfly nymph*). Some bugs and beetles and many larvae use 'paddles' which may be adaptations of limbs. Some creatures move on the surface and rely on surface tension to keep themselves skimming over the surface.

Some of the means of propulsion which will be observed include these:

Pond creatures moving on the surface
e.g. pondskater   whirligig beetle

Pond creatures moving under the surface

shelled creatures using a foot
e.g. pond snail
    ramshorn snail
    freshwater mussel
    pea-shelled cockle

swimming without proper legs
e.g. leech/horse leech
    nematode worm
    flatworm
    eel tadpole
    midge pupa
    gnat larva
    mosquito larva

crawling or clinging without proper legs
e.g. bloodworm
    flatworm
    hydra
    nematode worm
    various larva – blackfly
          midge
          hoverfly
          cranefly

swimming with oars
e.g. waterboatman
    lesser waterboatman
    fish louse
    water flea

crawling and swimming with legs
e.g. water mite
    water spider
    nymphs – dragonfly
         damselfly
         stonefly
         Mayfly
  larva – alderfly
      lacewing
      whirligig beetle
      silver beetle
      caddisfly

Frog spawn and tadpoles

Frogs mate and spawn is produced in the spring during March and April. The timing of the event will depend on the weather during that period. Once the air temperature starts to rise, the frogs migrate to the breeding sites. The same sites are used each year. Each female common frog will produce 2000 to 4000 eggs which she lays usually in shallow water. The time from laying to the development of the mature frog is about three months. In the following table, times are approximate.

day 0	spawn laid
day 4	eggs hatch
day 8	eyes develop; mouth starts to grow; external gills begin to disappear
1 month	increase in size; gills become covered
2 months	legs begin to develop; mouth continues to grow; tail gets smaller; comes to the surface more to breathe
3 months	frog able to emerge on to land; tail disappears

The frogs will not be able to breed until the following year.

Activity 1 — Creatures great and small

Objectives

At the end of this activity the children should be better able to:
1 observe in detail, looking particularly for similarities and differences;
2 classify into sets and sub-sets;
3 recognise patterns in what they observe;
4 use a simple key;
5 use reference books for identification purposes.

Preparation

Collecting a sample of pond water could be done by you before the lesson, but if it is at all possible the children themselves should do this. It will give much more purpose and meaning to the activity if they have been involved in the original collection. If you collect the pond water yourself, do a little sampling in different parts of the pond (with a pond net, if you have one) to try to ensure a rich mixture of creatures. If the children are collecting the sample, you may find it useful to visit the pond yourself beforehand to search out the most likely places for sampling. Choose an area of weed, if there is one. By dragging a bucket through this you are sure to collect a fair number of specimens. A piece of rope attached to the bucket handle will enable you to throw it into deeper water and retrieve it.

If you intend to pay several visits to the pond or spend a reasonable time collecting specimens, some more refined equipment would be useful. A sampling net can be bought or borrowed but you can make one with a broom handle, some strong wire and some nylon curtain mesh.

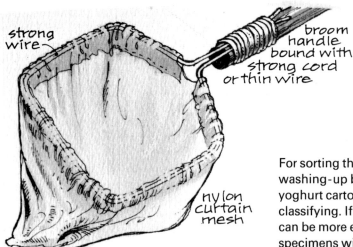

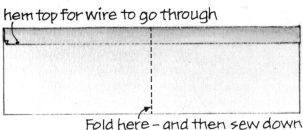

For sorting the catch back in the classroom small plastic fish tanks or old washing-up bowls are useful. A variety of small containers, such as yoghurt cartons, margarine cartons etc., are needed for further sorting and classifying. If you have white or light-coloured containers the creatures can be more easily seen. Spoons are needed for transferring the specimens without damaging them – plastic tea strainers are also useful, particularly for straining the mud and fine detritus which you may collect.

Teaching points

General points
The children are investigating the variety of life which is found in a pond. By sorting it they set up a simple system of classification.

Before you take children out to collect samples of pond water you will want to establish very firm safety procedures and warn the children of the dangers involved. You may want to make it absolutely clear that the children should, on no account, attempt to collect from a pond by themselves. They should always be accompanied by an adult.

Children should be given some basic guidance about how to handle living organisms before they begin. Whilst collecting they should disturb the surroundings as little as possible; they should only collect enough specimens for their needs. When handling them back in the classroom they should treat them with great care to avoid any damage. Small quantities of plant life can be removed, if the plants are common.

There may be a tendency for the children to overlook careful, close observation in the midst of the excitement of having living creatures in the classroom. The children are observing in order to carry out simple classification procedures so attention to detail in their observations is important.

Specific points
The children may try to describe the creatures they see in their own terms. Allow them to do this – do not discourage descriptions such as 'short and fat', 'long and wriggly' etc. or be too anxious to put names to what they see. The way the creatures move may indicate whether they are herbivores or carnivores. Close observation will enable the children to describe the creatures' methods of propulsion.

If you have collected some carnivores, the children may well observe them feeding on each other.

For section 2, sort the creatures using the tea strainer or a spoon. It may be easiest to start with two larger containers – one for creatures with shells and one for those without.

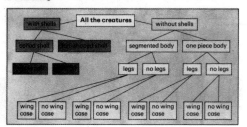

Smaller containers can then be labelled 'segmented body', 'one-piece body', 'coiled shell' and 'fan-shaped shell', so that further sorting can be done. At each stage of sorting have available labelled containers of a suitable size.

Once the creatures have been sorted, some recording can be attempted. This can be by identification using reference books, as suggested. This is not always easy but with a magnifying glass a fair attempt can be made at identifying most of the creatures.

Careful drawing of some specimens is a useful method of recording the catch. Some counts would establish which type of creature is most common in your sample.

The close observation and sorting may lead some of the children to recognise patterns of structure and behaviour. For example: carnivores are generally fast moving, have large eyes and long legs; whereas herbivores are usually slow moving, have reduced eyes and short legs or no legs at all.

They may also begin to recognise patterns of structure which lead to groupings, e.g. *mollusca* (generally with shells) – snails, mussels etc.; *arthropoda* (jointed body) – shrimps, daphnia etc.; *insecta* (6 legs) and the various stages of development of many common insects which may include larvae, nymphs and beetles.

Remember to return all the organisms you collected to their environment. Even the smallest is an essential part of a living community.

Further activities

1 Get the children to make their own simple key or punch card system to help identify pond creatures or plants. For example:

*Freshwater animals with shells –
a branching key*

water animals with shells

two hinged shell — one shell only

large shell (over 25mm long) — small shell — shell flat and coiled — shell coiled with a spiral

swan mussel
or
freshwater mussel — pea-shelled cockle — ramshorn snail — wandering snail
or
great pond snail

Freshwater animals with shells – a punch card system

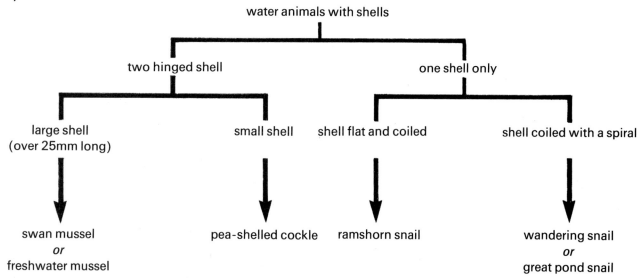

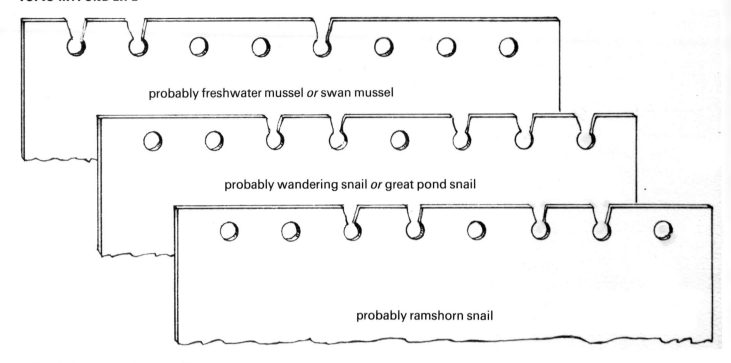

probably freshwater mussel *or* swan mussel

probably wandering snail *or* great pond snail

probably ramshorn snail

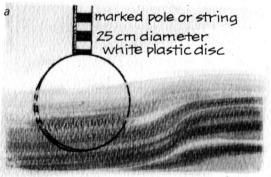

a marked pole or string
25 cm diameter
white plastic disc

b open tin can
with holes punched
in the bottom
line to surface

weight

c

needle on a piece of tissue

d

tissue sinks —
needle floats!

(Neither of these methods will give a definitive answer but they will help identification. Further and more precise identification can then be done using textbooks.)

2 Use these computer programs: FACTFILE (MEP), ANIMAL (MEP), SEEK (Longman).

3 Calculate the speed of movement of some water creatures. Put one in a clear container and stand the container on millimetre-squared paper. Measure the distance moved in a given time.

4 Test pond visibility – lower a white disc on a marked string into the pond on the end of a pole. Read the measurement when the disc disappears. See illustration (*a*).

5 Sample the bottom of the pond to see what lives there. This can be done with a tin can that has holes punched in the bottom, is then weighted and a line or handle attached. See illustration (*b*).

6 You could introduce the children to the systematic use of a series of questions when they are studying small creatures. These questions are general ones applicable widely. Not all of them will be pertinent to water dwellers.

a) Where does it live?
b) How does it protect itself?
c) What does it eat?
d) Where is its mouth?
e) Does it have teeth?
f) What does it do when it is touched?
g) How does it move?
h) How many legs has it got?
i) Where are its legs?
j) Does it have antennae?
k) What do they do?
l) How does it move?
m) How does it breathe?
n) How big is it?
o) Can you name it?
p) Does it prefer light or dark?
q) Does it prefer dry or damp?
r) What difference in its movement does roughness or smoothness make?
s) Are there a lot together or just one or two?

Draw several pictures of it and its different parts.
Find out more about it from books and magazines.

7 Investigate surface tension. Try to float a needle. See (*c*) and (*d*).

Activity 2—Eggs without shells

Objectives

At the end of this activity the children should be better able to:
1 select which observations to make and make these in appropriate detail;
2 plan and carry out an investigation;
3 recognise and control relevant variables;
4 record a sequence of events.

Preparation

Frogs usually mate and produce spawn from early March to the end of April. Exactly when frog spawn will be found will depend on the weather during this period. If you are familiar with a site which had frog spawn last year, it is almost certain that it will be found there again this year. The ravages of pollution and the draining and infilling of ponds in recent years have seriously reduced the frog population so only collect sufficient spawn for your study needs and return the hatched tadpoles to the same site.

The best containers for frog spawn are plastic or glass aquaria. If these are not available use old, clean washing-up bowls. You can fill the containers either with clean pond water or with rain water or with a mixture of pond water and tap water. If you are using tap water, leave it to stand overnight before transferring your frog spawn. This allows the chlorine to clear. No weed or other food will be needed until the spawn hatches.

Teaching points

General points

The children are observing the hatching of frog spawn and the metamorphosis from tadpole to frog. It will take about three months for the process to be completed although the initial changes happen quite quickly. The children will have to be systematic and persevering in their observing and recording if they are to follow the changes throughout.

Specific points

You can expect the tadpoles to emerge from the eggs in about a week under normal conditions. Indoors, in a warmer environment, this time could be reduced to a matter of a few days. By leaving one container outdoors and having one indoors, a clear difference in hatching time should be seen.

The amount of light can be governed by covering the outside and top of one container with black paper. Wherever the containers are kept, they should be out of direct sunlight.

Remove the 'jelly' a few days after the eggs hatch.

The questions concerning the amount of light and the temperature can both be answered at the same time if you have four containers.

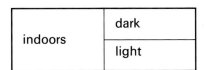

indoors	dark
	light

outdoors	dark
	light

The children should consider some variables which they may be able to control to make this investigation fair. These will include:
—frog spawn from the same batch
—same size and material for each container
—water changes at the same time
—same conditions for dark and light outside
—same conditions for dark and light inside.

In section 3, for children with poor written language skills, a pictorial chart of the daily changes could be used or could supplement the written record.

When the tadpoles hatch they will need food. They will feed on pond

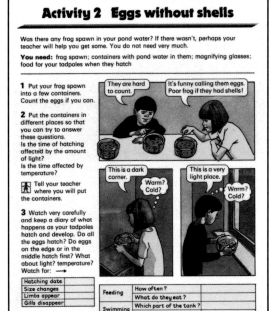

weed, if it is available. This can be left in the tank. Failing this, you can pour boiling water over a lettuce leaf and put some of this in the tank – but this needs to be changed every day. Tadpoles can also be fed raw meat. This should be suspended on a string and removed after about an hour. Do this each day.

Recording for section 4 might be done over a period of weeks. Spend a little time on it each day, producing a gradually changing pattern of observations consistent with the changes in the life style of the tadpoles as they develop. Alternatively, a chart like the one in the *Pupils' Book* could be used to record behaviour over a single session. If it is used in this way it may be difficult to establish any patterns in behaviour but it will draw attention to some of the ways in which tadpoles behave.

Further activities

1 If you are able to visit a pond every day, keep a daily record of water and air temperatures. Record when the frogs begin arriving, when the first spawn appears and when it begins to hatch. Is the spawn laid in deep or shallow water? Is it laid in one part of the pond or all over?

  If it is possible to take water temperatures in different parts of the pond and at different depths, a reason may emerge as to why the frogs favour one particular part of the pond.

2 Find out whether the background colour affects the colour of developing tadpoles.

3 Using a millimetre-square grid, is it possible to keep a daily record of the growth of a tadpole?

4 Set up a school pond.

Activity 3—Fishy goings on!

Objectives

At the end of this activity the children should be better able to:

1 select observations which are of significance and make these in detail;
2 look for patterns in their observations;
3 make suggestions based on observed evidence;
4 plan and carry out an investigation.

Preparation

The children will need some fish in a tank (minimum four). For all parts of this activity you can use a tank that has already been set up. You may have a tank in school or you may be able to borrow one or decide now is the time to have one of your own. (See page 71 for information about setting up aquaria.) If you are setting up a tank, goldfish are easily obtainable and very suitable; although for section 4 of the activity sticklebacks are especially interesting. You can use sticklebacks for the whole of the activity, if they are available. If you can find a male stickleback in breeding condition in the spring it will exhibit some quite aggressive behaviour patterns which will show up particularly in the first investigation suggested in section 4. Male sticklebacks at this time of the year are recognisable because of their red bellies and blue eyes. Only have one male in a tank along with a number of females. More than one male and you will have a fight on your hands!

  There is no need to beautify the tank with weed and pebbles etc. The fish will be quite happy for a while in a tank with only water in it. This will make observation much easier.

  If you transfer fish from one container to another always make sure that both containers have been left standing in the same situation for a while to equalise the temperature of the water. If you are using tap water, remember to let it stand overnight. Sticklebacks and goldfish can be fed on cold-water fish food.

Teaching points

General points

In this activity the children will be observing and investigating the way in which fish respond to their surroundings and to each other. Because animals are mobile their responses are often immediate and therefore reasonably easy to observe. However, animal responses vary from very simple movements to quite complex behaviour and caution should be exercised in interpreting what we think an animal is doing or to what it is responding.

The behaviour patterns of animals can be either instinctive or learned. All animals exhibit instinctive behaviour – the instinct to feed, to mate etc. Learning how to respond to a particular stimulus occurs frequently in animals – it can be seen in fish which have been kept in a tank for some time and are used to being fed at a certain time. Tapping on the tank at feeding time will cause the fish to respond, if this has been a normal pattern.

The fishes' responses to stimuli and their shoaling instincts are explored in this activity.

Specific points
Breathing rate can be recorded by counting the opening of the gills over a given time. The count should be made when the fish is at rest or has been undisturbed for some time. If there are several fish in the tank, the breathing rate of several could be counted and an average taken.

Gentle stirring of the water should be enough to show there is an increase in the breathing rate when the surroundings are disturbed.

A distinction should be made between the response to mechanical vibrations and the response to sound. If a bell was rung in the water, would the fish be responding to the disturbance created in the water or to the sound? Tapping the side of the tank could be seen as causing vibration. Keep any sound source – bell, buzzer etc. – away from direct contact with the tank.

The children will also have to consider other questions before they can draw any conclusions from their investigation: for example, if the fish respond are they responding to the sound or to the observer's ringing action? Are there stimuli other than the noise which are causing the fish to respond?

The problem for the children in section 3 will be measuring the small quantity of food given at a particular time. A very sensitive measuring device could measure, say, one gram. The resulting pile of fish food could then be divided and sub-divided to produce a $\frac{1}{2}$ g or a $\frac{1}{4}$ g. (Overfeeding will leave a lot of residue which will very quickly foul the water.) Fish food can be bought as pellets – in which case the number can be counted. Let the children try to find a solution to this problem. Some of them may remember making a straw balance.

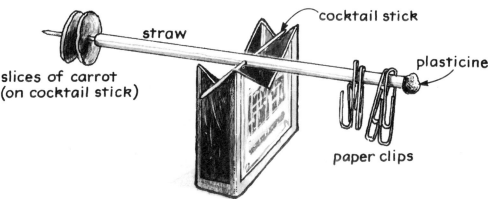

Activity 3   Fishy goings on!

Rosa and Tan Hing were interested in the fish they saw in the tank. See what you can find out about what fish do.

You need: some fish in a tank; a mirror; a stop clock; a bell; a transparent plastic bag; some fish food

1 Watch your fish. How often do they breathe? If you stir the water slightly, does the rate of breathing change?

If I tap the side, do they hear or feel?

Shall I ring the bell here or should I put it in the water?

2 Can fish hear? Make a fair test to find out.

3 How much do your fish eat? Do they feed on the surface? in mid-water? on the bottom?

4 Investigate the behaviour of your fishes. Place a mirror against one end of the tank. What happens? Make an accurate drawing of one of your fishes. Cut it out and stick it on the outside of the tank. What happens?

They don't seem to like my fish.

They like their own faces!

5 Some fish swim in shoals – do yours? Carefully place all but one of your fish in a plastic bag of water and suspend the bag at one end of the tank. What does the odd fish out do?

33

If flakes or fine-granulated fish food is used, it will probably float for a while before absorbing water and slowly sinking. Some pellets float for a short time before sinking quickly to the bottom where they break up. It may be difficult, therefore, for the children to introduce food to any one particular part of the tank – surface, mid-water or bottom. Close observation of how the fish feed after the food is introduced at the surface may be the only way of trying to answer the question. However, a little ingenuity might make it possible to introduce food at the different levels in an attempt to make the investigation as fair as possible. For

73

example, if pellets are used one can be broken up so that it will float and one can be pre-soaked so that it will sink immediately. The children may be able to devise a way of introducing food at different levels which does not cause too much disturbance in the tank.

If a male three-spined stickleback in breeding condition is used in the investigation in section 4, it will almost certainly react in an aggressive way towards its own reflection or a drawing. It may threaten the 'intruder' by swimming straight at it or adopt a threatening posture which may be tail up and head down towards the bottom. Remember, however, that no response at all is also worthy of note.

Further activities

1 If you can collect sticklebacks in the spring, set up an aquarium with some weed anchored in a gravel bottom. Introduce a male stickleback and watch how he builds a nest. Then put in two or three females. With luck, the fish will breed and the behaviour of the fish during this time can be observed closely. The male will perform a zigzag courtship dance and entice a female into the nest where she will spawn. The male will then enter to fertilise the eggs. He will care for the eggs and after hatching (7–8 days) care for the young fish – even gathering them into his mouth if they move too far away.

2 Which end of the tank do the fish favour? Stick a piece of tape on the outside to divide it in half. Over a five-minute period record how long the fish spends in one half. Repeat for the other half. Do this several times. Does a pattern emerge?

3 Buy a fresh fish from a fishmonger and look carefully at its various parts. Is anyone prepared to cut it open to look inside? Cooking will allow the bony skeleton to be uncovered.

4 If you know someone who is keen on fishing, ask him/her to come into school to show the children angling equipment and tell them how fish are caught. (What does an angler need to know and be able to do? Lots of science here!) Do the children think fishing is cruel? Is fishing a sport?

5 Record the behaviour of other pond creatures. How do they feed? How do they move? Do they prefer one part of the tank to another? What do they respond to – light, noise etc?

tape

Making and doing activity

There are two problems for the children.

i The problem for the children is:
   'Can you make a device which will enable you to find the temperature of the water in a pond at different depths?'

You need:
junk of all kinds; metre rules; long sticks or canes; washing line (plastic covered); wire; large nails; objects to act as weights; waterproof markers; tools.

1	The problem	To make a device that will tell you the temperature of pond water at different depths.
2	Exploring the problem	How can temperature be measured? Does a thermometer have to be used? Does the thermometer have to be sent down to different depths? How could the thermometer be read if it were underwater? Can the problem be tackled differently? Could a sample of water from a specific level be brought to the surface and its temperature measured?
3	Ideas for solving the problem	Arrange to collect samples at known depths, bring them quickly to the surface and measure the temperature. A container could be fastened to a pole

marked to measure depth. The container could be hung on a rope. Could the rope be marked to measure the depth? How can a container be arranged so that it only fills with water at the required depth? Could a stopper be lifted for a short interval and then replaced? Could the container be insulated so that the water sample stays at the temperature at which it was collected? Here are some ideas.

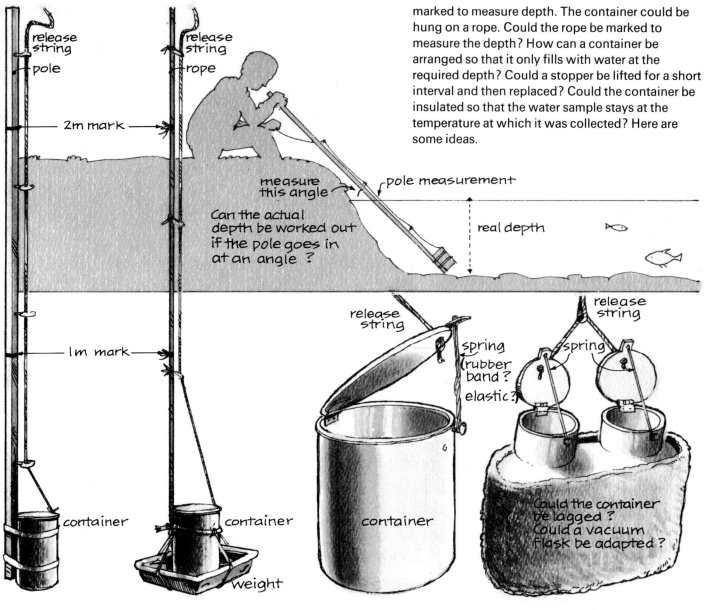

4 Making

The main problem is likely to be designing a lid mechanism so that the lid only opens when required. The children may find that it is easier to make two small openings than one large opening. A tub of water would be useful as a test ground for the container. Fixing the container to a pole or rope should be reasonably straightforward but the rope version will need adequate weighting. Field testing will be needed to decide whether the samples can be brought up quickly enough to give a true depth temperature measurement. Perhaps you could carry out your tests at a local swimming pool, if a pond is not safely and easily accessible.

5 Evaluating

Does the device work? Is it easy to use? Is the container the right size? Is it small enough to sample at close enough intervals? Is it big enough to collect a large enough sample of water?

ii The problem for the children is:
'Can you make a device that will drop a measured quantity of food from a storage container into a fish tank? Can you operate the device by remote control?' (There are two fish and the container should hold enough food for three weeks.)

You need:
junk of all kinds; string; twine; wire; pieces of wood; strips of metal packing case binding; batteries; nails; pulley wheels.

1 The problem

To make a device that drops food into a fish tank and can be operated by remote control.

2 Exploring the problem

How much food will be required? How often will the fish need to be fed? What sort of food do they eat? Does the food flow freely – like salt – or is it reluctant to flow? What ways are there of making something work by remote control?
—switching electricity on and off?
—making and unmaking an electromagnet?
—using a piece of string?
—using a pulley arrangement?
How can food be measured? weight? volume?

3 Ideas for solving the problem

A wide variety of approaches are possible. Here are some ideas.

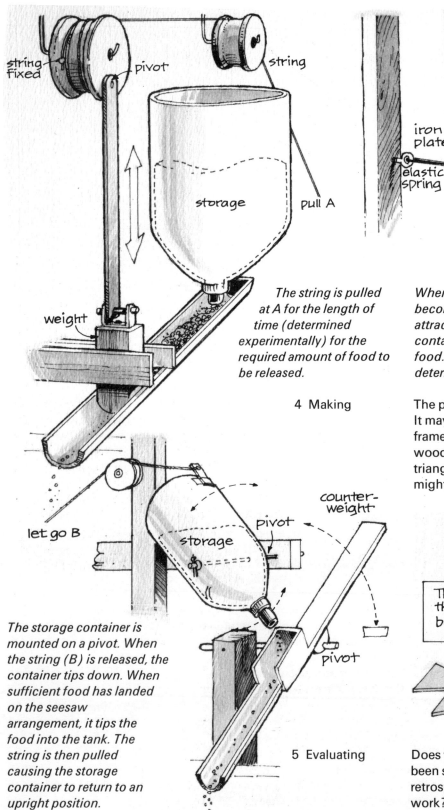

The string is pulled at A for the length of time (determined experimentally) for the required amount of food to be released.

When the circuit is closed, the nail becomes an electromagnet and attracts the iron cover of the storage container. This causes the release of food. The length of time for release is determined experimentally.

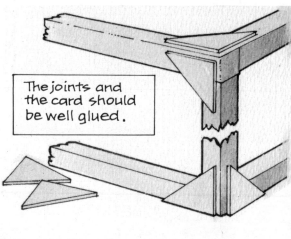

4 Making

The problems will be as varied as the solutions. It may be useful to remember that simple frameworks to support things can be made from wood of small, square cross-section using card triangles to reinforce the corners. Such a framework might be made to rest on top of a fish tank.

The joints and the card should be well glued.

The storage container is mounted on a pivot. When the string (B) is released, the container tips down. When sufficient food has landed on the seesaw arrangement, it tips the food into the tank. The string is then pulled causing the storage container to return to an upright position.

5 Evaluating

Does the device work? What problems have not been solved? Would different ideas be tried in retrospect? How do commercial feeding devices work?

Propagating

The story

(*Junior Pupils' Book 4* page 34)
Julie and Mark talk to the gardener who looks after a public garden about the ways in which plants can be produced on a large scale.

Science

People and their jobs and occupations

The work of landscape architects and gardeners is discussed, particularly their role in developing and reclaiming derelict land.
(*Teachers' Book* pages 78–9)

Concepts

Pupils will explore some aspects of these concepts:

7.3 Soil is a mixture of things which come from rocks as well as some material which was once living.
15.1 Living things have common properties: growth . . . reproduction . . .
16.3 Plants need food and water.
16.4 Plants get their food from the soil.
16.5 The food which plants take from the soil must be replaced.
18.3 Parents produce offspring of the same kind as themselves.
18.4 The life cycles of living things are often linked to seasonal change.

Making and doing activity

The problem for the children is:
'Can you devise a means of lowering a hanging basket weighing 5 kg from its hanging position at 3 m to 1 m so that it can be watered? You have only one hand free since the other hand is holding the watering can.'
(*Teachers' Book* pages 85–6)

Skills

Pupils will develop their scientific skills by:

Activity 1—Leave it to me   *TB* p81
Investigating the use and construction of a   *PB4* p35
lateral key

Activity 2—Multiplication   *TB* p82
Investigating ways of propagating plants –   PB4 p36
stem and leaf cuttings

Activity 3—Division   *TB* p83
Investigating ways of propagating plants –   PB4 p37
tubers and corms

Activity 4—Tomatoes for tea   *TB* p84
Investigating the growth and cropping of   *PB4* p38
tomato plants

The story

Few children will not at some time have visited a park or public garden where bedding plants provide a welcome splash of colour. Whilst the children probably see the open space as somewhere to play they may well have wondered at the vast numbers of plants and considered how these plants have been produced. Some parks and open spaces have existed for many years but in some inner city areas derelict land has been reclaimed and landscaped to provide places for children to play safely and pleasant places for people to enjoy.

The story page provides a background for discussion of a range of topics: for example, is this a newly reclaimed area or do the children think it has been like that for a long time? (The plants in the beds must be planted each year so they could all be quite new.) Do people really care about parks and gardens? Do they look after them? Are there parks in the country? Are they different from town parks? What about country parks? What is their purpose?

Another range of discussions can focus on plant propagation. What ways of propagating plants do the children know? *(Propagation from seed, cuttings, splitting, corms, tubers, plantlets etc.)*

Can the children tell the difference between desirable plants and weeds? What is a weed? How do gardeners tell the difference between seedlings they are trying to grow and weed seedlings? These discussions will lead the children into the activities and put these in a practical context.

People and their jobs and occupations

Creating a park or large garden (public or private) requires knowledge and skills of various kinds. The planning stages require consideration of the locality, the purpose of the park or garden, the kind of soil, the shape of the land and its contours. At the same time, people need to have imagination and knowledge of plants and trees and their habits so that they can consider how they can best clothe the park or garden landscape to produce pleasing vistas and views. Some of the finest gardens and parks were planned many many years ago so the planners never saw their ideas come to fruition. They saw them in the mind's eye because they had knowledge about plants and trees and their needs and habits plus the ability to picture what a planned landscape or garden would look like when all the plants and trees had grown to maturity. Many of the children will have visited great parks and gardens and you could use these visits as a focus for discussion.

Brilliant colour is often provided by the use of annual bedding plants – as in the garden in the story. These are produced on a very large scale. Many people are employed in the production of plants for public places and the nursery trade for private gardens is a thriving one.

There is a wide range of discussion points which can be pursued, depending on your own circumstances and the experience of the children. One point you might like to develop is the reclamation of derelict land in cities. Who plans the work? Who does the work? Who pays for the work? Who decides what flowers to grow? Who decides which trees to plant? Where are the plants raised? Is all the work in a reclamation programme paid or do some people work without payment?

The establishment of country parks is widespread and here people are needed who have knowledge and skills which enable them to understand the needs of people and other living things. They can all share and enjoy the countryside without conflict of interests. Again a wide range of discussion points can be picked up.

A key figure in all these developments is the landscape architect or landscape gardener who uses special knowledge and skills to work with the plant producer who, in turn, has particular knowledge and skills. They must work as a team. Points about their work which you might like to bring out include these:

2 Sometimes work is done in return for money. Sometimes work is unpaid (occupations).
5 The work of some people helps us indirectly – they work behind the scenes.
10 People may need special knowledge, expertise and skills in their work and hobbies.
14 Sometimes, people's enjoyment depends on the jobs being done by other people.
17 People need to use a scientific viewpoint in their jobs, occupations and hobbies.

Further activities

1 Ask someone from a local environmental planning department or parks department to come and talk about reclamation and planting of open spaces.
2 Visit a large house with landscaped and decorative gardens.
3 Visit a country park and ask someone to explain to the children what the park is attempting to do.
4 Visit a nursery where plants are grown on a large scale. Consider the economics of the business.

Science

Background notes

Gardens

Ornamental gardens and flower beds will be dominated by plants cultivated for their aesthetic qualities. They will have been grown from seeds, cuttings or by other means of propagation. A well-established garden may contain hundreds of species chosen for their form, habit or for the colour they provide. Weeds are not generally tolerated although, since a weed is merely a plant growing in the wrong place, the distinction can be a fine one. Increasingly, gardens contain a patch where native plants are encouraged to grow in order to preserve them and the creatures which are dependent on them. Much use is made of chemicals in controlling weeds and the range of weed-killers which chemists have made available enables gardeners to cultivate ground successfully with far less labour than was required previously.

Plant propagation

Many green plants can reproduce asexually – a single parent plant can produce new individuals. Thus cuttings from a geranium stem or the leaf of an African violet will produce new plants which will have characteristics identical to those of the parent plant. This is known as vegetative reproduction.

Fungi, such as mushrooms, exhibit a form of asexual reproduction: the parent plant produces spores which, like seeds, can produce new plants.

Sexual reproduction requires two parent plants. Most plants contain both male and female parts but in some plants both the male and female plants must play a part in reproduction. Most plants have the female egg cells (ovules) in an ovary which is at the base of the pistil. The male cells (pollen) are held on anthers. A grain of pollen must find its way to the stigma at the top of the pistil by some means (wind or insects). Fertilisation takes place when the pollen grows a pollen tube down the style and enters the ovule allowing male genetic material to intermingle with the female genetic material. If both come from the same flower, no new characteristics are introduced; however, if the male and female genetic material comes from different individuals, the fertilised seed will contain a mix of genetic material giving the seed and resulting plant a new combination of characteristics. Of course, there will be similarities in much the same way as there are in human reproduction. Occasionally, a genetic 'mistake' occurs producing a plant of unexpected form or flower colour. These 'sports' can lead to the production of new and improved varieties which are highly prized. The main characteristic of sexual reproduction is that the resulting plants will show a range of characteristics depending on how the genetic material from the parents is disposed. In vegetative reproduction the nature of the offspring is known – they will be exactly like the parent. There are advantages and disadvantages in the two systems. Vegetative reproduction gives no possibility of improvement or variation but it ensures continuity of what exists. Sexual reproduction is full of uncertainties but it offers variation and the possibility of improvement. It should, however, be noted that it is more likely that new forms will be worse rather than better.

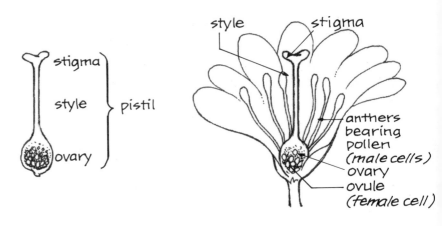

Reference has been made to stem and leaf cuttings but the underground parts of plants can also provide means of reproducing identical individuals. Some plants produce a type of underground stem with buds and shoots. Plants like the potato and dahlia produce underground stems that become swollen. These swellings, which are called tubers, contain food stored by the plant and may have several 'eyes' or buds present from which shoots will grow in succeeding seasons. Plants such as irises produce rhizomes in which food is stored for new plants which grow from them. Plants that are raised from tubers and rhizomes will reach a mature stage much more rapidly than plants grown from seed. Division is also possible, provided that each piece of the tuber or rhizome has a bud.

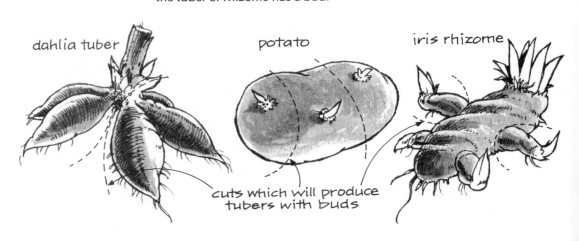

dahlia tuber   potato   iris rhizome

cuts which will produce tubers with buds

buttercup parent   offspring

ivy   stem rooting where it touches the ground

Other plants store food in bulbs and corms. Some plants produce plantlets which root at a distance from the parent; for example, buttercups. Ivy will root where a stem touches the ground. Dandelions and bindweed grow from root cuttings – any piece of root will produce new plants. In each case, the offspring are exactly like the parent plant – in contrast to sexual reproduction where the form of an individual may be quite different from that of the parents.

Some plants (e.g. roses) can be produced in very large numbers sexually and some of the plants produced may have desirable qualities but be unsatisfactory from the growers' point of view because they lack vigour or have unsatisfactory form. In such cases, methods of propagation – such as budding and grafting – are used. The desirable genetic material in the form of a small bud or shoot is grafted on to a rose stem which is growing from a vigorous root system. The natural stem and buds are then carefully cut away and the grafted material uses the stem and the root system for itself. Many modern roses are grafted in this way. Budding and grafting are fascinating processes which you may like to try yourself. There are many gardening books which explain the process in detail. (See under Topic 4.8 on page 159.)

Activity 1—Leave it to me

Objectives
At the end of this activity the children should be better able to:
1 use a given lateral key;
2 classify into sets and sub-sets using observed characteristics;
3 construct and use a lateral key independently.

Preparation
The children will need the items listed on page 35 of *Junior Pupils' Book 4*. The five tree leaves will need to match the given key, i.e. oak, sycamore, holly, horse chestnut and ash. As an alternative, you will need to give the children a modified key to fit the leaves you are able to obtain. It is possible to use the key by simply considering the drawings of the leaves but this is very much a second best approach. The weed leaves can either be collected by the children or provided by you. They will need to be identified to construct the key. Try to ensure that there are fairly marked differences amongst the five weeds. You may decide to let different children work with different weeds and then swap keys and try them out. For useful reference books see page 159.

Teaching points

General points
The children are using a given lateral key to identify tree leaves and they then go on to construct a key to identify lawn weeds. The lateral key is different from the branching key used in Topic 3.1 'Timber'. The branching key may be easier to construct but can be difficult to use since it relies on right answers at every stage – with a long key it is easier to go wrong. Constructing the non-sequential lateral key may be more demanding but in use it is quick and easy.

The children will have had considerable experience of classifying but you may find it useful to remind them, in discussion, of the variety of ways in which leaves can be classified, e.g. by colour, size, shape, texture etc.

Specific points
It is much better if the children can work from real leaves rather than the drawings.

The children should be aware that more than one of the characteristics may describe a particular leaf. For example, a leaf with a toothed edge may also have several leaflets arranged in pairs.

Accuracy is necessary in making the scanner (section 2). For some children, you may decide to duplicate it on paper which can then be stuck on to a piece of card. Scoring along the dotted lines will make folding down the tabs easier.

Activity 1 Leave it to me

The children collected some weed leaves to take back to school to make a key for the gardener. You make a key for your leaves. Start with tree leaves. Mark and Julie made a key like this.

You need: stiff card; ruler; five tree leaves; some weed leaves

1 These are the leaves from five trees. Look at them very carefully.

Look for these things.

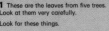

plain edge   toothed edge

several leaflets   lobed edge

(A leaf might have several of these.)

2 Next you need to make a scanner.

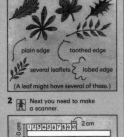

Make your scanner this size.

Cut down these lines to make small tabs.

3 Choose one of the tree leaves. Fold down any tab on your scanner with the same number as anything on Mark's list which fits the leaf you have chosen.

Mark's list

1	several leaflets
2	plain edge
3	toothed edge
4	lobed edge
5	leaflets arranged in pairs
6	leaves like a fan
7	leaf as wide as it is long
8	leaf shiny
9	leaf has prickles
10	irregular lobes

4 Now run the scanner down the key Julie made until there is a black dot in each space where you folded a tab down. Look at the end of the scanner. It tells you the name of the tree from which the leaf came.

Julie's key

1	2	3	4	5	6	7	8	9	10	
		•		•						horse chestnut
•	•					•				oak
							•			holly
•		•		•						ash
			•		•					sycamore

5 Now make a key for your weeds for other children to use.

35

Children are often so eager to find a name that they will pick out the first characteristic without due care. Remind them that caution is needed before a decision is made.

In order to make a key for their weed leaves, the children will first have to identify the weed plants from which the leaves come. Your reference book will help here (see page 159). If the children are using common weeds such as daisy, buttercup, dandelion, plantain and clover, they will find identification easier if they look at the whole plant before picking the leaf to construct the key.

They will then have to make a list (like Mark's) of identifiable features of their leaves. (It helps if you make sure that their choice of weeds gives at least one clear characteristic for each leaf.)

Ensure that the size of the key matches the scanner strip. To make this easier you could use squared paper or a prepared duplicated sheet. The children will enjoy trying out each other's efforts.

Further activities
1 Devise a punch card system to identify house plants.
2 Make a lateral key to identify fungi or bedding plants.
3 Make a lateral key to pick out individuals from a group within the class.
4 Use the computer programs FACTFILE (MEP), ANIMAL (MEP) and SEEK (Longman).

Activity 2 — Multiplication

Objectives
At the end of this activity the children should be better able to:
1 plan and carry out a simple investigation;
2 identify and control relevant variables.

Preparation
The children will need the items listed on page 36 of *Junior Pupils' Book 4*. Healthy and reasonably mature plants will be needed if propagation is to be successful. Geranium plants need plenty of light. Begonia rex prefers shade and a temperature of about 60°C. Plastic plant pots are best as they will retain moisture more readily than clay pots. The stems need to be cut cleanly with a sharp knife.

Teaching points

General points
The children are investigating plant propagation by using stem and leaf cuttings. They are trying to identify some of the criteria which lead to success. The children will need to be methodical in handling the stem sections and pieces of leaf, otherwise they will forget which way up they are.

Specific points
The best stem to choose is one that is hard and firm. When the stem has been cut into pieces, get the children to look at the pieces to see if there is a leaf or bud. (Pieces without a joint will not root – but this is something for the children to find out.)

The cuttings will tend to root better if they are put around the edge of the pot. Sealing the pot inside a polythene bag will help to conserve moisture and encourage rooting. The children must understand that rooting will take time and that patience will be needed. Warm, shaded conditions are best and the soil should only be watered if it looks dry. The polythene bag should be removed once it is apparent that growth has started from the stem above the soil.

To make the investigation in section 2 fair, the children will have to identify the variables which need to be controlled e.g. same plant stem, same soil/compost, same type of pot, same growing conditions etc.

Choose healthy leaves for section 3. Only leaves with the underside in

contact with the soil will root. The geranium will not propagate at all by this method. Begonia rex usually works well. To encourage the formation of a new plant, the main vein of the leaf can be nicked with a sharp knife before laying the leaf on the compost.

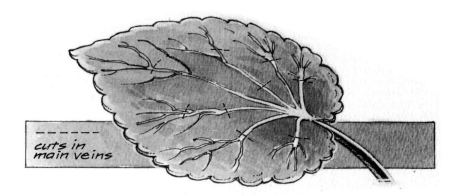

cuts in main veins

More than one plant will develop from a single leaf, particularly if you cut the main vein in a number of places. The leaf should be placed cut side down on a tray or pot of damp compost. A few pebbles can be placed on the leaf to hold it down.

Even a piece of leaf will root, particularly if the main vein is cut.

These means of propagation are vegetative and the new plants produced will have characteristics identical to those of the parents.

Further activities
1 Do cuttings root better in plastic or clay pots?
2 Do cuttings dipped in hormone rooting powder take more readily than those that are not dipped?
3 Do cuttings root more quickly in rooting gel than they do in compost?
4 What conditions are best for rooting cuttings successfully?
5 Try propagating other plants by stem and leaf cuttings.

Activity 3—Division

Objectives
At the end of this activity the children should be better able to:
1 observe in detail;
2 plan and carry out an investigation;
3 identify and control relevant variables;
4 make suggestions based on observed evidence.

Preparation
The children will need the items listed on page 37 of *Junior Pupils' Book 4*. The 'plant tuber' can either be a potato or a dahlia. Obviously a dahlia will provide extra interest. Tubers can be bought reasonably cheaply. Begonia corms can also be obtained at reasonable cost. They are more likely to be available in the spring but most garden centres will be able to supply them at any time. Any tuber will root if it is in good condition. Peat or potting compost are suitable but peat is cheaper.

Teaching points

General points
The children are investigating the propagation of plants from tubers and corms and, in particular, whether a part of a tuber or corm is able to produce a plant. They should discover that only a piece with a bud or 'eye' will grow into a new plant. Some patience will be required with this activity since it may be a matter of weeks before real results can be seen.

Specific points
Tubers can be grown without heat but some warmth will encourage more rapid growth. Even if no buds or eyes were apparent on planting, they will soon appear and both shoots and roots will develop rapidly. The tuber

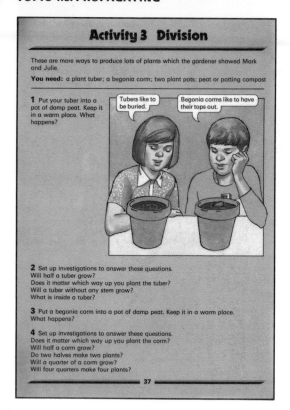

Activity 3 Division

These are more ways to produce lots of plants which the gardener showed Mark and Julie.

You need: a plant tuber; a begonia corm; two plant pots; peat or potting compost

1 Put your tuber into a pot of damp peat. Keep it in a warm place. What happens?

Tubers like to be buried.

Begonia corms like to have their tops out.

2 Set up investigations to answer these questions.
Will half a tuber grow?
Does it matter which way up you plant the tuber?
Will a tuber without any stem grow?
What is inside a tuber?

3 Put a begonia corm into a pot of damp peat. Keep it in a warm place. What happens?

4 Set up investigations to answer these questions.
Does it matter which way up you plant the corm?
Will half a corm grow?
Do two halves make two plants?
Will a quarter of a corm grow?
Will four quarters make four plants?

— 37 —

can be removed carefully from the peat or compost at intervals to have a look at the growth.

For section 2, potato tubers are cheap enough to be able to cut several in half to see if both halves will grow. Potato tubers do not have a right or wrong way up but only pieces with 'eyes' will grow. Shoots that emerge from under the tuber will find their way up – no problem!

Dahlia tubers will appear to have a right way up since there is usually a distinguishable remnant of the old stalk. Even if the tuber is apparently the wrong way up, the shoots will grow upwards to the surface. If a bunch of tubers is split, shoots will only appear from points where there are buds. A single tuber with a bud will produce a plant. In splitting a bunch of tubers, it may be necessary to split the old stem down the middle to divide the buds amongst the tubers.

In the case of the begonia corm, buds will appear on the upper surface if the corm has been planted the 'right' way up. There is a top and bottom to a begonia corm, although if planted the wrong way up it will sprout and the shoots will find their way to the surface. If a corm is cut into pieces, only those of reasonable size with a bud will sprout.

Further activities

1 Look at some flowering bulbs. Does it matter which way up they are planted? How are they different from tubers and corms? Will half a bulb grow?
2 Investigate other forms of propagation – division
                                      – layering
                                      – root cuttings.

Activity 4—Tomatoes for tea

Objectives
At the end of this activity the children should be better able to:
1 carry out an investigation;
2 identify and control relevant variables;
3 choose which observations to make for a specific purpose.

Preparation
The children will need the items listed on page 38 of *Junior Pupils' Book 4*. When in season, tomato plants are reasonably cheap and it should be possible to buy three different varieties. Alternatively, the plants can be grown from seed: the seeds need to be sown some weeks before the activity is to be started in order to have plants of a size which can be planted in the grow-bag. They do, however, grow quite easily from seed given indoor warmth.

Teaching points

General points
The children are investigating how tomato plants of different varieties grow and crop. They need to pay great attention to making sure that the plants are treated in identical fashion.

Once they are established, tomato plants grow rapidly given the right conditions of adequate warmth and moisture. The children will be making continuous observations as the plants grow, so a diary would be a good way of keeping an accurate record.

Specific points
Remind the children to label the plants. To treat the plants fairly the children will have to consider a range of factors e.g. amount of light, heat, water, fertiliser. Does the position of the plant in the bag matter?

It will be several weeks, even in the most favourable conditions, before some of the questions posed in the *Pupils' Book* can be answered. It will probably take about 12 weeks for the plants to fruit but interest can be maintained by regular observation of growth rates, plant condition, and the process of flowering and fruit formation. The children may become

interested in ways of producing bigger and better tomatoes. However, they must remember to treat all the plants in the same way if they are comparing varieties i.e. they must remember that the variable being investigated is 'variety of plant'.

It is quite possible to get seeds from a ripe tomato to germinate (section 2). Scrape out the seeds and wash in a fine sieve under running water. Dry out on a clean surface and plant in a standard seed compost. (Even a tomato sandwich has been known to grow!)

In section 4, the children might suggest alternatives to soil e.g. gravel, sand, sawdust etc. Why are these not suitable? How are they different from soil or compost? *(Soil and compost contain plant nutrients either naturally or by addition; the other media do not.)* Plants can be maintained in a barren medium if they are supported by adding nutrients. In general, this requires considerable skill and knowledge but given a proprietary product such as Phostrogen the children might like to follow suggestions for the use of this and try to match the results for ordinary, bought plant compost.

A leaflet obtainable from the company describes how to use Phostrogen as an additive to water to produce a growing medium. (See under Topic 4.8 on page 159.) The children could try this method of cultivation and compare the results with those obtained if they try to grow plants in water only.

Further activities

1 The children could investigate different varieties of other flower and vegetable crops. How do they differ?
2 Try growing other plants hydroponically i.e. in water with added nutrients. (See 'Hydroponics' leaflet on page 159.)
3 Plants can be watered automatically by using a bowl of water as a reservoir and a strip of material as a wick.
   The children could investigate which material makes the best wick. (Nylon tights work well.)

Making and doing activity

The problem for the children is:
   'Can you devise a means of lowering a hanging basket weighing 5 kg from its hanging position at 3 m to 1 m so that it can be watered? You have only one hand free since the other hand is holding the watering can.'

You need:
junk of all kinds; strong cord; wire; thin rope; wood; pulley wheels; nails; tools.

1 The problem   To find a way of lowering a hanging basket weighing 5 kg from 3 m to 1 m with one hand.

This would be difficult to hold with one hand.

The block and tackle make it much easier to hold the basket.

2 Exploring the problem

The hanging basket is heavy so that the device must lessen the work which the waterer has to do. It must hold the basket at the lower position whilst it is watered. It must be possible to hold it with one hand.

3 Ideas for solving the problem

The basket could be hung from a pulley system so that the effort required to move it is diminished. A block and tackle could be made. The cord from which it is hung could be looped round something whilst the basket is being watered, or a counterweight could be fitted. Do the children know how sash windows work? Do they remember the work they did on pulleys in Topic 3.7? Here are some ideas that the children may produce.

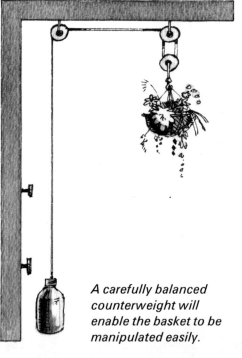

A carefully balanced counterweight will enable the basket to be manipulated easily.

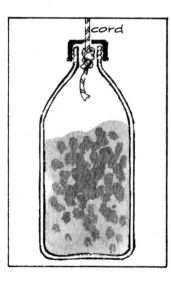

Counterweight – made by putting sand/gravel into a plastic bottle. The cord passes through a hole in the bottle cap.

4 Making

Some care will be needed in developing a final version and the children might be guided towards planning and designing the device they want to make and then making a small model before they attempt the final solution. Hanging baskets that want watering at least once a day are a real problem so that the children could be encouraged to work carefully to produce a reliable solution.

5 Evaluating

Does the device enable the basket to be lowered with one hand so that watering is a simple matter? Might there be other ways of solving the problem? For example, could a means of getting the water up to the hanging basket in situ be devised?

plastic tube buried in soil

washing-up liquid bottle 'pump'

OR

tube tied to supports for overhead watering

The story

(Junior Pupils' Book 4 page 39)
The setting for the story is Sports Day at Dalton Primary School which the Newton Street children attend.

Science

People and their jobs and occupations

Understanding how the human body works and investigating performance under controlled conditions helps athletes and their coaches to improve performance.
(Teachers' Book page 88)

Concepts

Pupils will explore some aspects of these concepts:

5.3 Measurement using standard units – time, distance, weight.

15.1 Living things have common properties: . . . respiration . . . movement.

19.1 People are living things. They exhibit variability.

19.6 The different life processes take place in different defined parts of the body.

19.7 Apart from the sex organs and those functions which are sexually controlled, the bodies of all people are the same and function in the same way.

Making and doing activity

The problem for the children is:
'Can you make something which will indicate by sound or light when a runner has left the starting line?'
(Teachers' Book pages 95–6)

Skills

Pupils will develop their scientific skills by:

Activity 1—Thump, thump!   *TB* p91
Investigating the effect of exercise on heart   *PB4* p40
beat and pulse rates

Activity 2—Puffed out   *TB* p92
Investigating lung capacity and the effect of   *PB4* p41
exercise on rate of breathing

Activity 3—Hop it   *TB* p93
Investigating leg strength and its relation to   *PB4* p42
running performance

Activity 4—Fast ones   *TB* p94
Investigating factors which might determine   *PB4* p43
whether someone is a good runner

The story

Sports day is a familiar part of the routine of many schools. For some children it is great fun; for others it is something to be endured. Children who are naturally good runners or jumpers enjoy competing but those who are not naturally endowed with speed or sprightliness can find sports afternoon a big disappointment mixed with feelings of failure. The story provides a good opportunity to explore all these feelings. It also creates an opportunity to reinforce the idea that although human beings have much in common, we all have our own special strengths and weaknesses. Not many people are going to be great athletes and only one person can win. Nevertheless, many people enjoy athletics, sports and games. We all need to keep our bodies as fit as possible even if we never win anything.

People and their jobs and occupations

The children will know many sporting personalities and you could encourage them to produce photographs of their favourites. Can they think of reasons why these people are successful in their chosen sports? Can you tell by looking at them? What do they have in common? *(Probably a large measure of natural gifts but mainly total dedication and motivation translated into a punishing training schedule.)* All the people engaged in sport at a high level – whether they are runners, jumpers, football players or skaters – need to understand how their bodies work, how to look after their bodies carefully and how to make themselves perform with maximum efficiency. Many of these people make a living by their sports performance but many more perform as amateurs. High-level performers are usually helped by a coach – someone who understands how to make a particular human body achieve its peak performance potential. It is a highly skilled job. The coach must observe the athlete's movements very carefully. He or she must consider which variables might be affecting performance and formulate ideas about changes which the athlete could make to improve performance. These have to be tested in a controlled manner so that the coach and the athlete will know whether the changes are beneficial. The coach and the athlete must tackle their tasks scientifically. They need knowledge and the skills to act scientifically.

In some countries the development of athletic and sporting performance is highly organised and scientific and there is massive support from a technological viewpoint. The fine detail of the equipment of ski teams is familiar to many children via the television, as may be the equipment of cycling teams.

It is a good opportunity to discuss with the children the importance of a healthy diet and the dangers of smoking, drug taking etc. Particular points which you might like to emphasise in discussion include:

15 What is a job for one person may be an occupation or hobby for another.
16 People use scientific information in their jobs, occupations and hobbies.
17 People need to use a scientific viewpoint in their jobs, occupations and hobbies.

Further activities

1 You may be able to get an athlete or sportsperson to come into school to talk to the children. The importance of practice and training would certainly be stressed. You may find someone who will coach the children.
2 The way in which some item of sports equipment has developed could

be investigated e.g. football boots, training shoes, tennis racquets, cycling equipment etc.

Science

Background notes

The body

The heart is a pump which continually sends the blood round the body so that tissues are supplied with nutrients and oxygen and waste products are removed and conveyed to those organs which cleanse and re-oxygenate the blood. Normally, the heart beats at a steady, comparatively slow rate but when the body is being used more intensely and requires more nutrients and more oxygen at key sites the heart-beat rate increases. The pulse, which can be felt at points in the body where arteries are near the surface, is a measure of the rate of heart beat. The wrist is the usual pulse point but the pulse can also be easily detected at the sides of the throat under the chin. The pulse can be detected by using gentle finger pressure. It is not quite as easy to feel and count heart beat and a stethoscope, even of the most rudimentary kind, will help.

The blood passes to the lungs where it is re-oxygenated and carbon dioxide is released and breathed out. When a person is at rest and the blood is being pumped round to supply normal requirements, the breathing rate is quite slow and the lungs are operating gently. When the body's requirements increase in exercise and the blood is being pumped rapidly, the lungs have to work harder to provide sufficient oxygen to oxygenate the blood and clear the carbon dioxide. Lung capacity becomes an important factor in determining the efficiency of athletic or sporting performance. Two incidental points: the air which is breathed out contains a considerable amount of oxygen; and the ability to take in a large quantity of air is largely controlled by making a considerable effort to empty the lungs rather than concentrating on the process of inhaling.

The strength of a person's legs depends on amount and tone of the muscular tissue. Exercise and use of the muscles are prime factors in building up tone, but nutrition has a key role in producing the muscular tissue. Endurance is associated with general fitness. In prolonged and intense exercise, muscles need nutrition and oxygen to release the energy necessary for their function. The more intense the exercise, the more energy is needed and the faster the blood flow and supporting breathing rate the better. Even so, problems can arise when the oxygen supply to the muscles is inadequate. Muscles suffer painful cramp in conditions of insufficient oxygen supply because the normal chemical reaction which results in release of energy is not possible and substances deficient in oxygen start to accumulate. It is these substances which cause the pain and condition of cramp. A period of rest allows the body to sort itself out and to convert the cramp-producing substances into the normal products which are moved from the muscles by the blood. So somebody may have strong legs but not be a very good runner. Of course, it also depends what is meant by 'a good runner'. Some people may be able to run a short distance very quickly (sprinters), whilst others will be able to run long distances at a steadier rate.

So many factors are involved in determining running performance that it is not possible to say by looking at someone that that person will be a good runner. It might be possible to spot a likely poor runner – unfit, flabby muscles, lacking exercise – but even that kind of prediction is likely to be wrong. We are all the same in having the same essential parts but in the detail we are all different. Each of us is unique – and amazing!

Fitness

The arguments about which sport needs the greatest fitness have been investigated scientifically. Dr Craig Sharp, co-director of the Human Motor Performance Laboratory at Birmingham University, analysed top performers in 33 different sports. The results of these tests are shown in

SCORES OUT OF TEN	cardio-respiratory fitness	muscle speed	strength	local muscle endurance	flexibility	low body fat	total
Olympic gymnastics	6	9	9	10	10	9	53
Stage dance	8	8	7	8	10	10	51
Karate	6	9	9	8	9	6	47
Swimming: 1500m	7	6	7	9	8	7	44
Slalom canoeing	8	7	7	9	6	7	44
Squash rackets	9	7	5	8	6	9	44
Cycle-cross	9	7	8	8	5	7	44
Basketball	9	8	5	7	5	8	42
Sprint canoeing	6	6	8	10	5	7	42
Rowing: sculls	8	7	7	9	5	6	42
Windsurfing	6	5	8	10	7	6	42
White-water canoe	7	7	6	9	6	6	41
Shinty	8	7	6	7	6	7	41
Sprint cyclist	8	10	6	7	1	8	40
Rowing: fours, eights	7	6	8	9	4	6	40
Football: 1st division	6	7	7	8	5	7	40
Hurling	7	7	6	7	6	7	40
Road cyclist	10	6	4	9	1	8	38
Rugby: back	7	8	5	6	5	7	38
Netball	8	7	5	6	5	7	38
Badminton	7	7	4	6	6	7	37
Athletics: sprinting	4	10	8	5	4	6	37
Lacrosse	6	7	5	7	5	7	37
Athletics: middle distance	8	7	4	7	2	8	36
Hockey	6	8	4	6	5	7	36
Volleyball	7	7	5	6	6	5	36
Speed-skating	7	7	6	6	4	6	36
Cross-country skiing	10	2	4	9	2	9	36
Tennis	5	5	6	7	5	7	35
Athletics: distance	9	4	2	9	1	10	35
Table tennis	5	7	4	7	5	6	34
Rugby: forward	6	5	10	5	4	4	34
Long distance swimming	7	2	7	10	3	1	30

the table above.

The *cardio-respiratory fitness* test monitors the oxygen delivery system of the body. Distance runners, cyclists and cross-country skiers score highest; sprinters do not have time to replenish much oxygen as they run so only score four out of ten. *Muscle speed* tests measure the time it takes for athletes to reach peak power. Sprinters and karate exponents score highly. The *strength* category is self-explanatory. For no apparent reason, however, there were variations of up to 10 per cent in athletes' performances of strength from day to day. The amount of work the athlete can do is registered under *local muscle endurance*. The tests measure how quickly work-rate falls off, the onset of fatigue and then recovery rate. *Flexibility* tests produced some interesting results: distance runners only scoring one out of ten; dancers and gymnasts reaching a maximum score. The thickness of skin at various points on the body was measured to determine the percentage of *body fat*. Young males average around 14 per cent and females around 26 per cent. For sportsmen the average is down to 10 per cent and for sportswomen down to 22 per cent.

These tests and the table of figures show some surprises. Which sport did you think requires the greatest fitness? You could ask the children the same question and provoke discussion on this subject.

Activity 1 — Thump, thump!

Objectives

At the end of this activity the children should be better able to:
1 plan and carry out an investigation paying particular attention to the reliability of their findings;
2 identify and control relevant variables;
3 look for patterns in their findings;
4 select in advance an appropriate recording method.

Preparation

The children will need a stop clock and a home-made stethoscope. Although the physical activities which the children are required to do are not unduly strenuous you should make sure that you are aware of any children with conditions which require special care e.g. asthmatic or overweight children. You should supervise the children and should keep a watch for any children who are exercising to the point of distress.

Teaching points

General points

The children are investigating how the heart reacts to cope with the demands of exercise on the body. They should be able to appreciate that in everybody the heart responds by beating faster. They should also be able to discover that normal and enhanced heart rate is about the same, but not exactly the same, for different people. Human beings are more or less the same but the way their bodies function varies in detail.

Specific points

The children can make a simple listening device from yoghurt cartons. They may remember an earlier activity and attempt to make a stethoscope of this kind.

They should discover in section 2 that the heart-beat rate and the pulse rate are the same.

The children need to work in groups and to organise their work as a group. Individual investigations may be done by pairs of children but the pairs should come together to compare results. This means that the children as a group will need to plan how to carry out the investigation and agree to follow the plan carefully so that all the results will be comparable. Careful recording is essential as a basis for the final written report.

The illustration beside section 3 suggests that the exercise variable is controlled by the number and size of steps as the subject runs on the spot, but the children will realise that they need to watch carefully to try to control the effort which their subjects make.

They will also have to take steps to ensure that they test their subjects immediately the exercise is finished. They will probably decide to measure pulse rates, if they have decided from their previous measurements that pulse rate is a measure of heart-beat rate. Some discussion of this point may be needed to clarify their ideas.

You could discuss with the children what kind of report they would like to write.

Further activities

1 The children could compare the effect on heart/pulse rate of various activities e.g. running, walking, skipping, jumping etc.

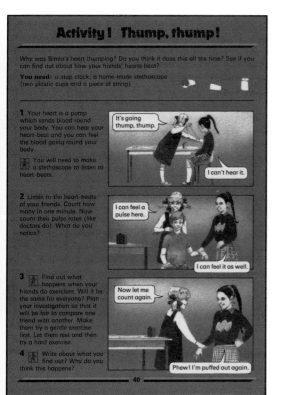

2 Is the heart/pulse rate the same when people are standing up, sitting down, lying down?

3 Does the heart/pulse rate alter for any other reason than physical exercise e.g. writing, reading an exciting book, watching a television programme?

Activity 2—Puffed out

Objectives
At the end of this activity the children should be better able to:
1 plan and carry out an investigation paying due regard to the need for repetition to improve reliability;
2 identify and control relevant variables;
3 recognise patterns in their results;
4 find a way to measure a volume of air;
5 record using mathematical representation, choosing in advance the most appropriate method.

Preparation
The children need the items listed on page 41 of *Junior Pupils' Book 4.* The sterilising solution is to rinse the balloon after each user. Check that the balloon can be blown up easily. The children have to find a way of measuring how much air there is in the balloon. They may decide that they need string, a measuring tape, a washing-up bowl, jam jars, plastic tubing, Blu-Tack etc. You should have such items in reserve.

Teaching points

General points
The children are investigating breathing rates and lung capacity. They should recognise that everyone breathes quite slowly and gently in resting condition and breathes more rapidly after exercise – some people more rapidly than others. Lung capacity can differ considerably from one person to another.

Do not allow the children to become involved in prolonged deep breathing activities/competitions. Deep breathing is harmless in small amounts but can cause problems for some individuals if there is over-indulgence. You should also watch for children trying to blow too hard when they are blowing into the balloon. Again, no problem if they work within their comfortable capacity.

Specific points
The children will need to work in groups and plan their investigation so that all the results at the end will be comparable.

If they are going to compare results within their group it would be easier if the group decides on a common method of recording. Can they devise a method of recording which shows their findings clearly – perhaps a graphical method? They should realise that counting for a single one-minute period is not reliable enough. It is quite difficult to breathe normally if someone is counting every breath and very difficult to count one's own rate of breathing. A number of one-minute counts should be made. Agreement on how to control the running is essential. They will also have to agree on how they can count the breathing rate after exercise, so that the results are comparable.

For section 1 the children may produce a range of ideas about how to measure the blown-up balloon so that it will provide a comparison of lung capacities. Some possibilities are shown on the opposite page.

If the children have any difficulty in blowing up the balloon from flat, they could inflate the balloon an agreed amount using a balloon pump and then measure how much more air is breathed in.

Are they satisfied that one measurement is a reliable indicator of lung capacity? Do they see a need to check their results or to carry out a number of measurements and take an average?

Activity 2 Puffed out

What does Anna mean when she says she's 'puffed out'? What does it feel like when you are out of breath? Why does it happen? Do we all get puffed out in the same way?

You need: a stop clock; some balloons; sterilising solution

1 Sit down quietly with your friends and see if you can answer any of the questions at the top of the page. Now start the stop clock and find out how many times each of you breathes in 1 minute. Is it fair to count only for 1 minute? Can you count your own breaths fairly?

Now all run on the spot and count your breaths in 1 minute again. Is there a difference among your friends?

You count my breaths.
Will that be fair?
Then you do mine.

2 Can some of them take in more air at one gasp than others? Ask each of them to take in a big gasp of air and then to blow it into a balloon, like this. Find a way to measure how much air is in the balloon. Keep a record of your results.

Blow hard.

3 Which of your friends can take in most air? Why do you think this is so?

41

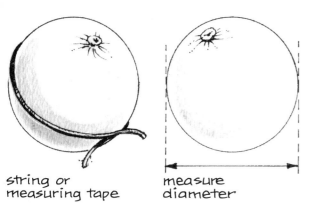

string or
measuring tape

measure
diameter

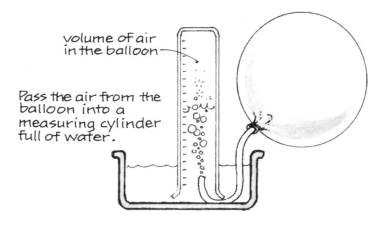

volume of air
in the balloon

Pass the air from the
balloon into a
measuring cylinder
full of water.

Is there any pattern if breathing rates and lung capacity measurements are compared? Is there any pattern if the lung capacities of the supposed good runners and the supposed bad runners in the class are compared? How could an answer to this question be investigated properly?

Further activities

1 Try using other methods for measuring the increase in volume of the balloon. The water methods provide opportunities for measuring volume in millilitres using a measuring cylinder. They also provide an excellent opportunity for a discussion about how accurately the volume needs to be measured if it is a measure of lung capacity. (How precisely measurable is the amount of air a person blows out from a particular lung intake?)
2 Is the breathing rate the same for sitting? standing? lying down? Is it fair simply to stand up or lie down and then measure the breathing rate?
3 How do swimmers have to breathe? This could be a useful investigation for children who are trying to improve their swimming performance. You may be able to arrange for a swimming coach to talk to the children. A visit to the swimming baths would be very appropriate.
4 Investigate the breathing rate of animals.

Activity 3—Hop it

Objectives

At the end of this activity the children should be better able to:
1 plan and carry out an investigation paying particular attention to the reliability of their results;
2 look for patterns in their results;
3 measure in kg and g reading a calibrated scale;
4 make suggestions and plan an investigation to test these suggestions.

Preparation

The children will need bathroom scales. Make sure that the children are able to read the scale.

Teaching points

General points

The children are investigating leg strength by measuring the push which they can exert with their legs on a bathroom scale. They go on to investigate who can do big hops. If those with strong legs are listed, does it coincide with the list of those who can do big hops? (Is there a pattern?)

Specific points

The children need to work as a group and agree on a plan for the investigation and on recording methods. They will have to decide on how to arrange the pushing so that the result for one child can be compared fairly with the result for another one. Are they sure that it is just leg strength they are measuring?

Activity 3 Hop it

How strong are your legs? Do the best runners in your class have the strongest legs?

You need: bathroom scales

1 Find out how strong your left leg is and then test your right leg. Your friends will test their legs as well. Plan your tests so that all your results can be compared.

I'm pressing as hard as I can.

I'll read the dial.

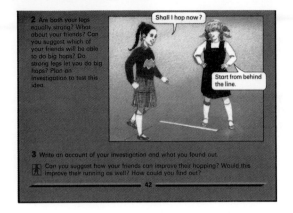

When they have tested one leg, ask them what they think the result for the other leg will be. Is the result what they expected? Is there a pattern? For instance, do all the children have both legs the same or do all the children have legs which are different in strength?

The children will have to consider a number of variables, e.g. how much arm action is to be allowed, starting position of the free leg etc. The children will probably realise that one hop is not a reliable measure of performance. If they repeat the measurement they must decide whether to take an average or whether to take the best result.

For section 3, does the method of recording which they have used show their results clearly? Have they chosen a useful recording method?

This should give rise to an interesting discussion. The children will no doubt suggest that hopping can be improved by practice. They may suggest that special leg-strengthening exercises could be used to improve muscle tone and improve hopping and running action. Do the children refer back to their investigations into lung capacity and realise that being a good runner depends on more than strong legs?

Further activities

1 The children could use a spring balance to find the pulling strength of their legs. A sponge or pad of material will stop the cord cutting into the children's feet.

   Do the results for pulling show the same pattern as the results for pushing?
2 Investigate jumps from a standing position. Do they correlate with the hopping results?
3 Investigate high jumps. Do the results correlate with any of the other results?
4 The pushing and pulling strength of arms can be investigated. Is there any correlation between the results for legs and arms?
5 Is there any correlation between the girth of legs and arms and their strength?

Note In each of these 'Further activities' the children should be asked before they start the investigation to suggest what they think they will discover and to explain why they have made a particular suggestion.
If the results are not what they expected they should be encouraged to consider why. On reflection, was the suggestion not well-founded? Is the investigation reliable? This kind of thinking should become 'part and parcel' of the children's way of working.

Activity 4—Fast ones

Objectives

At the end of this activity the children should be better able to:
1 distinguish between observations which are significant and those which are not;
2 plan and carry out an investigation;
3 use a graphical means of communicating results;
4 look for patterns in their results.

Preparation

The children will need a stop clock and a collection of multiblocks. They may need other measuring equipment depending on what they decide to investigate in section 4 of the activity.

Teaching points

General points
The children are trying to find out if it is possible to say what makes a

good runner. They establish an order of performance for running and then use multiblocks to see if they can find any other factor which shows the same form. They consider the various factors they have already investigated and are invited to look at any other factors which they think might be significant. They should realise that many factors contribute to the efficiency of running performance and it is very rarely that these are all optimised in one individual.

Specific points
It does not matter particularly how far the children run but you could use the opportunity to let them measure 50 metres (or 100 metres if you consider that appropriate). The children will need to record the times for the class carefully – or you can let them work in smaller groups and bring the groups together later. They will need to decide on a scale – 2 seconds ≡ 1 block would be appropriate. The block for each child should be labelled and the blocks put in order starting with the smallest time.

Graphs are then constructed for each of the other factors which have been investigated in previous activities. In each of these the name order of the running graph is used so that the shape of each of the graphs can be compared with the running graph. Are any of them the same shape? Is there a pattern?

There are a number of factors which could be investigated in section 4. Weight is suggested; others include height, leg length, length of stride.

By the time the children have finished building their block graph they will probably realise that there is no easy way of deciding what makes a good runner. It is unlikely that any of the graphs will have exactly the same shape as the running graph but the graphs for some factors may be closer in shape than for others. Again, it is an illustration of human variability and shows that we all have strong points and weak points.

Throughout this activity and the previous ones, the main concern is that the children should be working thoughtfully and with concern to obtain reliable and comparable results. Then they will feel confident that any patterns they detect really exist and that any they cannot detect really do not exist.

Further activities
Can the children devise tests of people's flexibility e.g. people's ability to touch their toes; do the splits; put leg round neck; assume various yoga positions etc? For what sports or athletic events do the children think flexibility will be very important? (See reference books on page 159.)

Making and doing activity

The problem for the children is:
   'Can you make something which will indicate by sound or light when a runner has left the starting line?'

You need:
junk of all kinds; wire; batteries; bulbs; pieces of metal; nails; blocks of wood; string; scissors; tools.

1 The problem	To make something which will indicate by sound or light when a runner has left the starting line.
2 Exploring the problem	What happens when a runner leaves the starting line? What does the runner do which might be linked to some alarm device? The children can discuss this in light of their own experience and observations. Do they know about starting blocks? Television coverage of athletic events has ensured

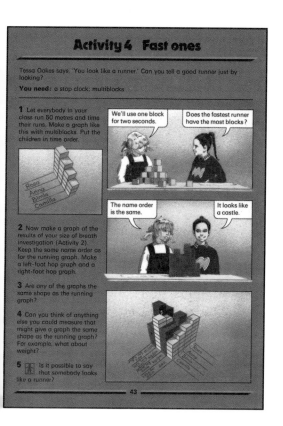

Activity 4   Fast ones

Tessa Ookes says: 'You look like a runner.' Can you tell a good runner just by looking?

You need: a stop clock; multiblocks

1 Let everybody in your class run 50 metres and time their runs. Make a graph like this with multiblocks. Put the children in time order.

We'll use one block for two seconds.

Does the fastest runner have the most blocks?

The name order is the same.

It looks like a castle.

2 Now make a graph of the results of your size of breath investigation (Activity 2). Keep the same name order as for the running graph. Make a left-foot hop graph and a right-foot hop graph.

3 Are any of the graphs the same shape as the running graph?

4 Can you think of anything else you could measure that might give a graph the same shape as the running graph? For example, what about weight?

5 Is it possible to say that somebody looks like a runner?

43

that few people have not seen a major race.

What kind of alarm devices do the children know e.g. lights which come on/go off; buzzers which start/stop; or mechanical noise makers? How can these be activated by the actions of the runner? When the runner leaves the starting line his/her feet move and this is probably the action which the children will decide can be used to activate an alarm. What sort of things might be made to happen when the runner's foot is lifted? For example, an electric circuit can be closed and the circuit can operate a buzzer or a light; a device might allow a weight to fall and either produce a noise or close an electric circuit and operate a buzzer or light.

Here are some ideas which might be similar to those produced by the children.

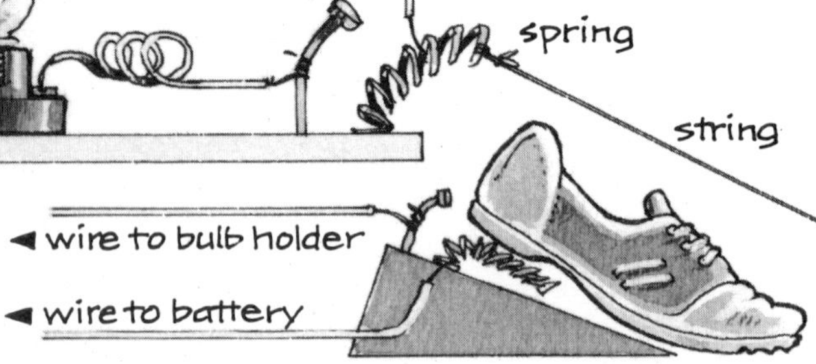

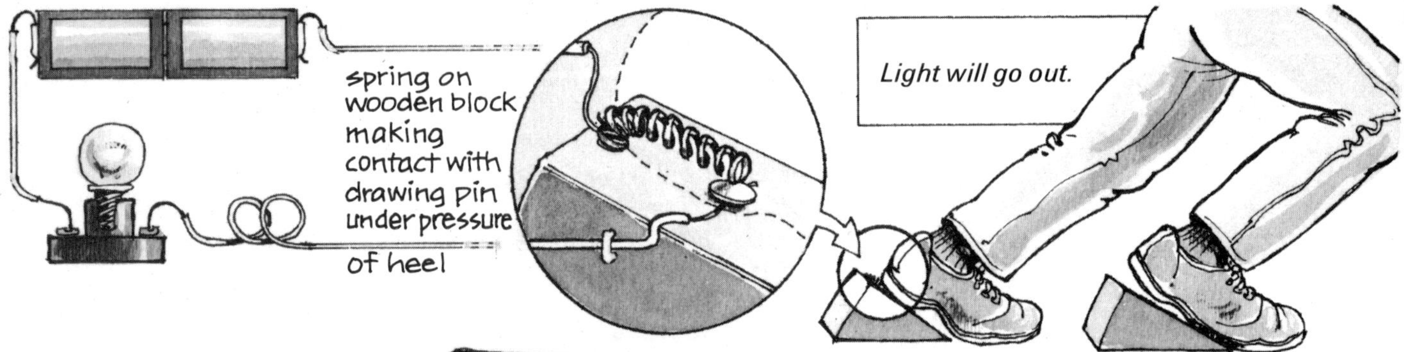

3 Ideas for solving the problem

4 Making

bulb in holder

nail

spring

string

wooden block

OR

◄ wire to bulb holder

◄ wire to battery

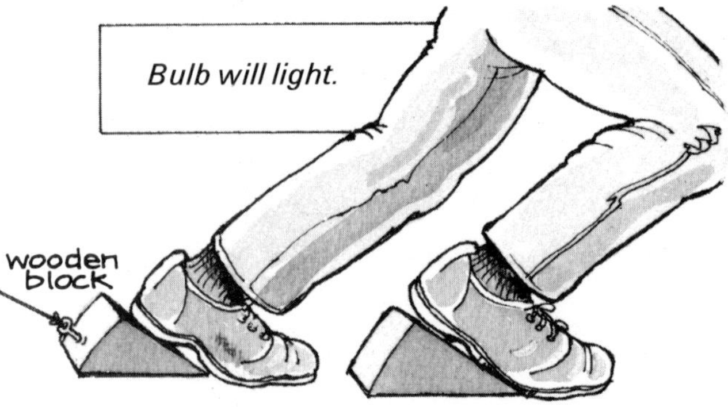

Bulb will light.

spring on wooden block making contact with drawing pin under pressure of heel

Light will go out.

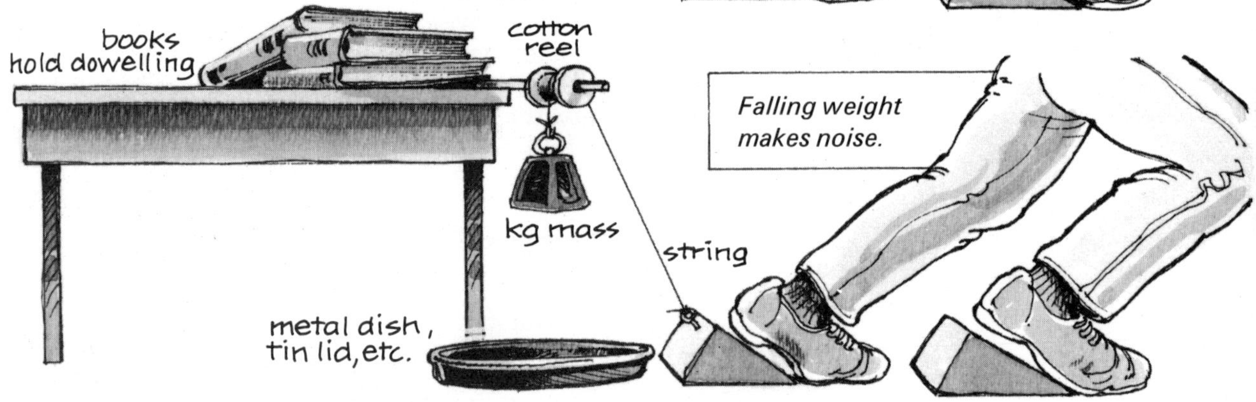

books hold dowelling

cotton reel

kg mass

metal dish, tin lid, etc.

string

Falling weight makes noise.

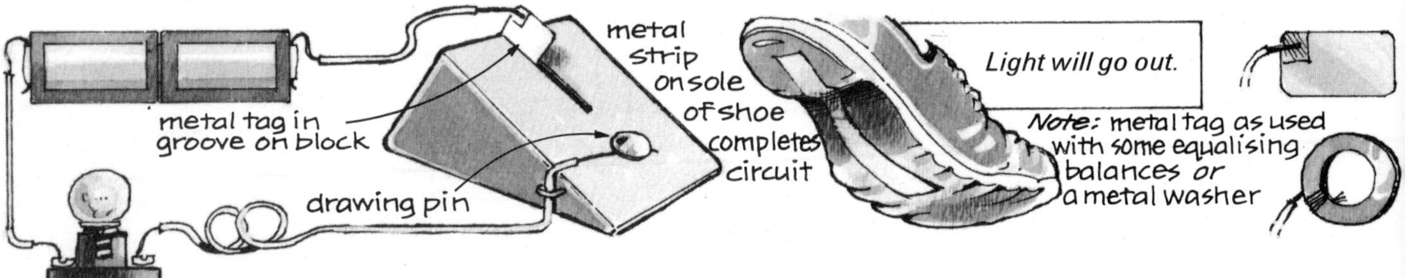

metal strip on sole of shoe completes circuit

metal tag in groove on block

drawing pin

Light will go out.

Note: metal tag as used with some equalising balances *or* a metal washer

5 Evaluating

Does the device work? Can the children suggest how it might be possible to use devices (electrical ones) to time the runner very accurately? Do the children know how major races are timed?

Moving on

The story

(*Junior Pupils' Book 4* page 44)
David, Camilla and the other Newton Street children visit Davy High School where they will be going next term. They meet Mrs Turner who will be their science teacher and try some sample experiments in the science lab.

Science

People and their jobs and occupations

Various aspects of photography are discussed, including photography as a hobby and photography as a scientific means of recording.
(*Teachers' Book* page 98)

Concepts

Pupils will explore some aspects of these concepts:
11.1 Light travels in straight lines.
11.2 Objects can be seen because of the light they give out or reflect.

Making and doing activity

The problem for the children is:
'Can you use two mirrors to see round a corner or over the top of a high wall?'
(*Teachers' Book* page 106)

Skills

Pupils will develop their scientific skills by:

Experiment 1—A thousand faces   *TB* p101
Investigating the number of reflections   *PB4*   p45
produced when two mirrors are put at
different angles to each other

Experiment 2—Beaming along   *TB* p102
Investigating the angles made when   *PB4*   p46
a beam of light is reflected at a plane mirror

Experiment 3—Make a camera   *TB* p103
Investigating the pin-hole camera   *PB4*   p47

Experiment 4—Magnificent   *TB* p104
Investigating how 'lenses' can be formed   *PB4*   p48
by using drops of liquids

The story

The story provides an opportunity for the children to discuss their feelings about moving on to their next school (or schools). How do they view the prospect? Many children will visit their new schools before the great move; other children will be less prepared for what can be an exciting but anxious experience. What will science at the new school be like? Will the children be able to work in an open-ended, investigative way as they have been doing? It is possible that the senior school science department will put greater emphasis on learning the agreed truths of science. Perhaps you could discuss with the children how in becoming better investigators they have also 'discovered' a great deal of information.

It would be very useful if you could arrange for the children to visit the science labs at their new school(s) and even better if they could sample work in the way the Newton Street children did. You might be able to arrange for the science teachers from the senior school(s) to visit your school and see the children working. It would be a great pity if the solid foundation of science which the children have acquired was not used and developed effectively at the next stage of their science education.

People and their jobs and occupations

The discussion suggested here arises from Activity 3 where the children make a pin-hole camera.

Children are always fascinated by the pin-hole camera. This serves to make clear the great refinement which is offered by commercially produced cameras at quite modest prices. Cameras can be very sophisticated and the intended use will determine the degree of refinement required. Can the children think of occasions when a camera would be nice to have and occasions when it is absolutely necessary? For example, people like to have photographs of each other. Scientific recordings often take the form of photographs e.g. satellite views of the earth. The children will have come across many examples of the use of photography, ranging from spies and microcameras to decorative views of the landscape, street scenes, sports, portraits and so on. It is very much part of modern life.

How do cameras work? What do you have to know and be able to do to use a camera well? What about the film to use? How are films made and how does the photographer decide which kind of film to use for a particular occasion? In producing a photograph, much of the skill is in the printing process and the quality of the print relies heavily on the quality of the printing paper and the quality of the developing process. Do the children know anyone who develops and prints his/her own photographs? Many people take photographs for a hobby. What sort of people earn a living by taking photographs? How have they acquired the knowledge and skills which they need? There is considerable scope for discussion but you could in particular develop these ideas:

3 Different people do different jobs and follow different occupations.
11 People have to acquire the special knowledge, expertise and skills which they need.
15 What is a job for one person may be an occupation or hobby for another.
16 People use scientific information in their jobs, occupations and hobbies.

Further activities

1 You could ask someone who is a photographer to come into school and talk to the children. The local photographic society may be able to help if there is not a parent enthusiast.
2 Get in touch with the photographic department at a local College of

Further Education. Perhaps you could arrange a visit.
3 Let the children do some developing and printing.
4 Do a topic about photography, including the history of photography.

Science

Background notes

Light

We can see objects because they reflect light. The light which strikes the object and the light reflected from it travels in straight lines so that the image is clear. So if the object is round a corner we cannot see it! Light travels at a measurable speed but so fast that, for ordinary purposes, we can consider the giving out or reflection of light and its reception by the observer as instantaneous. (Both light and radio waves travel at the same speed – 300,000,000 metres per second. Sound travels much more slowly – about 330 metres per second in air.)

Mirrors

When a flat (plane) mirror reflects a beam of light, the path followed by the beam going to the mirror (the incident beam) and the reflected beam are as shown in the sketch to the left.

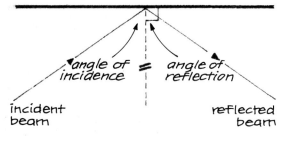

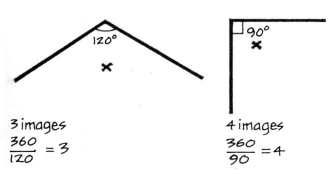

3 images
$$\frac{360}{120} = 3$$

4 images
$$\frac{360}{90} = 4$$

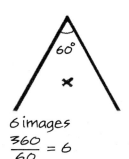

6 images
$$\frac{360}{60} = 6$$

12 images
$$\frac{360}{30} = 12$$

24 images
$$\frac{360}{15} = 24$$

If two plane mirrors are put at an angle, multiple reflections of an object placed in the angle between the mirrors can be seen. The number of images depends only on the angle between the mirrors. If the mirrors are parallel to each other the number of images becomes infinite – in effect, the angle between the mirrors is zero. ('Halls of Mirrors' use this to great effect.) It can be seen from the sketches that the number of images can be calculated by dividing the angle between the mirrors into 360° (the angle all the way round a point).

In a periscope (see 'Making and doing activity' on page 106), two mirrors are arranged so that the light is reflected twice.

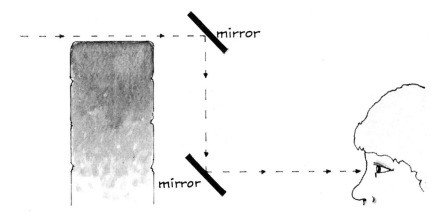

Lenses

Light can travel through any medium which is transparent to it. It can also travel through a vacuum. When it travels through a dense material, such as water or glass, it goes more slowly (although for all practical purposes instantaneously). This slowing down makes a beam of light bend as it goes from the air into the material. The effect is called refraction. A lens is shaped so that a beam of light going through it passes through different thicknesses of glass and the amount of bending for different parts of the beam is different.

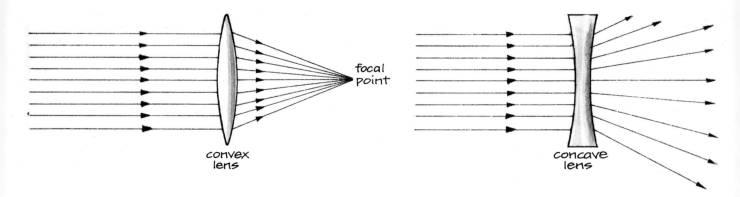

convex lens

concave lens

focal point

The beam is thus focused and brought to a point if the lens is convex or spread out if the lens is concave. The focusing effect of a convex lens is easily seen if the lens is held below a ceiling electric light and moved up and down. A position will be found at which a very bright image of the light is formed on a surface. The distance from the lens to the surface is the focal length of the lens.

If a convex lens is correctly placed in relation to an object, it acts as a magnifying glass. The object to be magnified must be nearer than the focal length of the lens.

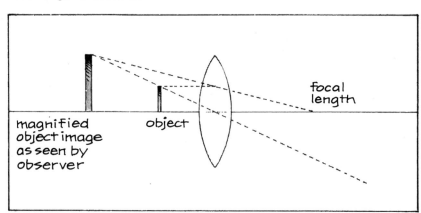

magnified object image as seen by observer

object

focal length

Pin-hole camera

The pin-hole camera works because light travels in straight lines. The sketch shows what happens when light reflected from an object or passing through a window goes through the pin-hole.

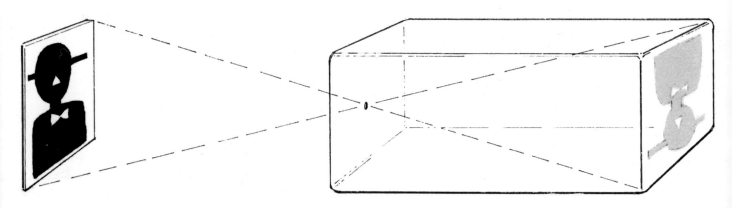

The image which is formed on the screen is upside down but quite sharp. If the hole is made larger, the image becomes brighter but less sharp. If the length from the hole to the screen is increased, the image gets larger. If more than one hole is used, the number of images produced is the same as the number of holes.

If you can arrange to black out a room completely and have a small hole in a blind over a window so that a tiny beam of light enters, an image will be formed on the wall opposite the hole. In effect, you are inside a pin-hole camera.

Experiment 1 — A thousand faces

Objectives
At the end of this activity the children should be better able to:
1 measure and draw angles;
2 carry out an investigation and decide in advance which observations to make;
3 recognise patterns in their observations;
4 make suggestions based on these patterns.

Preparation
The children will need the items listed on page 45 of *Junior Pupils' Book 4* (Experiment 1). The mirrors should be edged with sellotape (or similar) if they are at all sharp. Plastic mirrors are very suitable. Mirrors can be obtained from many sources, including DIY shops which sell mirror tiles. These can be used intact or cut into smaller pieces. Mirrors can be hinged together with sellotape, when they will stand up alone, or they can be wedged up with plasticine or Blu-Tack. A more permanent stand can be made by making a saw cut in a block of wood or by screwing clips to a block of wood.

If the children are likely to have trouble using a protractor and drawing angles with reasonable accuracy, you could prepare templates of the angles from stiff card.

Teaching points

General points
The children are asked to record what they see when a small object is placed between two mirrors which are at an angle to each other. The children are not told to count the number of images produced. They should recognise that this is a significant observation. They will need to explore the effect of changing the positions of the mirrors in a random way before they start the investigation proper in order to pick up this point. They should also recognise that there is a pattern in the number of images formed in relation to the angle at which the mirrors are placed. The simplest description will be that the number of images increases as the size of the angle decreases. With discussion, the children should be able to pinpoint the pattern more closely and realise that

$$\frac{360°}{\text{size of angle}} = \text{number of images.}$$

They should be able to use this pattern to suggest the number of images when the mirrors are arranged at stated angles.

Specific points
The object used should be small e.g. a pen top or small maths cube. The children should discover that for a given angle the number of images is always the same no matter where the viewpoint is or where the object is placed as long as it is between the mirrors.

It may help the children to put their results in a table.

In realising that the smaller the angle the greater the number of images the children will have difficulty testing their ideas (section 2). It is easiest if larger mirrors can be used, but the way in which parallel mirrors produce a theoretically infinite number of images can be seen.

Section 3 shows the basis of the kaleidoscope. If one end of the arrangement is covered with tracing paper and scraps of coloured and silver paper are introduced, pleasing symmetrical patterns will be produced when the kaleidoscope is held up to the light.

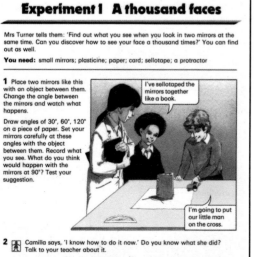

Experiment 1 A thousand faces

Mrs Turner tells them: 'Find out what you see when you look in two mirrors at the same time. Can you discover how to see your face a thousand times?' You can find out as well.

You need: small mirrors; plasticine; paper; card; sellotape; a protractor

1 Place two mirrors like this with an object between them. Change the angle between the mirrors and watch what happens.

Draw angles of 30°, 60°, 120° on a piece of paper. Set your mirrors carefully at these angles with the object between them. Record what you see. What do you think would happen with the mirrors at 90°? Test your suggestion.

'I've sellotaped the mirrors together like a book.'

'I'm going to put our little man on the cross.'

2 Camilla says, 'I know how to do it now.' Do you know what she did? Talk to your teacher about it.

3 Camilla says to David: 'Guess what would happen if we put three mirrors together.' Can you guess? Try it.

45

Further activities

1 Make a Pepper's ghost.

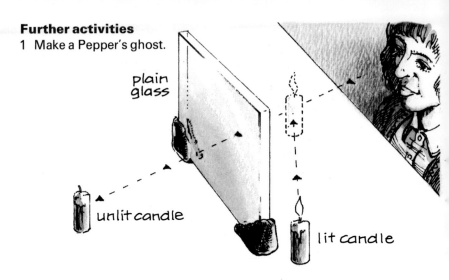

Looking at the unlit candle through the glass (which acts as a reflector) you can see the candle at the back as though it were alight. This was sometimes used as a special effect in Victorian theatre.

2 Explore the reflections from curved surfaces. If curved or flexible mirrors are unavailable, the inside of tin cans gives quite good reflection. The polished surface of a large metal spoon is also good. The children might be able to find examples of shaving mirrors, make-up mirrors, car rear view mirrors etc. They are all curved mirrors.

3 Try anamorphic drawing. This is drawing an apparently distorted image which when viewed through a curved mirror will appear as a normal undistorted image. For details see *Anno's Magical ABC,* listed on page 159.

Experiment 2—Beaming along

Objectives

At the end of this activity the children should be better able to:

1 carry out an investigation;
2 measure angles;
3 recognise and describe patterns in their findings;
4 make and test suggestions based on recognised patterns.

Preparation

The children will need the items listed on page 46 of *Junior Pupils' Book 4* (Experiment 2). If the torch produces a good bright beam it should not be necessary to dim the classroom lighting.

Teaching points

General points

The children are measuring the angle of incidence and the angle of reflection when a beam of light strikes a mirror and is reflected (see page 101). They should be able to discover that these are always equal. They do not need to know the formal names of these angles.

Specific points

The line of the mirror should be marked and the centre line should be accurately at right angles to the mirror.

In writing a description of the pattern, the children may be quite glad to have names for the angles of incidence and the angle of reflection. (The beam of light approaching the mirror is called the incident beam.)

Further activities

1 Investigate what happens to the reflected beam when the mirror which is reflecting it is turned through an angle.

The incident beam is kept in the same place and the mirror is turned so the incident beam strikes the mirror at the same point each time. If the angle through which the mirror is turned and the angle through which

---

Experiment 2   Beaming along

Mrs Turner says, 'Find out what happens when a beam of light from a torch is reflected by a mirror.' She shows Camilla and David what to do.

You need: a mirror; a large sheet of paper; a torch; two long cardboard tubes; a protractor

1 You can do the same. Arrange one tube so that the light from the torch goes along it to the mirror. Place the other tube so that the light from the mirror comes back along it. Draw a centre line at right angles to the mirror. Mark where the tubes are. Measure the angles. What do you find? Try with the torch at different angles. Can you recognise a pattern in your results?

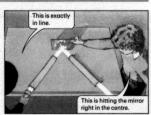

This is exactly in line.

This is hitting the mirror right in the centre.

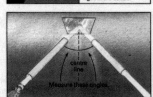

centre line

Measure these angles.

2 Make a table like this. Choose the angle for the torch and suggest what the angle for the light coming from the mirror will be. Write down your suggestions and then check them. Were you right? Did you recognise the pattern of your results correctly?

Write down a statement about the pattern.

Angle between torch beam and centre line	Angle between light beam from mirror and centre line	
	suggestion	measure
30°		
50°		

46

the reflected beam is turned are measured, it will be found that the reflected beam is turned through twice the mirror angle.

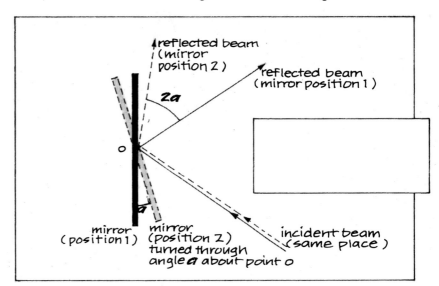

The reflected beam is turned through twice the angle that the mirror is moved through.

2 Find out about heliography – sending messages by reflecting the sun's rays from a mirror.

Experiment 3—Make a camera

Objectives
At the end of this activity the children should be better able to:
1 follow written instructions;
2 carry out an investigation;
3 recognise patterns and make suggestions based on these patterns;
4 test their suggestions.

Preparation
The children will need the items listed on page 47 of *Junior Pupils' Book 4* (Experiment 3). You will find it useful for a child to be able to stand in front of a brightly lit window that the children can view through their cameras. The child will appear as an upside-down image on the camera screens.

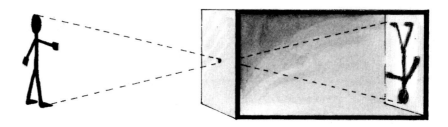

Teaching points

General points
The children should be able to make their pin-hole cameras and discover: the smaller the hole the sharper the image; as the hole is made bigger, the image becomes brighter but less sharp; if the distance from the hole to the screen is increased, the image gets bigger; if more than one hole is made, an image is produced by each hole and the pattern of the images is the same as the pattern of the holes; images are always upside down.

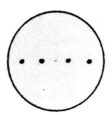
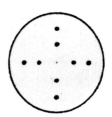
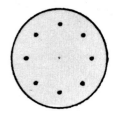

Experiment 3 Make a camera

Mrs Turner tells David and Camilla that they can make a camera. She shows them how to do it.

You need: a cardboard or plastic tube or a tin can with its top and bottom cut out; tracing paper; aluminium foil; a pin; sellotape; rubber bands; thread

1 This is what Mrs Turner tells them to do. Cover one end of the tube or tin with tracing paper pulled tight. Cover the other end with foil pulled tight. Make a pin-hole in the centre of the foil.

Make the pin-hole here.

Use tape or a rubber band to keep these tight.

2 Look through the tracing paper end and point the other end towards a window or a light. What do you see? (If not much light is getting through you may have to make the hole a bit bigger. Be careful!)

3 Try making a pin-hole camera, like David and Camilla have. The tubes must fit closely. What do you see as you slide the inner tube in and out?

This needs to fit snugly.

tracing paper

baking foil

4 Try other shapes and sizes of camera. Try holes of different sizes. Try more than one hole.

You have to watch carefully.

47

Specific points

The tracing paper and the foil must be stretched tightly. The size of the pinhole is difficult to judge to start with. The children should start with a very tiny hole and then gradually make it bigger, if the image is not bright enough. As the pinhole is made larger, the image gets brighter but it becomes less sharp. The children may overshoot the optimum size and decide to try again. It helps, if the room is fairly bright, to put an old blanket or a coat over your head – as photographers used to do when using plate cameras.

In section 3, the tubes must fit snugly one inside the other or the leakage of light will reduce the brightness of the image. As the body of the camera lengthens, the image on the screen gets bigger but its sharpness does not alter.

In section 4, each hole will produce an image. The images will form the same pattern as the holes.

Further activities

1 Take real photographs with a pin-hole camera.
   Get a biscuit tin and punch a large hole in the lid. This hole is then covered with foil in which a neat pinhole can be made. The cleaner the pinhole the sharper the picture.

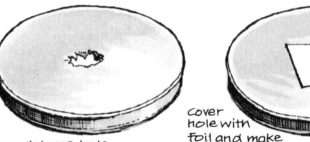

punch large hole

Cover hole with foil and make a small, sharp hole in the foil

   The inside of the box and the lid should be painted with matt black paint. Under darkroom conditions, a piece of photographic paper is cut and stuck to the inside of the bottom of the box. The lid is then put on the box and taped with insulating tape or similar to ensure that no light can leak in round the edges of the lid. The pinhole is covered with light-proof tape.

   The tin can then be taken outdoors and pointed at the object to be photographed. The pinhole is uncovered and the tin left absolutely still. An exposure of about two seconds may be adequate on a sunny day; an overcast day may require up to 10 seconds – it is a matter of trial and error. The pinhole should be re-covered at the end of the exposure time. The print will need to be processed in the normal way.

2 Examine an old camera and find out how it works.

Activity 4—Magnificent

Objectives

At the end of this activity the children should be better able to:
1 make observations in appropriate detail;
2 recognise patterns in their observations;
3 produce a written communication of their observations.

Preparation

The children will need the items listed on page 48 of *Junior Pupils' Book 4* (Experiment 4). Make sure that the glass does not have sharp corners. Tape it, if necessary. The piece of glass should not be bigger than about 25 cm square.

   A collection of lenses will be needed. It is possible to buy lenses singly or as collections from suppliers but you may be able to build up a fair selection from old spectacle lenses, discarded toys etc.

Teaching points

General points

The children should be able to discover that droplet lenses are convex.
The more curved the lens the more it bends the light and magnifies.
A concave lens will give an image which is reduced in size.

Specific points

The size of the hole is not critical but it is best to start with little more than a pinhole. If nothing can be seen, the hole should be gradually enlarged. The children may have several failures before they get a suitable combination of hole size and drop size. This is all good investigation so let them suffer a little frustration.

The children should be able to discover in section 2 that the curvature of the lens is significant. The more heaped up the drop is the greater the magnification. The glass should be cleaned thoroughly before being used and it is important that wax crayons (not ordinary crayons) are used. The children will need to keep careful notes to help them with their final written accounts.

In section 3, some of the liquids may dissolve the wax and refuse to stay in drops but the children should be able to see that different liquids will form drops with different degrees of curvature and this will affect the magnifying power.

Section 4 poses a problem for the children. Using their previous experience, they should be able to suggest which lenses will magnify and which will not; which might reduce the image; which will be the best magnifier; which will be the worst etc.

They could draw up a table so that their suggestions can be recorded and then tested. They could try to suggest an order for the degree of magnification produced and then test these suggestions.

Further activities

1 Make a magnifier from a curved glass shape filled with water, e.g. a wine glass, a coffee jar on its side, a watch glass etc.
2 Make a droplet miscroscope. A mirror can be angled underneath the glass or the whole thing can be mounted higher and a torch placed underneath. The microscope is focused by flexing the card/tin strip up and down.

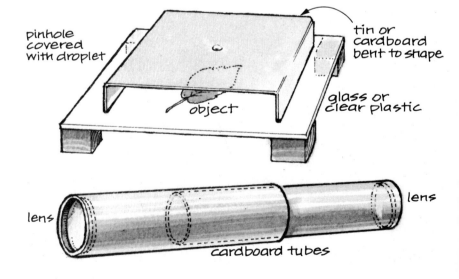

3 Make a telescope. Two cardboard tubes with lenses fixed in their ends are arranged so that the distance between the lenses can be altered. The tubes are arranged so that a focused image can be seen. A cruder arrangement is to mount the lenses on a board and move them about until a focused image is seen. The lens near the eye should be short focus and the other lens should have a long focus.

Experiment 4 Magnificent

Mrs Turner wants the children to make a magnifier which will help them to read very small print or see tiny creatures. She shows them what to do.

You need: small pieces of card, glass or clear plastic; water; cooking oil; washing-up liquid; white vinegar; wallpaper paste powder; an eye dropper; wax crayons; lenses

1 Make a small hole in a piece of card. Cover the hole with a drop of water. Look through the drop at a page of a book. What does the drop do?

> It's easier if you use an eye dropper.

> Hold it very close to the page.

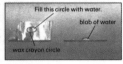

2 Take a piece of glass and draw on it a small neat circle with wax crayon. Fill the circle with water. Look through the water at your book. What happens? Try different sized circles. Try different amounts of water. Look at the shapes of the drops. Write about what you discover.

Fill this circle with water.

blob of water

wax crayon circle

3 What happens if you use different liquids instead of water?

4 Look at the shape of the lenses. Do you think they will make things look bigger or smaller? Make a suggestion and then test it.

> This lens is very fat.

> The sides of this are hollowed out.

5 Write an account of what you did and what you discovered.

48

---

lens	suggestion	test
1	magnifies	
2	reduces	
3		

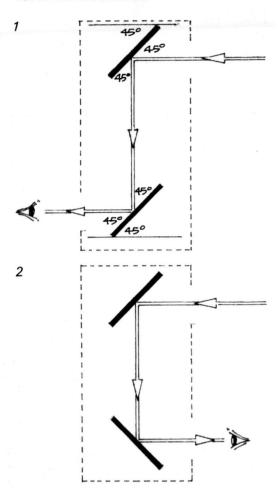

1

2

Making and doing activity

The problem for the children is:
    'Can you use two mirrors to see round a corner or over the top of a high wall?'

You need:
small plane mirrors with edges protected; cardboard inners of kitchen paper or foil; pieces of wood; plasticine; Blu-Tack; card; glue; parcel tape; sellotape; tools.

1 The problem	To use two mirrors to see round a corner or over the top of a high wall.
2 Exploring the problem	The children will want to investigate with the mirrors to find an answer to the problem in working terms. It is possible that they will already have a fair idea from the manipulations which they have been doing during the rest of the Topic 4.10 activities. The main problem will be to fix the mirrors so that the device which is produced stays together when it is used.
3 Ideas for solving the problem	In a periscope the mirrors are arranged in this way (1). Although an arrangement like number 2 will also work. The observer has to stand with his/her back to what is being viewed.

    How can the mirrors be fixed? A cardboard tube provides the easiest answer but a wooden holder might be constructed. |
| 4 Making | The children will need initially to find at what angle to each other the mirrors should be placed and they need to decide how far apart they can be placed. They will probably find it easiest to do this by fixing the mirrors on a horizontal surface with plasticine and then translating the arrangement to the vertical. |

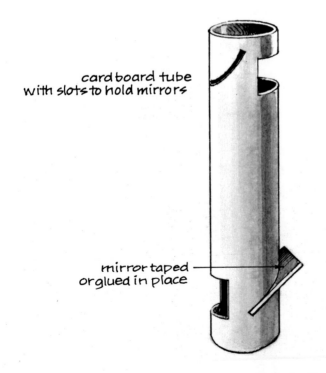

cardboard tube with slots to hold mirrors

mirror taped or glued in place

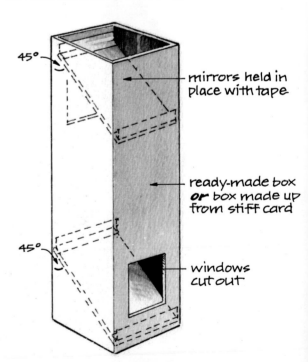

45°

45°

mirrors held in place with tape

ready-made box **or** box made up from stiff card

windows cut out

5 Evaluating	Can the children see over walls or round corners? What are the problems? Can the children make a periscope to see over a higher wall? Is there a limit to the height of the wall which can be tackled? Do the children know any real-life situations where people use periscopes? *(Submarines; great events to see over the crowd.)*

EXTENSIONS

Introduction

In the very early stages of developing *Longman Scienceworld*, it was recognised that there were areas of concern to which particular attention should be given. As a result of this, a series of guiding principles was drawn up, and this is set out below.

Principles

About science

1 Science is a way of looking at the world which is unique and therefore different from the view of the world provided by other disciplines.
2 Being able to look at the world scientifically requires the development of particular skills, abilities and attitudes.
3 By looking at the world in this way, a body of scientific knowledge has been produced.
4 Science is a major contributor to technological development.
5 Science is used in society in all sorts of ways. People use it in their work and hobbies. Everyone is confronted with it in everyday life.

About science for young children

6 Science for young children is an active process, which requires the development of those skills, abilities and attitudes which will enable them to explore their surroundings in a scientific way.
7 The scheme concerns itself with ideas and information – with scientific knowledge – because the children themselves will acquire ideas and information, as a consequence of their own active exploration of their surroundings. This information and these ideas will be relevant to the children since they will be the children's own.
8 It is probable that the information and ideas will be concerned with the immediate environment because that will be the context of most of the children's active exploration. Equally, if we are concerned to develop children's ability to work scientifically, it is likely that things and actions in the close environment will be most effective in arousing children's interest and encouraging their active involvement.
9 A particular scientific idea can be introduced in a wide variety of contexts. Scientific investigation and activity can be concerned with a wide range of subjects. It is, therefore, necessary to establish criteria for selecting contexts. The contexts chosen here reflect the following concerns:
   - interest for the children;
   - compatibility with the whole curriculum – the contexts must fit the normal curriculum pattern;
   - potential for the development of scientific skills;
   - provision of a wide range of experiences across the sciences;
   - provision of experiences of some major areas of understanding, e.g. life processes, energy conversion, etc;
   - potential for showing how a scientific perspective is useful and is relevant in a variety of circumstances – in everyday life, in jobs and in hobbies.
10 It is very important that children should develop an understanding of the relationship between science and technology. They should be provided with opportunities to engage in simple problem-solving activities. Working towards the solution of a problem is valuable in its own right; at the same time, it provides many opportunities for scientific investigation, and enables children to bring together their developing skills and abilities not only in science but also in other disciplines.
11 Evidence furnished by Piaget and others suggests that there is to some extent a developmental pattern which most children follow. This should be taken into account, but the scientific activities proposed should encourage development rather than just provide a passive response to this developmental pattern.

About teachers and science

12 The form of *Longman Scienceworld* and its classroom approach should be compatible with the normal patterns of organisation used by teachers in primary schools.

13 Many teachers feel that they have had little experience of science in their own education and believe that they do not have a solid enough basis from which to teach it. This science scheme should help these teachers to overcome their doubts and provide the information and encouragement necessary to give them the confidence to introduce science into the curriculum.

14 Teaching science involves careful attention to classroom organisation. The materials should provide the teacher with adequate guidance and advice.

15 Science has great potential for providing opportunities and stimuli for the development of language and the application of mathematics. These opportunities should be exploited.

16 Following children's progress in acquiring scientific skills and abilities is an important aspect of ensuring that children are given systematic help in developing their skills and abilities. Particular attention should be paid, therefore, to recording progress.

Some of these principles have been expanded to present a more detailed framework. They follow in the form of Extensions A–J.

Extension A   Scientific skills

Science for children in the primary school is essentially about observing, investigating and making sense of the world. The intention of *Longman Scienceworld* is to provide children with opportunities to carry out these investigations and to foster the development of the necessary skills, abilities and attitudes.

First, it must be made clear that 'investigating' is not the same as 'experimenting' as conventionally used in describing scientific activity. Our investigating differs from experimenting in a way which is best made clear diagramatically. In essence, conventional science works like this:

Diagram 1

Observing ⟶ Classifying ⟶ Recognising and stating patterns

Making predictions based on these stated patterns

Designing experiments to test these predictions

Controlling variables

Carrying out the experiments

Analysing the results, recognising the significance of these results

Opinions differ about the order of the early stages of this sequence but it remains that experimenting is about careful planned testing of a formally stated prediction based on a formally stated recognition of a pattern. The sequence involves a high level of understanding and the ability to manipulate and communicate ideas. In the planning of experiments, it is necessary to be able to recognise and plan the control of a range of variables. Again, this involves thinking in a highly sophisticated way.

Manipulation of ideas at this level is inappropriate for most children of primary school age (and indeed for many older children). It is probably the complexity of thinking which is implied in this approach to science that has led to the non-acceptance of a number of primary science curriculum developments.

What then is meant by 'investigating'? Firstly, some investigations are an extension of observing. Instead of just observing what is, the child carries out some action and finds out what happens when . . . , or what happens if . . . . Observing the sound when an object is tapped, planting seeds, or adding water to salt are investigations at this simple level. An event is provoked and what happens is observed. No prediction is being tested but observation is being directed towards looking for some change. (Simple observation is concerned with observing what is there. No change is provoked although a change may be observed, e.g. changes in nature.)

At this simple level of investigation, no attempt may be made to recognise or control variables. The investigation is concerned with what happens on a particular occasion. The investigation requires planning; the results are observed, communicated and recorded. Measurement may be involved and there will be discussion of what is observed. It is the nature of this discussion which will probably determine what happens next. Children may be content with the information they have acquired or, with encouragement, they may begin to frame questions of the sort, 'If that was what happened when we did that, I wonder what would happen if we did this?' It is this kind of thinking which leads to a more refined pattern of investigation, which can best be described diagramatically.

Diagram 2

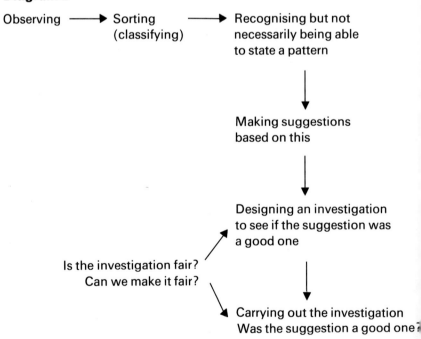

This differs significantly from the statement about experimenting in Diagram 1. Children are not expected to be able to make formal statements of patterns, or recognise and control a range of variables. Expectations are pitched lower and chances of success are greater. Progress to the more formal sequence of experimenting may develop over the years. The objective is to help children to develop the skills needed at a pace which is possible for them. It must be realised that being able to

(continued on page 118)

Table 1   Development of the science skills

	Children starting the scheme	Children at the end of the infant years	Children at the end of the junior years
Observing	The children can observe using the senses individually as suggested by the teacher. They can compare simple objects.	The children can observe using the senses in combination, aided by a range of measures and magnifiers and over a period of time (change, behaviour, etc.). The most appropriate observations to make are determined by the children prompted by the teacher. The children can, in retrospect, identify the most appropriate observations.	The children can observe using the senses in combination aided by a range of measures and magnifiers used with skill and over a period of time (change, behaviour, etc.). The children can decide which will be the most appropriate observations to make.
Communicating	The children can communicate in simple oral statements assisted by the teacher's prompts.	The children can communicate in detail using a range of methods. In retrospect, they are able to choose the most appropriate from a number of possible methods tried.	The children can communicate in detail using a refined range of methods and can choose for themselves the most appropriate method to use.
Measuring	The children can compare two objects placed side by side.	The children can measure using a range of equipment including some standard measures. They can exercise judgement about the level of accuracy/approximation which is appropriate. They can measure with precision.	The children can measure using a range of equipment. They can use their own judgement about what should be measured and how accurately the measurement should be made.
Recording	Some children can record by simple picture or mathematical representation.	The children can record using a wide range of methods including mathematical representation. With prompting they can choose retrospectively, from a number of methods tried, the most appropriate for a particular purpose.	The children can record using a wide range of methods including mathematical representation. They can choose in advance the most appropriate method for a particular purpose.
Classifying	The children can classify according to one characteristic suggested by the teacher.	The children can classify into sets and subsets using complex criteria if prompted by the teacher.	The children can classify into sets and subsets using complex criteria selected by themselves. They can use and construct simple keys.
Recognising patterns	The concept is not appreciated.	When making observations, the children may seek patterns if prompted by the teacher. They can recognise common factors in the information obtained by observing a number of instances. They are not able to describe the pattern formally. They may or may not be able to identify other instances which fit the pattern.	When making observations, the children seek patterns in the information obtained. They recognise common factors in the information obtained by observing a number of instances. They are able to recognise other instances which fit the pattern.
Predicting	The children make suggestions, guesses or predictions based indiscriminately on experience and fantasy.	The children make reasonable suggestions based on observations which may be carried out over a period of time. Some causal relationships are recognised.	The children base their suggestions on firm evidence including recognised patterns. There is increasing recognition of causal as distinct from casual relationships. They use known concepts in making suggestions.
Controlling variables	There is little appreciation of the existence of variables, and minimal recognition of causal relationships.	The children start to identify one or two obvious variables. These may or may not be relevant. The children are able to find out whether or not they are relevant. When a variable is identified, the children are able to find a way of controlling it if prompted by the teacher.	The children are aware of a wide range of variables and can, on most occasions, identify and control those which are relevant.
Investigating	With clear directions from the teacher, the children can carry out and understand simple investigations.	The children may suggest what they would like to investigate or test. They can design and carry out simple investigations with only minimal help with practicalities. They start to notice the more obvious variables and can suggest ways of testing whether they are relevant. With some help, the children can control one or two of the variables they have identified.	The children can design and carry out simple investigations with confidence. They can identify and control most relevant variables. They can review their investigations critically and check results by repetition.

Table 2(i)   The infant years

	Year 1		Year 2	
	Level 1	**Level 2**	**Level 1**	**Level 2**
Observing	The children can observe differences and similarities using the senses individually as specified by the teacher. One attribute at a time is observed and direct comparisons are made.	The children can observe using more than one sense and can cope with more than one attribute. Observations are still immediate and teacher prompted.	The children choose appropriate senses to observe changes, behaviour and movement. Arbitrary measures are used to refine observation.	The children can observe movement in relation to time. They are able to select increasingly appropriate arbitrary measures and start to see some need for standard measures.
Communicating	The children can make simple oral statements describing and naming in terms of one property. They can use pictorial representation suggested by the teacher. They ask questions.	The children use more accurate oral descriptions for more than one property. Sets can be described pictorially.	The children can include in their oral descriptions the time sequence of events related to change. They can use a very simple block graph as a means of communication.	The children can now extend their oral descriptions to include comments on results. They can make statements and justify these with reasons. They can use block graphs and pictorial representation more freely.
Measuring	The children can describe length and weight orally. They can make direct comparison of unequal lengths and use their hands to compare unequal weights directly. They can describe capacity (non-relative). They can time-sequence in simple fashion.	The children can match objects of the same length or use several objects to make up the length. They can decide whether containers hold more or less by judgement and by counting. Weighing and time sequence are as at Level 1.	The children can measure length using repeated units and limb measures. They can use balance scales to balance and order weights. They can compare capacity by emptying or filling. They can compare fast and slow.	Length, weight and capacity are as at Level 1. The children are now able to measure time, e.g. with an egg timer.
Recording	The children can make classroom displays of sets by grouping actual objects. They can use simple pictorial representation and show relationships using arrows provided by the teacher.	The children can use simple tallying and pictorial representation. They can match words and sentences to appropriate sets. The recording method is suggested by the teacher.	The children can use simple charts relating to behaviour and movement. They are able to indicate by ticking in appropriate columns. They can use double-ended arrows for balances etc. and simple graphs. They are able to do their own drawings and copy simple sentences. The method of recording is suggested by the teacher.	The children are able to write their own sentences, use greater than and less than signs, and use a simple matrix. They exploit their improved accuracy in drawing and cutting out. If the teacher suggests two methods of recording, the children are able after discussion to choose the more appropriate.
Classifying	The children can sort for one attribute by matching an example provided by the teacher.	The children can sort for two attributes decided by the teacher; if the teacher sorts, the children can identify the criteria being used.	The children are able to suggest more than one way of sorting a given collection and decide their own criteria. Sorting criteria may include purpose, movement and behaviour if these are identified by the teacher.	The children can sort according to the properties of materials using very simple keys. They are able to notice and match several common features of different materials.
Recognising patterns	The children are unlikely to be able to appreciate the idea.		The children are now better able to recognise similarities and describe these.	With prompting, the children can look for patterns in their observations.
Predicting	The children can suggest what will happen next. There is some evidence that the suggestions are based on experience, but reality and fantasy overlap considerably.		The children can make reasonable suggestions about likely outcomes based on the observations made in the course of an activity.	
Controlling variables	The children generally have little appreciation of the variables. The teacher controls the variables by providing restricted sets of materials and guiding investigations.		The children generally have little appreciation of the variables. The teacher controls the variables by providing restricted sets of materials and guiding investigations.	If the teacher suggests that a variable may be affecting the outcome of an investigation, the children may or may not recognise this as significant.
Investigating	The teacher can set a problem of the 'What happens when . . .?' type. The teacher provides a restricted set of materials and suggests the method. The children are able to carry out the investigation and make the necessary observations.		The teacher can suggest a problem. The children make suggestions about approaches and solve some of the practical problems. They need support and guidance and practical help. The teacher draws attention to related features but does not refer directly to cause and effect.	In the practical design of the investigation, more than one method may be tried by the children and a comparison made. The children begin to notice related features and some will recognise cause and effect relationships. Investigations include 'Which is best?' as well as 'What happens when . . .?'

Year 3

	Level 1	Level 2
Observing	The children can make observations at different times which are related to each other in sequence, so that they are able to observe gradual changes. They can use some standard measures to refine observations.	The children can make judgements about the level of detail and accuracy needed in their observations. They can appreciate to some extent the concept of approximation. They can increase the accuracy of their observations by using standard measures. In retrospect, they can choose which observations are most appropriate for the task.
Communicating	The children can make detailed observations orally and can express their reasons for choices. They can produce simple written accounts including mathematical representation and, orally, they can discuss the appropriateness of the means of communicating which they have used.	Orally, the children are able to give a detailed account of what was done and why, what happened and in what order. They can take part in a discussion of their results and draw some conclusions. Their written communications are increasingly appropriate.
Measuring	The children appreciate the need for a standard measure and can use the metre. They can now weigh, using $\frac{1}{2}$ kg and kg. They can balance against gram weights. Capacity and time are as at Year 2, Level 2.	The children can measure using rods marked in cm and 10 cm. They can measure straight and curved lines. They can weigh using grams, measure capacity in litres and half litres, and can calculate time intervals.
Recording	The children are able to record some measurements by using more detailed graphs. They are able to produce their own representational and observational drawings. They are able to attempt their own written records and can record over a longer period of time, noting and interpreting development. If the teacher suggests methods of recording, the children are able to comment on the usefulness of these and decide which to use.	The children's ability to draw proportions more accurately and to match colours more precisely is used in recording; this reflects their increasingly precise and accurate observational skills. Written accounts are more detailed and orderly, and records can be kept competently over a period of time. The children can suggest different methods of recording and use these. In retrospect, with prompting, they can choose which was the most suitable method and give reasons for their choice.
Classifying	The children can sort into sets and subsets. Sorting criteria may include characteristics of plants and animals.	The children can sort using more complex and less evident criteria. They can use simple keys.
Recognising patterns	The children can now recognise patterns. They will probably not be able to describe the pattern formally. They may or may not be able to identify other examples which fit the pattern.	
Predicting	The children can make reasonable suggestions based on observations over a period of time. They can recognise some causal relationships.	
Controlling variables	If the teacher suggests one variable, the children can discuss its implications and test whether it is or is not affecting the outcome of the investigation.	The children start to identify one or two variables. These will not always be relevant but the children will be able to investigate their relevance. When a relevant variable has been identified, the children should be able to find a way of controlling it.
Investigating	The children make useful suggestions about the design of investigations and carry them out with help. The teacher suggests one variable and the children can find out whether or not it affects the outcome. The children see more cause and effect relationships if the teacher points out related features which the children have not noticed.	The children may suggest what they would like to investigate. They design and carry out investigations with minimal help with practicalities. They start to notice one or two more obvious variables and with help can suggest methods of controlling these. They can carry out an agreed controlled investigation.

Table 2 (ii)   The junior years

	Year 1		Year 2	
	Level 1	**Level 2**	**Level 1**	**Level 2**
Observing	The children can observe using the senses in combination, aided by a range of measures and magnifiers and over a period of time. They are able to observe change, behaviour, etc. as well as the more obvious features, such as colour. The most appropriate observations are determined by the children, prompted by the teacher. The children can make judgements about the level of detail and accuracy needed in their observations. They can appreciate the concept of approximation to some extent. They can increase the accuracy of their observations by using standard measures. In retrospect, they can choose which observations are most appropriate for the task.	The children are increasingly able to observe detail. Independently, they recognise in advance that some observations may be of more significance than others.	With prompting, the children will seek to observe in detail and will select the appropriate equipment to do this. They are able to suggest in advance that certain observations may be of greater significance than others. With some prompting, they are able to view a sequence of observations as a whole.	Without prompting, the children observe in detail with accuracy. They can select in advance which observations to make and begin to observe for purpose, e.g. they look for similarities and differences in form.
Communicating	The children can communicate in detail using a range of methods, including mathematical ones. In retrospect, they are able to choose the most appropriate from a number of methods tried. Orally, the children are able to give a detailed account of what was done and why, what happened and in what order. They can take part in a discussion of their results and draw some conclusions. Their written communications are increasingly appropriate.	The children can give clearer accounts of their work both orally and in writing. Their oral work is more confident, and after discussion they can choose an appropriate form of written communication. With prompting, they include mathematical communication of various kinds among the methods of communication which they consider.	The children are able to communicate in detail, which parallels the increasing detail they are able to observe. With prompting, they are able to suggest different methods of communication, and after discussion will choose an appropriate method. They include mathematical communication among the methods they consider as a matter of course.	The children's ability to communicate develops in parallel with a more sophisticated approach to observing and investigating. Orally, the children are able to explain the plans and decisions which they make prior to and during observation and investigation. They can state their plan clearly. They can write a clear detailed account of their observations and investigations. They choose mathematical means of communication as appropriate.
Measuring	When directed, the children are able to use an appropriate measuring instrument. Length, Weight, Capacity – comparative, arbitrary, and standard measures where appropriate: metres and half metres, kilograms and half kilograms, litres and half litres. Time – intervals of time using timers and stop clocks Temperature – using a thermometer with easy-to-read scale	The children can measure using the most appropriate measuring instrument for the task within the limits of their conceptual understanding of quantity. Length – metres and centimetres Weight – kilograms and parts of kilogram Capacity – litres and parts of litre	The children can measure using the most appropriate measuring instrument within the limits of their conceptual understanding of quantity and can measure to finer limits. Length – metres and centimetres Weight – kilograms and grams Capacity – millilitres (multiples of 10) Time – minutes and parts of a minute	The children can measure to a finer degree of accuracy using the most appropriate measuring instrument. They can attempt to decide what to measure. Length – metres and centimetres Weight – kilograms and grams Capacity – millilitres (multiples of 10) Time – minutes and seconds
Recording	The children can record using a wide range of methods, including mathematical representation. They are able to draw in more detail and with more accuracy. Written records are more detailed and orderly and can be maintained over a period of time. The children can suggest different methods of recording and use these. In retrospect and with prompting, they can choose which was the most suitable and give reasons for their choice.	The children extend the range of recording methods which they use. They can write short accounts, and suggest the use of tables and block graphs which they construct with help. With prompting, they can consider in retrospect their success in recording.	The children are able to make notes and write a clear account based on these notes. They are able to record a sequence of events. They attempt to choose the most appropriate recording method in advance and for a simple record can proceed independently. They use tables, block graphs and diagrams.	The children begin to consider more carefully in advance the recording method(s) which will be most appropriate for the task in hand. With help, they make a choice and can then proceed.

	Year 3		Year 4	
	Level 1	Level 2	Level 1	Level 2
Observing	The children can identify which observations are likely to be significant and can make these in detail. They make less significant observations in less detail. In embarking on a sequence of observations, they are able to decide which observations are likely to be significant without prompting. They observe for purpose, e.g. they look for similarities and differences in form and behaviour. With prompting, they notice patterns in form and behaviour.	The children are increasingly able to make decisions about what to observe and in what detail to make the observations. They look for similarities and differences in form and behaviour. They look for change and can observe it in detail. With prompting, they observe patterns of behaviour and change.	They are able independently to select which observations are likely to be significant and make these in appropriate detail. They look for similarities and differences in form and behaviour. They look for, and are increasingly able to discern, patterns in their observations of form, behaviour and change.	The children can observe using the senses in combination. They can observe in detail. They can distinguish in advance between more and less significant observations, determine the level of detail which will be appropriate and make their observations accordingly. They look for and observe similarities and differences; with some prompting, they recognise observational patterns of form, behaviour and change, as well as of more obvious qualities such as colour.
Communicating	The children appreciate more clearly that the communications should be suited to the audience for whom they are intended. With help both orally and in writing, they can produce different kinds of communication and, in retrospect, can decide which would be suitable for an identified audience.	With prompting, the children can attempt to match the communication to the identified audience. They are able to describe their investigations and observations clearly and sequentially.	Without prompting, the children attempt to match their communications to the audience. They are able to describe and discuss their observations and the observational patterns they discern. They are increasingly able to convey clear statements about these observational patterns. With help, they can make suggestions connected with these recognised patterns.	The children can communicate in detail, using a refined range of methods, and can choose for themselves the most appropriate method to use.
Measuring	The children can read and record using decimalisation. Length – metres and centimetres, e.g. 1.32 m Weight – kilograms and grams, e.g. 1.250 kg Capacity – litres and millilitres, e.g. 1.625 l They can read scales and dials after selecting the appropriate measuring instrument for the task. They can read different calibrations on a variety of instruments.	The children can select the most appropriate instrument to give an accurate reading, e.g. force meter, spring balance, stopwatch, etc. They can read these instruments competently.	The children can measure, using their own judgement about what should be measured. With guidance, they can decide how accurate the measurement should be.	The children are able to use appropriate standard measures with confidence: (m, cm, mm, cm^2, cm^3, kg, g, l, ml, min, sec, $newton$). They can record using decimal notation. They can estimate with a reasonable degree of accuracy. They can select the appropriate measuring instrument to suit a particular purpose and read a variety of scales, e.g. thermometer, kitchen scales (both dial and linear), force meter and spring balance.
Recording	The children plan their recording method(s) in advance and include methods such as flow charts, block graphs and tables. They write accurate notes and produce a detailed orderly account. They can consider their efforts critically but may need prompting to act accordingly.	They give increasing consideration to mathematical recording methods and with help use a widening range. They draw and colour more accurately. They begin to consider for whom the record is intended and become aware that different recording methods may be appropriate for different audiences, e.g. self, teacher, other children.	The children plan their recording method(s) in advance, including the recording of a series of events over time. They can keep an observational diary and write an orderly sequenced account from this. They can consider critically the record which they have produced and suggest how it might be improved.	The children can record using a wide range of methods, including mathematical representation. They can choose in advance the most appropriate method for a particular purpose.

Table 2(ii)   The junior years (continued)

	Year 1		Year 2	
	Level 1	Level 2	Level 1	Level 2
Classifying	The children can classify into sets and subsets, using complex criteria if prompted by the teacher. They are able independently to sort, using simple criteria. They can use keys for simple criteria and, with help, for more complex criteria.	The children are aware that there are different criteria for sorting which could be used. Using simple criteria they are able to sort in different ways. With help, they extend the range of criteria to include, for example, behaviour and origin. With help, they can construct keys using simple criteria.	The children can confidently sort in different ways, using simple criteria. With help, they can use more complex criteria such as origin, behaviour and change. They use keys more confidently.	In retrospect, they recognise that of a number of methods of sorting used in any particular case one may be more productive and useful than the others.
Recognising patterns	When making observations, the children may seek patterns if prompted by the teacher. They can recognise the common factors in the information obtained by observing a number of instances. They are not able to describe the pattern formally. They may or may not be able to identify other instances which fit the pattern.	When making observations, the children look for patterns and recognise the more obvious patterns in their observations. With help, they describe the patterns orally. They will consider whether a new instance fits the pattern.	The children look for patterns, and with prompting are able to recognise patterns based on more complex observations. The process is assisted if the observations are made concurrently (or nearly so). Their oral description of the pattern improves and with prompting they consider whether new instances fit the pattern.	The children look more systematically for observations which form patterns, and become aware of the wider range of observations which may form patterns. Most patterns which they discern are in static properties, e.g. colour, shape, form, etc. With help, they describe these patterns and consider whether new observations fit the pattern.
Predicting	The children can make reasonable suggestions based on observations over a period of time. They can recognise some causal relationships.	The children make reasonable suggestions based on observations and when causal relationships are recognised they can, with help, make suggestions about effects that the cause will produce. They can suggest immediate and also future changes.	The children can base their suggestions on a number of observations viewed as a whole. They recognise a relationship but may not be able to give a clear oral description.	The suggestions which the children make are increasingly consistent with all the observational evidence. The children become aware that the reliability of their suggestions about future events or changes depends on the reliability of the observations on which they are based.
Controlling variables	The children start to identify one or two obvious variables. These may or may not be relevant. The children are able to find out whether or not they are relevant. When a relevant variable is identified, the children are able to find a way of controlling it if prompted by the teacher.	The children look for variables and notice more possibilities which may or may not be relevant. They can decide whether the more obvious are relevant and, with the help of the teacher, can find means of control.	The children look for variables and begin to draw on their experience in considering whether or not the variables are relevant. They are increasingly able to identify relevant variables and, with help, to find means of control.	The children are concerned to look for variables. They recognise that there cannot be a fair test if the relevant variables are not controlled. They can investigate two or three of the obvious ones and, with help, control those found to be relevant.
Investigating	The children can design and carry out simple investigations with minimal help with practicalities. They notice the more relevant variables and investigate them as part of their overall plan. With help, they suggest ways of controlling the variables and include this control in the design and execution of their investigations.	In designing their investigations, the children become increasingly aware of the possible wide range of variables. With help, they suggest means of identifying and controlling relevant variables and include this in the design and execution of their investigations. In discussion, they will agree that repetition is desirable and with prompting will repeat investigations.	Their range of investigations includes those of the type 'What happens when ...?', 'What happens if ...?' and 'Which is best?'. They start to consider investigation of suggestions based on recognised patterns.	They become better at formulating suggestions and questions for investigation. They are more aware of the possible range of variables and this awareness is increasingly reflected in the design and execution of their investigations.

	Year 3		**Year 4**	
	Level 1	**Level 2**	**Level 1**	**Level 2**
Classifying	The range of sorting criteria which the children can use independently and with confidence becomes wider, to include origin, behaviour and change. The children begin to consider in advance which sorting criteria will be most useful for a particular purpose, and with help they can make an appropriate suggestion. They are increasingly aware of the need to use keys, and with help they can construct them.		They make decisions about which sorting criteria to use with increasing independence, and the methods suggested are increasingly appropriate. In retrospect, the children are able to comment on the appropriateness of their choice. They use simple keys with confidence, and more complex keys with help. They are able to construct simple keys with little help and can attempt more complex keys.	The children can classify into sets and subsets using simple and complex criteria selected appropriately by themselves. They can use and construct simple keys.
Recognising patterns	The children use appropriate observations to seek patterns. They consider not only static properties but also dynamic ones, including, for example, behaviour and change, and they consider observations over a period of time. They recognise these patterns with help and can describe them orally. They can attempt to produce a written statement of simpler patterns and are increasingly able to decide whether new observations fit the pattern.	The children recognise patterns of various kinds and with help can describe them orally and in writing. They are increasingly able to use the patterns as the basis for suggestions about future happenings. They can look for patterns in derived data, particularly mathematical data, and with help can discern patterns in this data.	The children are able more readily to recognise patterns in simple data, and with help to recognise patterns in mathematical data presented in both graphical and tabular form. They are increasingly able to describe the patterns clearly, both orally and in writing. They are able to identify other instances which fit the pattern and to discuss their reasons.	When making observations, the children seek patterns in the information obtained. They recognise common factors in the information obtained by observing a number of instances. They are able to recognise other instances which fit the pattern.
Predicting	With help, the children increasingly make suggestions based on the recognition of an observational pattern. With help, the children can give a clearer oral description of the pattern and consequently, their suggestions become more consistent with the recognised pattern. They use not only observations and derived data but also known concepts.	The children base their suggestions on more complex patterns, including change and behaviour.	Increasingly, the children are able, with help, to make suggestions based on derived data. Their suggestions are more precise and take in all the evidence. They attempt to assess the likely reliability of their suggestions.	The children base their suggestions on firm evidence, including recognised patterns. There is increasing recognition of causal, as distinct from casual, relationships. They use known concepts in making their suggestions.
Controlling variables	The children attempt to identify variables and investigate two or three of the most obvious. With help, they control those that are found to be relevant. They start to consider in retrospect whether they have identified all the relevant variables and whether they have effectively controlled those that have been identified.	The children are increasingly able to identify variables and use their accumulating experience in eliminating non-relevant ones. They can find means of controlling simple variables and with help tackle more complex situations.	As for Year 3 Level 2. In retrospect, the children are increasingly concerned with whether relevant variables have been completely identified and whether they have been effectively controlled.	The children are aware of a wide range of variables and, on most occasions, can identify and control those which are relevant.
Investigating	With help, they start to investigate suggestions based on recognised patterns. They are increasingly concerned with the reliability of their investigations. They appreciate the need for repetition and when prompted repeat observations and measurements.	With help, they can investigate suggestions based on mathematical data. They can work with care and accuracy. They are aware of the need for repetition to check accuracy, and carry out checks without prompting.	The children can investigate simple suggestions and questions with minimal help. They design and carry out simple investigations, paying regard to obvious variables and their control. They consider the level of accuracy required and can use ideas about estimation and approximation.	The children can design and carry out simple investigations with confidence. They can identify and control most relevant variables. They can review their investigations critically and they check their results by repetition.

recognise and state a pattern of behaviour or being able to recognise and plan the control of a range of variables is a complex task. Some children of primary school age will possess the required degree of maturity but many will need a good deal of help. Nevertheless, many children will, on occasion, show an understanding which is apparently out of phase with their general level of development. This should be noted with pleasure but great care should be exercised in assessing its significance. *Longman Scienceworld* helps children to develop the skills required to carry out investigations. The sophistication of the methods they use will increase as their skills mature.

In the early part of the scheme, the prime concern is to develop the skills of observing and communicating information about what is observed. Measuring is introduced as a refinement of both observing and communicating. Recording and classifying are other skills which are introduced at an early stage. Recognising and describing patterns is recognised as a high level skill which will be developed gradually from the simple standpoint described in Diagram 2. Again, the skill of predicting will be developed by starting with the idea of good suggestions – although for the sake of simplicity and lack of a more appropriate word, the word 'predicting' will be used for 'making a good suggestion'. Controlling variables is another skill to be developed within the limits described, concentrating largely on the idea of making investigations fair.

Development of the skills needed to carry out scientific investigations is brought about in two distinct ways. In some of the suggested activities, one or two particular skills are considered in isolation, e.g. observing or sorting. In other activities, an investigation is suggested that requires a range of skills to be used and developed.

Table 1 on page 111 describes the development of skills in the primary years in *Longman Scieneworld*.

Each of these skills will be developed in a structured way through the scheme. This step by step progression is set out in Table 2 (pages 112–17). The table not only indicates the stage of development of the skills in the work at the different levels, but it also provides a guide as to what the children should be able to do when they have completed the work of a particular level. It should be noted that in going from one level to the next, the skills are cumulative and the skills taught at each level build on those acquired earlier.

The *Record Sheets* for *Longman Scienceworld* are based on this table of skill development.

Table 2 is in two parts. Table 2 (i) covers the infant years and Table 2 (ii) covers the junior years. Children who start using *Longman Scienceworld* for the first time when they enter the junior classes of primary school will require more help in the initial stages than children who have progressed through 'Science through Infant Topics'. For some time their skills will be much more teacher dependent and the descriptions of the skill objectives should be read with this in mind.

Extension B   Scientific ideas

These are the ideas to which we would like children to be exposed and which we would like them to explore. As stated already, they will meet these ideas in their own environment, and so will be able to experience and explore them in a familiar setting. It is difficult to indicate briefly the depth of understanding which it is hoped children will acquire, but as the ideas arise in the science activities the depth of treatment intended will be clearly explained. Indeed, in most cases, the activities themselves will tell the story.

It will soon become clear to teachers using the materials that it is necessary to return to ideas time and time again, each time probing them more searchingly and using the children's developing skills and abilities to help them towards greater understanding. The role of language in this process is crucial and this aspect is taken up in Extension D, Language in science.

Children's exposure to scientific ideas
The basic ideas are listed below and on pages 120–1. Table 3(i) on pages 122–3 shows at which point in the scheme in the infant years particular scientific ideas are explored. Table 3(ii) shows how scientific ideas are introduced in the activities described in *Junior Pupils' Books 1–4*. The ideas are presented in a way that will enable children working at a particular level to gain appropriate experience and understanding. In Tables 3(i) and 3(ii), the numbering of the scientific ideas corresponds to the numbering used for the statements in the following list. The topic letters and activity reference numbers denote the specific activities in which the ideas are introduced. The keys to the topic letters appear on pages 124–5.

Basic ideas

1 Sets – the concept of a set as a group of items sharing a common feature.

2 Colour – primary, secondary, black, white, shades, etc.

3 Shape
    3.1 2D – square, rectangle, circle, ellipse, triangle.
    3.2 3D – cube, cuboid, sphere, ellipsoid, cylinder, triangular prism.
    3.3 Symmetry – mirror images.

4 Concept of quantity

5 Measurement of quantity
    5.1 Direct comparison.
    5.2 Arbitrary units.
    5.3 Standard units.
    5.4 Approximation, estimation.

6 Spatial relationships and direction, e.g. under, behind, backwards, etc.

Ideas about the physical world

7 The world around us
    7.1 There is air round the earth.
    7.2 Air contains water vapour.
    7.3 Soil is a mixture of things which come from rocks as well as some material which was once living.
    7.4 The apparent movement of sun, moon and stars follows a regular predictable pattern.
    7.5 The seasons follow a regular pattern related to the position of the sun.
    7.6 Water flows to a common level.
    7.7 Floating and sinking depend on both the kind of material and on the shape.

8 Movement and energy
   8.1 The (average) speed of an object depends on the distance it travels in a certain time.
   8.2 Force is needed to move a stationary object or to alter the direction of travel of a moving object.
   8.3 Objects are pulled towards the earth; weight is a measure of how hard that pull is.
   8.4 The greater the force, the more energy is required.
   8.5 Energy can be supplied in many ways: by burning fuel, by eating food, or by doing work and storing the energy, e.g. in an elastic band, in a stretched spring, etc.
   8.6 The faster an object moves, the more energy it has.
   8.7 A moving object is stopped or slowed down by energy being removed from it.
   8.8 This energy may appear as heat (as in braking).
   8.9 An object moving on a surface must overcome friction.

9 Structure and forces
   9.1 Forces are needed to change the shape of an object.
   9.2 The strength of an object or structure depends on its shape and on the material from which it is made.
   9.3 For a given force, the pressure is greater the smaller the area on which it is exerted.

10 Magnets and electricity
   10.1 Magnets can attract or repel each other.
   10.2 Some materials are attracted by a magnet and some are not.
   10.3 Some materials can be magnetised and some cannot.
   10.4 Some materials conduct electricity and some do not.
   10.5 For an electric current to flow, there must be a complete circuit of conducting material.

11 Light and sound
   11.1 Light travels in straight lines.
   11.2 Objects can be seen because of the light they give out or reflect.
   11.3 Sound comes from vibrating objects.

12 Change
   12.1 Change may be reversible or irreversible.
   12.2 Change of state is reversible.
   12.3 Cooking usually produces irreversible changes.
   12.4 During a change of state, the substance itself does not alter, it merely changes its form.

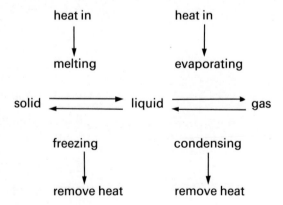

13 Properties of materials
   13.1 Different materials have different properties.
   13.2 Materials are used for purposes for which their properties make them appropriate (paper, wood, metals, plastics, wool, cotton, synthetic fibres, glass, brick, stone, rubber).
   13.3 Materials can be classified by consideration of their properties, e.g. metals, plastics.
   13.4 Some substances are soluble in water and some are not.
   13.5 Some substances do not dissolve in water but dissolve in other liquids, e.g. cooking oil.

13.6 Substances can be classified as liquids, solids or gases according to their properties, e.g. water, cooking oil, washing-up liquid; ice, wood, glass; steam, air.

14 Weather
14.1 The sun provides us with warmth.
14.2 Rain falls when there are clouds.
14.3 Clouds can stop the sun's rays (light and heat) from reaching us.
14.4 The type of weather we have is associated with the seasons.

Ideas about the living world

15 Living/non-living
15.1 Living things have common properties: growth, respiration, reproduction, nutrition, excretion, and possibly movement.
15.2 Non-living things do not have these properties.
15.3 Some non-living things were once alive.
15.4 Some non-living things occur naturally, e.g. rocks, and some are man-made.

16 Food chains
16.1 Living things must eat; they need water and air.
16.2 Big animals may eat little animals; eventually down the chain animals eat plants.
16.3 Plants need food and water.
16.4 Plants get their food from the soil.
16.5 The food which plants take from the soil must be replaced.

17 Living together
17.1 Plants and animals are very diverse in form.
17.2 Their form fits their environment: animals, fish, birds and plants.
17.3 Plants and animals are sensitive to their environment and respond to it.
17.4 Plants and animals in a particular environment are dependent on each other.

18 Life cycles
18.1 All living things have a fixed life cycle.
18.2 The life cycle of all members of the same species is the same.
18.3 Parents produce offspring of the same kind as themselves.
18.4 The life cycles of living things are often linked to seasonal change.

19 People
19.1 People are living things. They exhibit variability.
19.2 They share the common properties of all living things.
19.3 They are able to explore the environment by using their senses.
19.4 They are able to protect themselves from the environment.
19.5 Children must spend many years learning to care for themselves; this contrasts with other animals.
19.6 The different life processes take place in different defined parts of the body.
19.7 Apart from the sex organs and those functions which are sexually controlled, the bodies of all people are the same and function in the same way.

Table 3(i)   Children's exposure to scientific ideas in *Science through Infant Topics*

Basic ideas		Teachers' Book A Level 1	Teachers' Book A Level 2	Teachers' Book B Level 1
Sets	1	H^{1,2,7} C^{2,3,7} Cl^{1,7}	S^6 B^{2,3,4,5} Co^2 Ca^1 Sc^3	Sh^2 Su^{1,7} P^4 Sw^1 K^4
Colour	2	H^{1,6} Wh^4 C^{1,2,5,6,7} Cl^1 W^{2,4}	S^{1,2,3,4} B^{2,3} Co^1 Sc^{1,3,6}	Sh^1 P^{2,3} Sw^{1,4} Pt^4 K^{4,5}
Shape	3.1	H^3 Bo^{1,2} Wh^4 C^{2,4} Cl^4 W^{1,3}	S^1 B^{2,4,6} Co^{5,6} Sc^{4,7}	P^2 Pt^{1,2,3}
	3.2	H^3 Bo^{1,2} C^{2,7} Cl^4 W^3 C^4	S^{1,2} B^2 Co^{5,6} Sc^4 Co^{3,8}	Su^{1,5,7} Pt^{1,2,3}
	3.3	Cl^5		Sh^1 Pt^1
Concept of quantity	4	H^7 Bo^{1,2,3} Wh^{1,2,3} C^{2,4,6} Cl^{1,3,4,5,6} W^{1,2,3}	S^{3,5,6} B^{2,3} Co^{2,6} Ca^1 Sc^{2,3,6,7}	Su^{1,3,5} P^{2,3,6} Sw^{3,4} Pt^4 K^{1,2,7}
Measurement of quantity	5.1	H^7 Bo^{1,2,3} Wh^{1,2,3} C^{2,4,6} Cl^{1,3,5,6} W^{1,2,3}	S^{3,5,6} B^2 Co^{2,6} Ca^1 Sc^{2,3,6,7}	Sh^3 Su^1 P^{2,3,6} Pt^4
	5.2		Co^4	Sh^1 Su^5 Sw^{3,4} K^{1,2,7}
	5.3			
	5 4			
Spatial relationships	6	H^3 Wh^{1,4} Cl^5	S^1 B^3 Sc^8	P^{1,2,3}
The world around us	7.1		Sc^4	
	7.2	W^4	B^6 Sc^5	
	7.3		S^6 Sc^3	
	7.4			
	7.5	W^1		
	7.6		Co^8 Sc^8	Su^3
	7.7	W^3	S^6 B^5 Sc^{4,6}	P^1 K^3
Movement and energy	8.1			
	8.2	Wh^{1,2}	Ca^1 Sc^7	
	8.3	H^3 Wh^2		
	8.4	Wh^{1,2}	Ca^4	
	8.5		S^2 Ca^1 Sc^7 Ca^4	
	8.6			
	8.7			
	8.8			
	8.9			
Structures and forces	9.1	C^2	Sc^4	Su^7
	9.2			Su^7
	9.3			Sh^4 P^1
Magnets and electricity	10.1			
	10.2			
	10.3			
	10.4			
	10.5			
Light and sound	11.1	W^1		Sw^1
	11.2			
	11.3	Bo^4 C^{3,4}	Co^7	P^{4,5}
Change	12.1	H^6 Bo^3 W^{2,3,4}	S^2 B^6 Sc^{4,6}	Su^{4,5} Sw^4 K^{1,3}
	12.2		S^2 B^6 Sc^6	Su^4
	12.3	Bo^3 W^4		Su^5 K^1
	12.4	Bo^3 W^{2,3,4}	S^2 B^6 Sc^{5,6}	Su^{2,3,4,5}
Properties of materials	13.1	Bo^4 C^{4,5} Cl^{6,7,8} C^7	B^4 Co^{1,2,3,4,5,6} Ca^{1,2,3,4} Sc^{1,3,4}	Sh^4 Su^1 P^5 K^{1,2,3,4,6,7}
	13.2	C^{4,7} Cl^{6,7,8}	B^4 Co^5 Ca^{2,3,4} Sc^4 Co^6	Sh^4 Su^{1,2,7} K^6
	13.3		B^5 Co^{1,2,4,7}	Su^1 P^5
	13.4			Su^{2,6} Sw^2 K^{2,3,4,5}
	13.5			
	13.6		B^2 Co^{3,8} Sc^{1,6}	Su^3 K^3
Weather	14.1			
	14.2			
	14.3			
	14.4	W^{2,3}		
Living/non-living	15.1	H^8 Wh^{1,3,4} C^6	S^{1,3,5} B^1	Sh^1
	15.2		S^3 B^1	
	15.3		S^3	
	15.4			
Food chains	16.1		S^2	P^{1,3,6}
	16.2		S^2	
	16.3	H^8	S^{1,5}	
	16.4	H^8	S^{1,5}	
	16.5			
Living together	17.1	H^{1,2,3,4,5,6,7,8} C^{3,6}	S^{1,2,3,5}	P^{1,2,3,6}
	17.2			P^{1,2,3,6}
	17.3			P^{2,3}
	17.4			
Life cycles	18.1			
	18.2			
	18.3	H^8 C^6	S^5	
	18.4		S^{1,5}	
People	19.1	Wh^{1,2,3,4}	B^{1,3}	
	19.2	Wh^{1,2,3}	B^{1,3}	P^3
	19.3	H^{1,2,3,4,5,6,7} Bo^{3,4} C^{1,2,3,4,5,6,7} Cl^{1,2,6} W^4	S^{1,2,3,6} B^{2,4} Co^{1,3,4,7}	Sh^4 Su^{2,3,4,5,6} P^5 Sw^2 Pt^4 K^{4,5}
	19.4	Cl^{6,7,8}		Sh^4
	19.5		B^3	
	19.6			
	19.7			

Basic ideas		Teachers' Book B Level 2	Teachers' Book C Level 1	Teachers' Book C Level 2
Sets	1	E^1 $Po^{1,2,4}$ Pa^5	N^1 G^4 Hn^5 Sg^3	T^4
Colour	2	$E^{1,2}$ F^1	$G^{2,5,6}$ $Ce^{2,3,4,5}$ G^1 N^5	A^2 $Fa^{1,4}$ Fm^2 We^3 A^3 Fa^5
Shape	3.1	M^1 $Pa^{1,2}$	Hn^1 $Hs^{2,3}$ G^1	T^7
	3.2	$E^{2,5}$	Hn^1 $Sg^{2,4}$ G^4 Ce^1	$T^{1,2,3,6}$
	3.3	E^2 Po^3	G^6 Hs^3 $Sg^{2,6}$	A^3
Concept of quantity	4	$E^{1,4,6,7}$ $F^{2,3,4}$ Pa^3		
Measurement of quantity	5.1	E^1 Po^2 $Pa^{3,4,6}$	G^1 Hn^3 $Ce^{1,3}$ $N^{2,5}$	
	5.2	E^4 $F^{2,3,4,6}$ M^2 $Pa^{3,6}$	G^4 Ce^1 G^5 N^1	$T^{1,5}$ $A^{2,3,5}$ $Fa^{2,3}$ $Fm^{2,4,5}$ $We^{2,3,5,6}$ A^1
	5.3	$E^{6,7}$	G^3 $Hn^{1,3}$ $Ce^{1,4}$ Hs^1 $N^{1,2,3}$ $Sg^{1,2,3,4,5,6}$ $G^{1,2,4}$ Hs^2	
	5.4		Sg^6	A^1 $Fm^{2,5}$ We^1
Spatial relationships	6	$E^{2,4}$ $F^{5,6}$ M^4 $Pa^{1,2,7}$	$Hs^{1,2,3}$ $Sg^{1,2,6}$ G^2	$T^{1,2,3,4,5}$ $We^{1,7}$
The world around us	7.1	F^4	$G^{1,3}$ Hn^1 Sg^1 G^4 $Ce^{1,4}$	$We^{3,4,7}$ Fa^3 Fm^4
	7.2		G^1 $Ce^{1,4}$ Sg^1	
	7.3			
	7.4			We^1
	7.5			
	7.6	F^5		
	7.7	E^2 F^5	Sg^2 Hn^3	$T^{6,7}$ A^5 Fm^1
Movement and energy	8.1	Po^1 $F^{2,3}$ Pa^3		$T^{3,7}$
	8.2	F^4 M^2 $Pa^{1,2,7}$	Hs^1 Sg^5 G^3	$T^{1,2,3,4,5,6,7}$ We^7
	8.3	E^2 $Pa^{2,4,7}$	$G^{3,4}$ Hs^2 $N^{1,2}$ $Sg^{3,4}$ Hs^3	$T^{2,5}$ Fa^2
	8.4	$Pa^{1,7}$	Hs^1	$T^{2,3,5,7}$ Fa^1
	8.5		G^3	$T^{4,5}$ $Fm^{1,3}$ $T^{2,3,7}$ We^7
	8.6			$T^{4,5}$ Fm^1
	8.7			T^4
	8.8	Pa^1		T^4
	8.9	Pa^1	N^4	$T^{2,3,4}$ Fa^1
Structures and forces	9.1	E^2	Hn^1 Ce^4 $Sg^{2,3}$	$T^{5,6,7}$ Fa^2 $Fm^{3,5}$
	9.2		Hn^3 $Hs^{1,4}$ $N^{1,2,3}$	$Fa^{1,2}$ Fm^3
	9.3		Hn^3	
Magnets and electricity	10.1	Po^1	Hn^5	
	10.2	Po^1	Hn^5	
	10.3		Hn^5	
	10.4	Po^4		
	10.5	Po^4		
Light and sound	11.1	M^4	Ce^5 Sg^6 Hn^4	$We^{1,2}$
	11.2		Hn^4	
	11.3	M^2	Hs^5	
Change	12.1	E^2 M^2 Pa^5	G^6 $Hn^{1,3}$ $Ce^{1,2,3,4}$ Sg^1 G^1	$T^{6,7}$ $A^{1,3,4}$ $Fa^{3,4,5}$ $Fm^{1,2,3,5}$ $We^{2,4,6,7}$
	12.2		Ce^2	Fa^3
	12.3	M^4	G^6	$Fm^{2,5}$
	12.4		G^1 $Ce^{2,4}$ Sg^1	A^1 $Cs^{3,4}$ Fa^5 Fm^2 $We^{3,4,5}$
Properties of materials	13.1	$E^{2,4}$ $Po^{1,4}$ $M^{2,4}$ $Pa^{1,5}$	$Hn^{1,2,3,5}$ $Ce^{1,2,3,4}$ $Hs^{1,4}$ $N^{1,2,3,4}$ $Sg^{1,3,4}$	$T^{3,4,6}$ $Fa^{1,2,3,4}$ $Fm^{1,3}$ $We^{2,4}$ Fa^5
	13.2	Po^4 $M^{2,4}$ $Pa^{1,5}$	G^6 $Hn^{1,2,3}$ $Ce^{1,2,3,4}$ $Hs^{1,4}$ $N^{1,3,4}$ $Sg^{1,3,4}$	$T^{3,4,6}$ $Fa^{1,2,3,4}$ Fm^3 Fa^5
	13.3	$Po^{1,4}$ F^1 M^2 Pa^5	Hn^5 N^4	T^4 Cs^4
	13.4		Hn^3	A^1 Fm^5 We^4
	13.5			
	13.6	M^3	Ce^2	Fm^1
Weather	14.1		Sg^1	$We^{1,2,4}$
	14.2			We^5
	14.3			We^7
	14.4			
Living/non living	15.1	$E^{3,4,5,6,7}$	$G^{1,2,3}$ Hn^4 G^4	$A^{1,3,4,5,6}$ Fm^4 A^2
	15.2			
	15.3	F^1		
	15.4			
Food chains	16.1	F^4	Hn^4	$A^{1,2,3,4,5}$ Fm^4 A^6
	16.2			$A^{2,4,5,6}$
	16.3	$E^{3,4,5,6,7}$	$G^{1,2,3}$	Fm^4
	16.4	$E^{3,4,5,6,7}$		Fm^4
	16.5			
Living together	17.1	$E^{1,3,4,5,6,7}$ F^1 M^4	$G^{1,2,3,4,5,6}$ Hn^4	$A^{1,2,3,4,5,6}$$Fm^4$
	17.2		$G^{3,4}$ Hn^4	$A^{1,2,3,4,5,6}$
	17.3	$E^{3,4,5,6,7}$	$G^{3,4,5}$ Hn^4 $G^{1,2}$	$A^{1,2,3,4,5,6}$ Fm^4
	17.4			$A^{2,3,4,5,6}$
Life cycles	18.1	$E^{3,4,5,6,7}$	$G^{3,4}$	$A^{1,3,5}$ Fm^4
	18.2	$E^{3,4,5,6,7}$	$G^{3,4}$	$A^{1,3,5}$ Fm^4
	18.3	$E^{3,4,5,6,7}$	$G^{3,4}$	$A^{1,3,5}$ Fm^4
	18.4	$E^{3,4,5,6,7}$	$G^{3,4}$	$A^{1,3,5}$ Fm^4
People	19.1	$Po^{2,3}$ $F^{2,4}$ M^1		$A^{2,4}$
	19.2	$Po^{2,3}$ $F^{2,4}$ M^1		
	19.3	E^4 Po^1 $M^{1,4}$	$Hn^{3,4}$ $Hs^{4,5}$	Fm^2
	19.4			Fa^3
	19.5			
	19.6	F^4 M^1		
	19.7			

Table 3(ii) Children's exposure to scientific ideas in *Junior Pupils' Books 1–4*

Basic ideas		J1 Level 1	J1 Level 2	J2 Level 1	J2 Level 2
Colour	2	MU[1,2,3]			
Shape	3.3				AG[1]
Concept of quantity	4				
Measurement of quantity	5.1	HF[2]			
	5.3		KW[1,2,3,4]		
The world around us	7.1		KW[2,3,4]	WF[3,4]	
	7.2				
	7.3				
	7.6				LL[3]
	7.7				LL[1,2]
Movement and energy	8.2		WT[1,3]		
	8.3			WF[3,4] SY[1,2,3]	
	8.4		WT[1]		
	8.5		HT[2]		
	8.6				
	8.7		WT[1,2,3]		
	8.8		WT[1,3]		
	8.9		WT[1,3]		
Structures and forces	9.1			WF[1] CC[1,2,3]	
	9.2			WF[2] CC[2,3,4] SY[1,2,3]	
	9.3			CC[1,2,3]	
Magnets and electricity	10.1			ST[1,2,3,4]	
	10.2			ST[1,2,3,4]	
	10.3			ST[3,4]	
	10.4				WU[3,4]
	10.5		HT[3]		WU[3,4]
Light and sound	11.1				DO[1,2] AG[2]
	11.2	LH[1,4] MU[2]			DO[2]
	11.3	CT[1,2,3,4]			WU[1,2]
Change	12.1				
	12.4				
Properties of materials	13.1		WT[1,2,3]	BW[1] SY[1,2,3]	LL[1,2]
	13.2		KW[2,3] WT[1,2,3] HT[2]	SY[1,2]	
	13.3				
	13.4				
	13.6				LL[1,2,3]
Weather	14.1		KW[1,2]		DO[1]
	14.2				
	14.3		KW[1,2]		
	14.4				DO[1]
Living/non-living	15.1		MS[1,2,3,4] UI[1,3,4]		
	15.2		UI[1,2,3,4]		
Food chains	16.1				
	16.2				
	16.3		MS[1,2,3,4]		CH[1,2,3,4]
	16.4				
	16.5				
Living together	17.1		MS[1,2,3,4] UI[1,2,3,4]	WF[1,2,3] BW[1,2,3]	
	17.2		MS[1,2,3,4] UI[1,2,3,4]	BW[1,2,3]	
	17.3		UI[1,2,3,4]	BW[2,3]	CH[1,2,3,4]
	17.4				
Life cycles	18.1		MS[1,2,3,4]	WF[1,2,3]	
	18.2				
	18.3			BW[2,3]	CH[1,2,3,4]
	18.4			WF[1,2,3]	
People	19.1	HF[1,2] LH[1,2,3,4]			
	19.2	HF[1,2]			
	19.3				
	19.4		KW[1,2,3]		
	19.5				
	19.6				
	19.7				

Key to Table 3(i) on pages 122–3

Topics

Year 1: Harvest H; Bonfire night Bo; What can I do? Wh; Christmas C; Clothes Cl; Winter W; Spring S; The bathroom B; The cook Co; The caretaker Ca; School holidays Sc.

Year 2: The shoe shop Sh; The supermarket Su; Pets P; The sweet shop Sw; The post Pt; Jobs in the kitchen K; Easter E; The police Po; The firefighter F; Milk M; The park Pa.

Year 3: In the garden G; Hallowe'en Hn; Celebrations Ce; Jobs in the house Hs; The newsagent N; Sports and games Sg; Transport T; Animals A; Fabrics Fa; The farm Fm; Weather We.

Basic ideas		J3 Level 1	J3 Level 2	J4 Level 1	J4 Level 2
Colour	2				
Shape	3.3				
Concept of quantity	4	TT[1,2,3]			
Measurement of quantity	5.1				
	5.3	TT[1,2,3]			SD[1,2,3,4]
The world around us	7.1	SW[1,2,3]	FH[1,2,3,4]	AB[1,2,3,4]	
	7.2	SW[2,3]			
	7.3	EM[1,2,3]			PG[4]
	7.6				
	7.7				SS[1,2]
Movement and energy	8.2		FH[1,2,3,4] OW[1,2,3]	FT[1,3,4] AB[2,3,4]	
	8.3	TT[1,2,3]	OW[1]		
	8.4		OW[1,2]		
	8.5	TT[1,2,3]	FH[2] OW[2,3]	FT[1,2,3,4] AB[3,4]	
	8.6			FT[2,3,4]	
	8.7	TT[1,2,3]		FT[1,2,3,4] AB[1,2]	
	8.8				
	8.9			FT[1,2,3]	
Structures and forces	9.1			BL[1,3]	
	9.2			BL[1,3,4]	
	9.3				
Magnets and electricity	10.1				
	10.2		DH[3,4]		
	10.3		DH[3,4]		
	10.4		DH[1,2,3,4]		
	10.5		DH[1,2,3,4]		
Light and sound	11.1				MO[2,3]
	11.2				MO[1,3,4]
	11.3				
Change	12.1	EM[1]	CK[1,2,3] DH[1,2,3,4]	PP[1,3] BL[1] HL[4]	SS[2,3]
	12.4				SS[3]
Properties of materials	13.1	TR[3] CS[1,2,3]	FH[2,3]	HL[4]	SS[2]
	13.2	EM[1,2,3]	FH[2]	BL[1,2,4]	SS[2]
	13.3				SS[1,2]
	13.4		CK[1,2,3]	PP[1,2,3]	
	13.6				
Weather	14.1	SW[4]			
	14.2	SW[2,3]			
	14.3	SW[4]			
	14.4				
Living/non-living	15.1	TR[2,3]		HL[3]	PL[1,2,3] SD[1,2,3,4] PG[2,3,4]
	15.2				
Food chains	16.1	ST[1,2,3]		HL[3]	PL[1,2,3]
	16.2	ST[1]			
	16.3				PG[2,3,4]
	16.4				PG[2,3,4]
	16.5				PG[4]
Living together	17.1	TR[1,4] ST[1,2,4]			PL[1,2,3]
	17.2	TR[2] ST[1,2,3,4]			PL[1,2,3]
	17.3	TR[2] ST[1,2,3,4]			PL[2,3]
	17.4				PL[1]
Life cycles	18.1			HL[2]	PL[2]
	18.2				PL[2]
	18.3			HL[2]	PL[2] PG[2,3,4]
	18.4				PL[2] PG[2,3,4]
People	19.1		RR[1,2,3,4]	HL[1,3]	SD[1,2,3,4]
	19.2				
	19.3		RR[1,3,4]		
	19.4				
	19.5			HL[2,4]	PL[2]
	19.6				SD[1,2,3,4]
	19.7				SD[1,2,3,4]

Key to Table 3(ii) above

JPB1: Happy families HF; Carnival time CT; Look Here LH; Mixed up MU; Hair raising! HR; Keeping warm KW; A mouldy story MS; Which tiles? WT; Home-made toys HT; Uninvited UI.

JPB2: Windfalls WF; Stick together ST; Bird watch BW; Spin a yarn SY; Circus time CC; Cheap seeds? CH; At the garage AG; Lots of liquid LL; A day out DO; Wired up WU.

JPB3: Timber TR; Snail tale SN; Earthy matters EM; Thinking time TT; Stormy weather SW; Flying high FH; Off to work OW; Café talk CK; Dolls' house DH; Rally round RR.

JPB4: Fair tests FT; Airborne AB; Paul's party PP; Built to last BL; Hospital HL; Seaside SS; Pond life PL; Propagating PG; Sports day SD; Moving on MO.

Extension C   Summary of experiences provided by the activities in Longman Scienceworld Junior Pupils' Books 1–4

Introduction

This summary identifies the main ideas which are explored in each activity in *Longman Scienceworld* Junior Pupils' Books 1–4. As the scheme progresses, teachers will need to check the children's record sheets to see which activities individual children have carried out; of course, the extent to which children retain the ideas they have encountered will vary. Teachers should always be prepared to adjust the level of discussion as the children reveal their thinking through the comments they make and the ideas they express. In Tables 3(i) and 3(ii) (Extension B, pages 122–5), the activities which contribute towards the development of children's understanding of particular concepts are identified.

Junior Pupils' Book 1 : Level 1

Happy Families

HF1   People have different and generally unique appearances. There are common factors in external appearance which provide criteria for grouping (classifying) e.g. hair colour. Of greater significance than external differences are internal similarities.

HF2   There are no relationships between external characteristics of the human body (e.g. height and arm span) than can be predicted with certainty. Some relationships are, however, more likely than others (e.g. tall people are more likely to have a wide arm span but arm-span measurements will not provide a basis for predicting hair colour).

Carnival time

CT1   When objects with a hard surface are tapped, a sound is produced. Better sounds are produced by hollow objects. The sound is improved if the object is hanging rather than standing on a surface.

CT2   When a tightly-stretched rubber band is plucked, it vibrates and a sound is produced. The sound is amplified if the rubber band is stretched across the mouth of a hollow container.

CT3   The length of a string (stretched rubber band) affects the pitch of the note produced. Shortening the string raises the pitch of the note. Lengthening the string lowers the pitch of the note.

CT4   A column of air in a bottle or jar will produce a note when the bottle or jar is tapped. The pitch of the note is altered if water is gradually poured into the container. The note becomes higher. Identical bottles or jars containing different amounts of water will produce notes of different pitch. A tuned set of containers can be produced.

Look here

LH1   Everyone has eyes with the same basic parts. The iris differs in colour from one person to another but the colour differences are limited and eyes can be classified according to colour. The pupil reacts to light intensity; becoming smaller in bright light and larger in dim light.

LH2   Brown- or black-skinned people always have brown eyes. The eyes of pink-skinned people vary in colour.

LH3   Some people have more acute eyesight than others. There may be differences between the right eye and the left eye of an individual.

LH4   Juxtaposition of certain colours produces a contrast which aids visibility. Other colour combinations lack contrast and make visibility difficult. A sharp contrast is useful for signs. Some insects use lack of colour contrast as a way of being inconspicuous.

Mixed up

MU 1 Primary colours produce secondary colours when mixed in pairs. Secondary colours cannot be mixed to produce primary colours. Black is produced by mixing three primary colours or possibly two secondary colours. Brown is produced by mixing three primary or two secondary colours.

MU 2 If a disc is coloured so that different colours are fed to the eye in succession as the disc is spun, the eye sees a colour resulting from the mixing of the colours on the disc.

MU 3 Water-based inks may be single colours or they may be made by mixing two or more colours. The colours can be separated by the process of chromatography. Spirit-based inks will not separate out when water is used.

Hair raising!

HR 1 When a balloon (or comb) is rubbed through the hair, it becomes charged so that it will attract hair and be attracted to a wall. The hair becomes charged so that individual hairs repel each other.

HR 2 When rubbed through the hair, a plastic pen becomes charged. The strength of the charge depends on a number of variable factors. The charge will gradually leak away.

HR 3 Different materials vary widely in their ability to receive or produce charge. Metal will not hold or produce a charge. Plastic and nylon hold and produce charge effectively.

Junior Pupils' Book 1: Level 2

Keeping warm

KW 1 Within a building temperatures can vary considerably. The temperature inside can differ greatly from the temperature outside. Temperature is measured by using a thermometer. A thermometer records its own temperature so that time must be allowed for the thermometer to reach the temperature of the surroundings.

KW 2 In a heated building there are temperature variations. Warm air moves to cooler areas and cold air to warmer areas. This process has to be controlled to create comfortable conditions for the occupants of the building.

KW 3 The air trapped between sheets of glass acts as an insulator so that double glazing will slow down heat loss from a heated building.

KW 4 A liquid will cool more rapidly if a larger surface area is exposed to cooler air.

A mouldy story

MS 1 A mould is a kind of plant – it grows and requires food and water. The spores (seeds) from moulds are always in the air so that food which is left exposed will provide a place where spores which land on it will grow.

MS 2 Moulds grow on moist bread in warm conditions. They do not grow on dry bread and only grow slowly when it is cold.

MS 3 Food preservation depends on creating conditions which are inhospitable for mould spores (and bacterial growth).

MS 4 Bread that has been handled or exposed to dirty conditions is likely to go mouldy before bread that has not been handled or contaminated with dirt.

Which tiles?

WT 1 Some surfaces are more resistant to wear than others. Energy is required to move a brick across a surface. Some of the energy is used in overcoming friction and the surface may feel warm as a result.

WT 2 Different materials have different properties. Some materials are more resistant to denting than others. Materials are chosen to suit their purpose.

WT 3 Different materials have different properties. Some materials give a surface offering greater friction than others. These provide a less slippery surface.

Home-made toys

HT 1 A mixture of washing-up liquid and water in certain proportions will form a stretchy film which will hold air so that bubbles can be produced. A bubble is always spherical, producing distorted images of the observer. Colours are produced similar to rainbow colours.

HT 2 The energy expended in twisting a rubber band is stored in the band. The energy can be made to do useful work by releasing the energy in a controlled way (e.g. in a cotton reeler).

HT 3 In an electric circuit a current, as demonstrated by the lighting of a bulb, will only pass if the components of the circuit are joined by a complete circuit of conducting material.

HT 4 If air is displaced suddenly so that pressure differences are produced, air movement to restore uniform pressure will cause a bang.

Uninvited

UI 1 Many small creatures are adapted to blend with their surroundings. Their form fits their environment.

UI 2 Creatures are sensitive to their environment and show preference for particular conditions e.g. damp or dry places. Their form fits their environment.

UI 3 Small creatures show variety in form and movement. This variety is found throughout the natural world. Aspects of it (e.g. differences in the number of legs) are used to classify creatures.

UI 4 Creatures have food preferences. These foods are found within their chosen habitats.

Junior Pupils' Book 2: Level 1

Windfalls

WF 1 Some seeds are protected by a hard cover. The hardness will differ for different kinds of seeds. Within the same kind of seed there will be some variation in hardness.

WF 2 Plants wrap up their seeds in fruits. These show great variety but the purpose is common, i.e. to disperse the seed from the parent. The variety of forms of fruits means that this is achieved in different ways e.g. by wind dispersal, by being eaten and excreted.

WF 3 Objects which weigh the same will take the same length of time to fall provided that their shapes are compact. If the shape offers resistance to the air (e.g. a seed with wings), the fall takes longer giving the possibility of transverse travel propelled by the wind.

WF 4 The time taken for an object to fall can be increased by increasing its resistance to the air by altering its shape. The longer the time of fall the greater the possibility that the descent will not be directly vertical.

Stick together

ST 1 Some objects are attracted by a magnet; some are not. Objects which are attracted are made of iron or have an iron component. A bar magnet has poles at each end – both of which will attract iron objects. If one pole of another bar magnet is held close to this bar magnet, one end will be attracted and one end repelled. Magnetic attraction is not affected by thin sheets of paper or plastic.

ST 2 Magnets vary in strength. Bar magnets attract most strongly at their ends (the poles). If two bar magnets are brought together, end to end, one pair of poles will attract and one pair will repel.

ST 3 Iron objects, such as needles, can be magnetised by stroking them with a magnet. The strengths of the magnets produced can be compared. The strength depends on the strength of the stroking magnet and on the number of strokes.

ST 4 The needle of a compass is a magnet which reacts to the magnetic field of the 'earth magnet'; both have North and South poles.

Bird watch

BW 1 Feathers are of different forms according to their function, e.g. flight feathers and body feathers. Flight feathers are perfectly adapted to their function. The insulating properties of body feathers can be investigated.

BW 2 Birds have food preferences. Their bodies have adaptations related to these food preferences (e.g. beaks).

BW 3 Hunger provides the motivation to learn new behaviour. Birds will often mimic the successful behaviour of one of their kind. This helps birds to survive in adverse conditions.

Spin a yarn

SY 1 The strength of a length of line is related to the material from which it is made.

SY 2 Lines made from different materials will stretch different amounts. The increase in length may be permanent due to a structural change in the line or temporary whilst the line is under tension.

SY 3 Hair will stretch considerably before breaking. Wet hair is weaker than dry hair.

Circus time

CC 1 If a number of blocks (10) are made into a pyramid, this will be more stable than tower arrangements of the blocks. The pyramid distributes the weight over a wider area – the pressure on the ground is less.

CC 2 A triangle is a very rigid structure which resists deforming forces. Other shapes (e.g. squares) are less rigid and can be deformed easily.

CC 3 The strength of a structure is related to the kind of material from which it is made and to the way the material is shaped, e.g. paper structures can be made stronger by folding or rolling the paper.

CC 4 Lowering the centre of gravity of an object will increase its stability. Three forces acting at a point can be made to balance.

Junior Pupils' Book 2: Level 2

Cheap seeds?

CH 2 In order to germinate, seeds need warmth and moisture. The germination properties and growth qualities of the same kind of seeds at different prices are compared.

CH 2 The size of a seed is not necessarily related to the size of the plant it produces.

CH 3 Seeds germinate more readily if they are given optimum conditions of warmth and moisture.

CH 4 Seeds are allowed to germinate and the resulting plants grow in light of different colours. The effects of the different colours of light are investigated.

At the garage

AG 1 A mirror reflects light so that the image is a laterally inverted version of the object.

AG 2 The casting of sharp shadows suggests that light travels in straight lines. The nearer an object is to a light source the larger will be its shadow on a fixed screen.

AG 3 An object with a low centre of gravity is more stable than one in which the centre of gravity is high. Stability can be increased by lowering the centre of gravity of an object.

AG 4 Air is difficult to squash but it can be moved about easily in a closed system and can be made to do useful work (e.g. lifting). Such a system is a pneumatic system.

Lots of liquid

LL 1 The thickness of a liquid (its viscosity) affects the way it behaves. It affects the rate at which an object will fall through it.

LL 2 The rate at which a liquid will flow from a container depends on its viscosity.

LL 3 The surface of water is always horizontal. It finds its own level so that in a U tube the levels in the two tubes will lie along the same horizontal. Water can be moved from one container to another by setting up a siphon.

LL 4 Water exerts a pressure. The pressure increases with depth.

A day out

DO 1 Shadows change in size and direction during the day. The shadow is shortest at midday when it is cast towards the North. Its size and direction are determined by the position of the sun in the sky.

DO 2 An object seen through water appears to be nearer than it is. An object which is half in and half out of water appears to bend where it enters the water (refraction).

DO 3 A wet garment will dry if the water can escape easily into the surrounding air (evaporation). Warmth and free circulation of air assist the process.

Wired up

WU 1 Vibrations cause sound which in turn can cause objects to vibrate. Some materials can deaden sound by absorbing the vibrations.

WU 2 Hard and/or taut surfaces are best at transmitting vibrations; soft or slack surfaces do not do this.

WU 3 For electricity to pass in a circuit there must be a complete circuit of conducting material. The coil of a light bulk in the circuit is a component of the completed conducting circuit.

WU 4 A number of batteries can be used in an electric circuit. The brightness of a bulb in the circuit is increased if the batteries are joined in series; but not if they are joined in parallel.

Junior Pupils' Book 3: Level 1

Timber

TR 1 Trees show great diversity in form as demonstrated by their leafy twigs. Trees can be classified by using their various distinctive characteristics.

TR 2 The rate of growth of trees and the symmetry of their growth is affected by factors such as the weather from year to year, the availability of light, competition from surrounding trees.

TR 3 By observing the grain in a piece of timber evidence can be gained about the structure, type and growth patterns of the tree from which it came. The direction of the grain greatly affects the strength of a piece of wood. Metal and plastic do not have grain and their strength is uniform in all directions.

TR 4 The hardness of a piece of wood depends on the type of tree from which it came and on the direction of the grain.

Snail tale

SN 1 Snails prefer cool, moist conditions. Generally, they will be found where their preferred food is readily available. Suitable conditions and food must be provided if they are to be kept.

SN 2 Snails eat plant material. They prefer soft plants but their diet can be varied.

SN 3 The amount a snail eats can be measured.

SN 4 Snails can move over a variety of surfaces – sometimes for quite long distances. They are unwilling to cross certain surfaces. Since they are plant-eaters they do not need to be able to move quickly.

Earthy matters

EM 1 Clay contains water. If the water is removed, the clay loses its plastic The change is reversible. It can be made permanent by firing the clay

EM 2 Soil is a mixture of things: some of these are organic in origin, some are mineral. The moisture-retaining properties of soil depend on its composition.

EM 3 The draining properties of soils depend on their compositions.

Thinking time

TT 1 When a pendulum is allowed to swing freely, the size of the swings diminishes gradually but the number of swings it makes in a given time remains the same.

TT 2 In a given length of time a long pendulum will make fewer swings than a short pendulum, i.e. the time of swing increases as the length increases.

TT 3 The weight of the bob on a pendulum of fixed length can be changed but the number of swings it makes in a given time remains the same.

Stormy weather

SW 1 Wind produces a variety of effects depending on how fast the air is moving. The speed of the wind can be measured with a home-made anemometer.

SW 2 There are many traditional indicators which people use in attempting to predict the weather. Fir cones are used in this way. An investigation is set up to test their reliability as weather predictors.

SW 3 A device is made which will show that the pressure of the air changes. An investigation is set up to find out how these changes relate to weather patterns. Lower pressure is associated with rainy weather; higher pressure with fine weather.

SW 4 Darker colours absorb and give out heat more quickly than lighter ones. We can make use of this knowledge in a number of ways.

Junior Pupils' Book 3: Level 2

Flying high

FH 1 A piece of paper can be made to fly by altering its shape in certain ways. Very small changes can produce great differences in the flight pattern. The effect of a variety of changes is investigated and the idea of 'lift' is explored.

FH 2 A model glider is made. Its flight characteristics are investigated and the effects of changes are explored and predicted. The flying efficiency of the glider can be improved by using the findings of the investigations.

FH 3 A model glider is made from a ceiling tile. The effect on flight of alterations in the size of the wing area is investigated. The area of the wings can be determined.

FH 4 The performance of a paper dart is affected by a number of factors. Some of these factors (variables) are isolated and investigated.

Off to work

OW 1 A pulley is a useful machine. It enables a load to be lifted by exerting a pull downwards. A moveable pulley system reduces the effort required to raise a load. The greater the number of moving pulleys the less effort is required to lift a given load.

OW 2 Running water can exert a considerable force which can be controlled so that useful work can be done. A simple water wheel is made to illustrate this.

OW 3 When two meshed gear wheels turn, the speed at which each turns is related to the numbers of teeth on the wheels. In a meshed pair the wheel with the fewer teeth will turn more quickly than the wheel with the greater number of teeth. When two unequal pulley wheels are joined by a belt, the smaller one will turn more quickly.

Café talk

CK 1 Salt is produced in a variety of different forms. The solubility of all these forms is the same but the rate of dissolving depends on the particle size. If a salt solution is allowed to evaporate, the resulting crystals will be the same regardless of the form of the salt which was originally dissolved.

CK 2 Sugar is produced in many different forms. The rate at which these dissolve depends on particle size and on temperature. The claim for 'quick dissolving' sugar is investigated.

CK 3 Coffee, tea and beetroot juice will stain (dye) cloth quite effectively. Their efficiency as dyes is investigated. Some materials (fibres) take dye more easily than others.

CK 4 Coffee, tea and beetroot stains may be removed by washing. The effectiveness of different cleansing agents is investigated. Some materials (fibres) are more difficult to wash than others.

Dolls' house

DH 1 In a simple electric lighting circuit containing more than one bulb there are alternative ways of arranging the bulbs. If the bulbs are arranged in series the light from an individual bulb becomes less as more bulbs are introduced. A parallel arrangement produces undiminished brightness. A missing 'series' bulb breaks the circuit; a missing 'parallel' bulb does not.

DH 2 A dolls' house wiring circuit is devised so that each light can be turned on and off independently. The switches are introduced into a parallel circuit.

DH 3 An electromagnet can be made by wrapping insulated wire around a large nail. The strength of the electromagnet is investigated and the effect of changing the variables in making the electromagnet is investigated.

DH 4 A buzzer is made by using an electromagnet in a circuit which is made and broken very rapidly.

Rally round

RR 1 The ability of people to react quickly to observed stimuli varies. Practice may effect improvement in reaction times, but fatigue is also a factor. Most people have one hand which will respond faster than the other in reacting to an observed stimulus.

RR 2 Some people have better coordination between eye and hand than others. Practice can improve performance in following a maze seen through a mirror.

RR 3 People have a wide range of vision. They see out to the sides as well as straight ahead. The range of people's vision is investigated.

RR 4 We use our senses to take in information which we remember. An investigation is set up to find out what difference the mode of presentation makes to ease of remembering. Whether it is possible to learn to remember is explored.

Junior Pupils' Book 4: Level 1

Fair tests

FT 1 The energy which is used in twisting a rubber band is stored in the twisted band and can be released in a controlled way to do useful work – to drive a cotton reeler. A smooth surface offers less friction than a rough surface. Friction is important in making it possible for things to go forward by pushing on the surface.

FT 2 A ball at the top of one side of a dip has potential energy. As it rolls downhill its potential energy decreases but it gains kinetic energy. At the bottom of the dip it has lost its potential energy but has maximum kinetic energy. It will reach a height on the other side of the dip lower than its starting height. Energy has been dissipated in overcoming friction.

FT 3 The energy possessed by a ball which is rolled down one side of a dip to collide with a ball released on the other side is related to how much the ball weighs. A heavy ball has more energy than a light ball. This can be demonstrated by observing collisions.

FT 4 When a moving vehicle is stopped by a barrier, its load if not secured will continue to travel forward until it falls to the ground.

If a toy car is allowed to travel down a slope it can be seen that the distance travelled from a stopping barrier by an unsecured load (a table tennis ball) is greater when the angle of the slope is greater.

Airborne

AB 1 Air resists the movement of objects through it. Air has substance. These properties make it possible to use a parachute to slow the fall of an object to the ground. The variables involved in making a parachute are investigated.

AB 2 The resistance of the air to the passage of an object is investigated by exploring how pieces of card of different sizes will slow down the descent of an object tied to a wound reel of thread.

AB 3 The jet of air emerging from a blown-up balloon is used to drive the balloon along a taut line to which it is attached. Ways of improving the balloon's progress are investigated.

AB 4 Air confined in a plastic bag is heated. The bag of hot air will rise if the surrounding air is cooler.

Paul's party

PP 1 Gelatine is a substance which, with water, will produce jellies of varying degrees of stiffness depending on the proportions of water and gelatine. The optimum stiffness is agreed and the proportions determined by investigation.

PP 2 A branching key is used to identify a number of white powders found in the kitchen which have lost their labels.

PP 3 Cooking oil floats on water. When it is shaken with water, it forms an emulsion which may not be stable. Egg yolk and mustard will help to stabilise the emulsion.

Built to last

BL 1 Cement powder is mixed with sand to produce a mixture used for sticking bricks together in building. The proportions of sand and cement which will produce a strong but economic mixture are investigated by preparing different mixtures and testing these.

BL 2 Common building bricks are porous and allow water to pass through them and to rise through them by capillary action. Other building materials are non-porous. The porosity of different materials is investigated and materials which will be suitable for a damp course are identified.

BL 3 Arches are often used in buildings to make strong openings. The shape of a piece of card can be altered to demonstrate that the arch shape enhances the weight-supporting properties of the card. The effectiveness of different shapes of arch is explored.

BL 4 Using paper of the same dimensions, it is shown that a cluster of slender columns will support a greater weight than a single fat column.

Hospital

HL 1 People have approximately the same body temperature but the 'normal' temperature for an individual may be slightly more or less than the conventional 'normal' temperature. The temperature of an individual may vary slightly. These ideas emerge from an investigation of people's temperatures.

HL 2 A very small baby has a greater problem keeping warm than an adult. This is because the small baby has a proportionately larger surface area through which cooling occurs. This is investigated by using hot water bottles of appropriate sizes.

HL 3 Diet is very important in maintaining health. The children plan and investigate their own diets.

HL 4 When plaster of Paris is mixed with water it sets. The process is irreversible. Optimum proportions of water and powder and optimum conditions for setting are determined by investigation.

Junior Pupils' Book 4: Level 2

Seaside

SS 1 An object suspended in water will weigh less than when it is weighed suspended in air. It will weigh even less if salt is added to the water. The weight loss will be related to the amount of salt which is dissolved.

SS 2 Salt water is corrosive. It is more corrosive than fresh water. The effect of fresh water and salt water on various materials is investigated. The effect of temperature is investigated. Increase in temperature speeds up the chemical reaction.

SS 3 The impurities in sandy salt water can be removed to produce water which is drinkable. Makeshift ways by which the sand and salt can be removed are explored. Sand can be removed by passing the solution through a filter – the holes of which are smaller than the sand particles. The salt must be removed by evaporating the water to form water vapour and then condensing the vapour to produce pure water.

Pond life

PL 1 A pond can support a wide variety of life. The creatures in the pond can be classified according to chosen attributes.

PL 2 Frogs develop from eggs hatched in water. The rate of development and the time taken for hatching to occur may be affected by various conditions – some of which can be investigated.

PL 3 The behaviour of a number of fish in a tank is explored. It can be demonstrated that certain factors will affect their behaviour.

Propagating

PG 1 A lateral key is used to identify tree leaves. A key is constructed to identify weeds.

PG 2 Plants can be propagated in various ways. Some plants can be propagated by stem and leaf cuttings. Success depends on certain conditions being met. These conditions are investigated.

PG 3 Plants can be propagated in various ways. Some plants are propagated by corms and tubers. Ways in which these can be divided successfully are investigated.

PG 4 Different varieties of tomato plants will have different growth and cropping characteristics even though they are grown under exactly the same conditions. These characteristics are investigated. Seeds from ripe tomatoes are germinated. The possibility of growing tomatoes using a nutrient solution without soil is investigated.

Sports day

SD 1 The rate of heart beat and pulse rate are the same. The rate under resting conditions is about the same for all children, but there is variation. Exercise increases the rate by about the same amount for each individual but there is variation as in all human characteristics.

SD 2 Normally people breathe quite slowly and gently. Exercise speeds up breathing and the lungs work harder. This process is investigated. Some people respond more easily to the demands of exercise than others. The lung capacity of people can be measured. It differs from one individual to another.

SD 3 Differences exist amongst individuals in the strength and spring which their legs can exert. Investigation also shows that a person's right leg and left leg may behave differently – one being more effective than the other.

SD 4 The ability to run fast is related to a number of characteristics. Since all these characteristics vary from one individual to another it is those individuals in whom a number of these characteristics are optimised who are good runners.

Moving on

MO 1 If two mirrors are set at an angle and an object is placed in the angle formed, multiple images are produced. The number of images produced depends on the angle between the mirrors.

MO 2 If a beam of light is shone on to a mirror and is reflected from it, the angles made by the beam and its reflection with a line at right angles to the mirror are equal.

MO 3 In a pin-hole camera the quality of the image can be improved by varying the camera. If multiple holes are used multiple images are produced. The pin-hole camera demonstrates that light travels in straight lines.

MO 4 'Lenses' can be formed by using drops of water (or other liquids). The lenses produced are convex; they magnify. The greater the curvature of the water drops the greater the magnification.

Environmental education in the school curriculum

In *Longman Scienceworld* the science is presented in the context of Topics which can be appreciated readily by young children. The Topics centre around themes which are associated with the children's familiar environment. The introduction of ideas about 'People and their jobs and occupations' and of technological activities further strengthens the environmental links. Teachers may find it useful in planning the curriculum for their classes to extend the Topic to include a wider range of studies and disciplines.

The table on pages 136–7 is based on work reported in *Handbook of environmental education*, edited by R. N. Savelands (published by Wiley 1976). Some modifications have been made in the light of a draft discussion document prepared by the Walsall Primary Support team (February 1983). The table provides guidelines for the extension of the Topics. Areas where the activities initiated by *Longman Scienceworld* contribute are indicated.

Overall objectives
Building basic vocabularies and skills leading to an appreciation and awareness of the varieties and similarities in the environment.

Key to abbreviations in table on pages 136–7

Junior Pupils' Book 1: Level 1 – HF Happy families; CT Carnival time; LH Look here; MU Mixed up; HR Hair raising!; *Level 2* – KW Keeping warm; MS A mouldy story; WT Which tiles?; HT Home-made toys; UI Uninvited.
Junior Pupils' Book 2: Level 1 – WF Windfalls; ST Stick together; BW Bird watch; SY Spin a yarn; CC Circus time; *Level 2* – CH Cheap seeds?; AG At the garage; LL Lots of liquid; DO A day out; WU Wired up.
Junior Pupils' Book 3: Level 1 – TR Timber; SN Snail tale; EM Earthy matters; TT Thinking time; SW Stormy weather; *Level 2* – FH Flying high; OW Off to work; CK Café talk; DH Dolls' house; RR Rally round.
Junior Pupils' Book 4: Level 1 – FT Fair tests; AB Airborne; PP Paul's party; BL Built to last; HL Hospital; *Level 2* – SS Seaside; PL Pond life; PG Propagating; SD Sports day; MO Moving on.

Contribution of Longman Scienceworld

Study area	Broad, differentiated objectives	J1 Level 1					J1 Level 2				
		HF	CT	LH	MU	HR	KW	MS	WT	HT	UI
Area and location	Experiences basic orientation within the local and national environments. Perceives the Earth as the home of mankind. Observes how people use and influence the environment.				√						
Atmosphere and cosmos	Can describe and measure climatic factors in the local environment. Recognises the role of the atmosphere in the life of plants and animals (special storms, evaporation and precipitation and fire).						√				
Landforms, soils and minerals	Knows that soil is dynamic: a) it forms b) it contains living things and supports plant growth c) it erodes. Can identify different kinds of landforms. Sees the interaction between landforms and living things.										
Plants and animals	Knows from first-hand experience various kinds of plants and animals in their own environment. Recognises interdependence among soil, atmosphere, plants (producers), animals and people (consumers).							√			√
Water	Knows the necessity of water for life and its importance as a natural resource.							√			√
People	Recognises the varieties and similarities among people. Knows how people live in and use different environments. Learns the inter-relationships between beliefs and rituals and the environment.	√	√	√							
Social organisation	Recognises ways in which people organise themselves. Learns individual and group responsibility concerning environment.	√	√		√						
Economics	Relates food, clothing and shelter needs to available resources. Finds that specialisation of labour increases efficiency.				√	√	√	√			
Aesthetics, ethics, language	Builds a basic vocabulary of environmental terms. Names and classifies plants, animals, water features, soils, minerals. Acquires basic skills in using visual arts and music to express feeling for the environment in an elementary way.	√	√		√						√
Built environment	Appreciates that people construct appropriate buildings to provide homes and services for an interdependent community. Recognises advantages/disadvantages of a built environment for the inhabitants. Recognises the need for an effective transport and communications network.					√	√		√		
Energy	Recognises that energy is needed to make things happen and that there are different sources and forms of energy. Knows from first-hand experience that energy can be converted from one form to another. Appreciates that in converting energy from one form to another some energy is always dissipated in a non-useful way.					√	√		√	√	

J2 Level 1					J2 Level 2					J3 Level 1					J3 Level 2					J4 Level 1					J4 Level 2				
WF	ST	BW	SY	CC	CH	AG	LL	DO	WU	TR	SN	EM	TT	SW	FH	OW	CK	DH	RR	FT	AB	PP	BL	HL	SS	PL	PG	SD	MO
√								√		√			√		√	√		√		√			√	√	√	√			√
√		√			√			√		√				√						√		√				√	√		
				√	√					√	√	√										√					√		
√		√			√					√	√	√		√										√	√	√			
		√			√		√			√	√											√			√	√	√		
		√	√		√										√	√		√				√	√	√			√		
																√		√					√	√				√	√
						√			√						√	√						√							
		√								√	√	√										√				√			
				√		√			√	√		√			√	√	√			√			√	√					√
	√					√	√	√	√	√		√			√	√	√	√		√	√		√						√

137

Extension D   Language in science

The relationship between science and language for young children is two-fold. Firstly, the rich variety of experiences which science offers requires a wide range of language to describe it, to comment on it and to report it. Secondly, if the observations and the information acquired are to be understood, language is the means by which teachers and pupils can explore their common experience and extract from it their individual understanding.

Spoken language is of crucial importance. Some of the children who are enthusiastically participating in the science activities, particularly in the early stages, will not yet have come to grips with the intricacies of the written word. They are encouraged to talk about what they are doing and what they are observing. Children are encouraged to work together and share their thinking. During these interactions they will be discussing, ordering and exchanging information and ideas and above all speculating and suggesting what might happen if . . .   Much of the talk will involve the teacher who will wish to use the opportunity to help children to develop their language usage in a variety of ways. For children who are proficient in written language, talking helps to clarify thinking and expression and it plays an important role in shaping the final written record.

Spoken language is the language mode which is closest to thinking and ideas. It provides the bridge between activity and understanding even after children have a firm and fluent grasp of reading and writing. Spoken language allows us to 'um' and 'ah' and change our minds; it allows us to say 'Do you mean this or is this what you really mean?' We can listen to alternative ways of making statements and again question these. Each of us must make sense of our experiences in our own terms. We are all different and each of us observes against a unique background. The interpretation of a new experience depends on the previous experiences which we bring with us. One of the tasks of the teacher in introducing science is to help children to explore these new experiences and to relate these to themselves. It is a rewarding task and an open-minded approach will help teachers quickly to become aware that there are no subject barriers in children's minds. They will bring together experiences from a wide variety of sources in interpreting their scientific activities.

The encouragement of talking towards understanding is a crucial part of learning science and learning to act scientifically. Writing can help children to probe their own thoughts and ideas, but it is a lonely substitute for talking. It must be pointed out that very little use is made of writing as a means of letting children explore their own thinking. We have suggested in a number of places that you might like to let your children write in this way.

Within the activities of *Longman Scienceworld* much of the writing is concerned with reporting observations and commenting on these observations. We have suggested a variety of levels of response, ranging from the short phrase to the full description. We have taken appropriate opportunities to encourage children to use and extend their vocabulary. Science can provide an incentive for children to develop reading skills. We have tried to write the Pupils' Books so that they can be read independently by the large majority of the children for whom they are intended. We hope that the children will want to read them and find out what to do next.

The science and technological activities also provide potential as starting points for encouraging the development of information skills – finding out about . . . Looking at people's jobs and occupations also provides a variety of opportunities for further research and the development of more wide-ranging projects.

In spite of this richness of opportunity for language development, the last words must be these: language is the means by which understanding is derived from experience. Each of us must come to individual understanding and language is the means by which we can achieve it. It is language in this guise that it is most important to develop in the classroom.

Extension E   Using mathematics in science

In scientific activities mathematical skills are constantly being used in estimating, measuring, recording and interpreting. An understanding of shape, length, area, volume and capacity is essential for many scientific investigations. Evidence from the DES Assessment of Performance Unit monitoring of mathematics indicates that measuring skills are often deficient even amongst older pupils. A serious lack of appropriate experience and opportunities for making use of developing skills is revealed. Science can be an important vehicle for the development of mathematical skills since it provides a wide variety of opportunities to apply these skills and to break down the isolation of mathematics from the rest of the curriculum which sometimes occurs. The HMI paper 'Curriculum Matters 3 – Mathematics from 5 to 16' draws attention to the artificiality of even practical activities if they set children 'measuring tasks for which they see no purpose'.

In *Longman Scienceworld* particular attention has been given to these concerns and teachers will find many examples of measuring for purpose. At the same time, detailed consideration has been given to the children's mathematical development and progression. For example, in Topic 1.9 each child constructs a small, moving toy which may travel in a straight line or may take a curved path. The children are required to measure and record the distance travelled in centimetres using either a metre stick or a shorter rule, as the task requires. In testing the toys they have made, the children are also practising measuring skills with which many of them should be familiar. Most of the activities throughout the junior years require the use of skills and concepts which the children will previously have encountered in their mathematics programmes. The main focus is on the scientific aspects of the activities. Mathematics is used as an essential tool in the scientific investigations.

In some cases, however, the scientific activity has been used as a vehicle for the development of mathematical ideas and skills. For example, Topic 1.6 involves using a thermometer to measure and record temperatures – an activity which many published mathematical schemes introduce at upper junior level (e.g. *Nuffield Maths 5–11* Book 6). In Topic 1.5 a stop clock is used to time thirty-second intervals. Seconds as a unit of measurement of time and the use of the stop clock are more usually introduced at a later stage, but in this case the scientific activity provides a motivating and appropriate context for the development of this particular mathematical skill and its associated concepts. In 'Mathematics from 5–16' science is included by the writers in the list of activities which provide 'excellent opportunities for the development of skills in appropriate contexts'.

Science also presents numerous situations in which children's ability to communicate mathematically can be developed. In many of the activities it is suggested that children should use a variety of forms of mathematical recording, such as tables, charts and graphs. The children are encouraged to use mathematical forms of communication and to develop the skills required to extract information from mathematical forms of presentation. The development of mathematical literacy is seen as a key factor in the development of scientific competence.

Extension F The development of technological ability and understanding (Making and doing)

A lot has been written about technology and what it is. For many non-specialist teachers, the picture which emerges is a daunting one; how can they translate the grand ideas into action? *Longman Scienceworld* tries to demystify technology and suggest activities which will enable children to acquire some technological skills. The children should have opportunities to investigate in situations where they really do need the information which the scientific investigation can produce.

Firstly, what do we mean by technology, and more importantly what do we mean by technology in the Making and doing activities suggested? Technology is a way of thinking which is useful in solving problems of a particular kind. Generally, these problems are expressions of some particular need. In real life, these problems may be very complex and complicated. In the classroom, where our concern is with how to set about solving the problems, our examples are simpler. For example, one of the first problems is 'Can you make a bag to carry fruit home from the fruit shop?' (*Infant Teachers' Book A* pages 9–10) Another feature of technological problems which this illustrates is that they do not have right and wrong answers: some solutions are just better and some are worse. Often, one solution will be better in some ways than another and worse in other ways, and there has to be a balancing of desirables and undesirables. There is a strong element of optimisation.

Another salient feature of technological problem solving is that we have to think about the problem from all sorts of points of view. For example, in making a bag, we have to think first of all about what the bag must do – what properties it should have. It will have to carry a fairly heavy weight, it may get wet and it must not collapse if it does, it must look attractive and the cheaper it is the better. So, even with this simple problem, we are able to pursue a variety of channels – the scientific, the aesthetic and the economic. It really is important that the material used is strong enough for the job, even when it is wet. A fully technological approach would require the setting up of scientific investigations to produce the information we need. However, the scientific investigation is only being used to support the technological problem solving activity. That is how scientific activity is related to technological activity: it provides vital information which is fed into the problem solving process, along with the information which comes from looking at the problem with the eye of the artist or that of the economist.

Sophisticated technological problem solving is very demanding: children can only be introduced to the ideas and be helped to acquire in some measure the skills needed to set about a task. As soon as the task is within the children's grasp, they should use their increasing scientific skills to produce information needed to make decisions within the problem solving sequence. It should be clear that the kind of scientific information required will depend on the problem and the materials which might be used. A question about what kind of paper to use or whether plastic sheet would be better than paper can be answered from the scientific viewpoint by setting up an appropriate investigation. For some problems, the children might need information about whether to use wood or metal, or what kind of wood or metal. Again, the information can come from a scientific investigation. How to make something move is another question which can be tackled, or how to cut a sleeve so that the arm can move freely requires an investigation of how our limbs work. All these are examples of scientific investigation being used within the context of technological problem solving.

Technological problem solving or Making and doing can best be tackled systematically and in each of the activities suggested, the same structured but simple approach has been used. It is not intended, however, that this should be regarded as prescriptive; rather, it is indicative.

1 The problem
  The statement of the problem to be solved.
2 Exploring the problem
  Examining the nature of the problem and identifying the various facets of it; being quite sure that the nature of the problem is understood; ensuring that the problem statement expresses the need.
3 Ideas for solving the problem
  a) Producing ideas without, at this stage, being concerned with whether they are practical; thinking creatively and openly; letting original thinking loose; brainstorming.
  b) Sifting the ideas; looking for obvious snags; comparing the ideas.
  c) Deciding which idea to pursue.
4 Making
  Planning how to implement the chosen solution; collecting and, if necessary, investigating methods of construction and materials. (Of course, it is possible that unforeseen snags will be found which will require that the solution chosen should be reconsidered. This illustrates another aspect of technological problem solving – it is not a straightforward sequence. As the problem and its solution are pursued, there will be snags, new bits of information and new ideas which will require that steps be retraced and new and different decisions made.)

  Finally, craft skills are exercised in the making of the solution. The skills of young children will be limited and imperfect but the aim is that they should produce their solution to the best of their ability. Often, the idea will be far better than its execution. Our main interest is in the development of technological thinking. At this stage, lack of craftsmanship is, therefore, a secondary consideration although teachers will undoubtedly wish to give children every help and encouragement to improve their craft skills. Equally, teachers will be concerned to ensure that every child experiences success, however modest.
5 Evaluating
  Does the chosen solution solve the problem? In the light of experience, would a different solution have been implemented? Might any of the ideas which were rejected have been better? Do the children want to try again? How have other people tackled similar problems?

  At first, children will not find it easy to evaluate their own work. Looking critically comes with maturity and for young children the sense of the product being right because it is a personal achievement is understandably overwhelming. Later, the children are able to look at their own work and the work of others more circumspectly, and then the teacher can (by question and discussion) help children to look at their own work and the work of others in a more analytical fashion. They are able to learn from each other and support each other's thinking. It is a field rich in opportunities.

Monitoring making and doing activity

It has not been suggested that teachers should attempt to record formally the development of children's making and doing skills; however, it may be useful to have in mind some questions which will help in monitoring the children's progress. More importantly, the questions may be of assistance in guiding the children's work. The questions are to some extent ordered so that they indicate a developing competency, but they should be regarded as no more than indicative. Tackling making and doing problems has so many facets that it is not possible to identify a right way or even a best way.

It is difficult also to suggest how children will progress. Some will move slowly, some rapidly. Young children can be surprisingly innovative and imaginative, particularly when they are interacting with construction materials. However, the level of thinking suggested by some of the questions is sophisticated and may be reached by only a few children. Nevertheless, the questions will provide a useful guide to progress in making and doing activity.

1 The problem

2 Exploring the problem
Do the children make little or no attempt to explore the problem?
Do they ask one or two isolated questions?
Do their questions go beyond what is immediately apparent?
Do the children begin to ask questions more systematically and to identify criteria which must be met?
Do the children, as a matter of course, ask a wide range of pertinent questions and assemble the criteria thus identified in an ordered manner?
Can the children reframe the statement of the problem if the criteria identified indicate that this is necessary?

3 Ideas for solving the problem – choosing a solution to implement
Do the children provide no ideas of their own and wait for ideas to be provided?
Do they produce no ideas of their own but respond to and develop ideas that are provided?
Do they produce one or two ideas of their own?
Do they think freely and creatively if they are encouraged to do so?
Do they attempt to evaluate ideas according to their understanding of the problem?
Are they able to evaluate the ideas in relation to the material and skill resources which are available?

4 Making
(The development of the ability to produce the chosen solution will depend on the nature of the artefacts being produced. Craft skills appropriate to the materials being used will be developed. Their development will relate closely to the development of attitudes to the work, as well as to the understanding and knowledge associated with the materials and solution chosen.)
Do the children choose appropriate materials?
Do they work neatly and safely with these materials?
Do the children use appropriate tools in the correct manner, thinking of their own safety and that of others?
Do they work accurately?
Do they use materials imaginatively?
Are they able to improvise?

5 Evaluating
Do the children make no attempt to evaluate their own work?
Do they attempt to evaluate their own work in some measure?
Do they view their own work with some detachment and examine it with some degree of analysis?
Do they consider criticisms of their own work by others?
Do the children look at their products critically and consider whether they meet the criteria identified in exploring the problem?
Are they able to suggest how the product might be improved?

Extension G   People and their jobs and occupations

On page 108 you will find this statement:
'Science is used in society in all sorts of ways. People use it in their work and hobbies. Everyone is confronted with it in everyday life.'
A variety of people who do different work and have different hobbies are introduced in the scheme, in order to show how science is important for them all. The kinds of work and hobbies they have were chosen with the following criteria in mind:
1 relevance to children of this age range and breadth of experience;
2 the relative importance of science in the particular work or hobby;
3 potential as a context for the development of science activities and understanding of ideas.
'Work' refers not only to paid work but also to all that work which is given little recognition because it is not financially rewarded. Therefore, the word 'job' has been used to signify paid work and 'occupation' to signify unpaid work. What are jobs for some are occupations or hobbies for others, and this might have to be pointed out. Here are parts of the original lists:

Jobs
School caretaker, school cook, lollipop man or lady, policeman or woman, detective, forensic scientist, firefighter, optician, hairdresser, health visitor, school doctor, general practitioner, nurse, dentist, medical auxiliary, engineer (aeronautical, electrical, electronic, etc.), chemist (plastics, fibres, food, etc.), pharmacist, public analyst, gardener, electrician, joiner, painter, decorator, motor mechanic, shop assistant, jeweller.

Occupations
Housewife, mother, father, DIY activities . . .

Hobbies
Fishing, flower arranging, pottery, athletics, pop music, playing the guitar (piano, violin, etc.), swimming, games . . .

It was after drawing up the lists that it became apparent that a good opportunity would be missed if there was no discussion about what jobs, occupations and hobbies are and what people do when they are pursuing their various interests. What is it that makes people want to do these things? What is it that makes them worthwhile?

Below are points which the children should be made aware of; these points have been used in drawing up the suggestions for discussions. The points listed are very basic ones because very many children have little idea about jobs and occupations. Often, even parents do not talk to their children about the work they do in their jobs and occupations.
1 People work.
2 Sometimes work is done in return for money (jobs). Sometimes work is unpaid (occupations).
3 Different people do different jobs and follow different occupations.
4 The work of some people helps us directly.
5 The work of some people helps us indirectly – they work behind the scenes.
6 Some work is done just during the day. Some work has to be done at special times.
7 Some work has to be done all the time.
8 Some jobs are not very pleasant but they serve the community.
9 People take pride in their work.
10 People may need special knowledge, expertise and skills in their work and hobbies.
11 People have to acquire the special knowledge, expertise and skills which they need.
12 People only work in jobs for part of the time.

13 When people are not working at jobs, they do other things and follow other occupations and hobbies which they enjoy.
14 Sometimes, people's enjoyment depends on the jobs being done by other people.
15 What is a job for one person may be an occupation or hobby for another.
16 People use scientific information in their jobs, occupations and hobbies.
17 People need to use a scientific viewpoint in their jobs, occupations and hobbies.

Extension H Recording progress in science

There are two aspects of children's progress which should be recorded:
1 their experience of scientific ideas – ideas which they have encountered in their activities;
2 their progress in acquiring the skills being developed in the activities.
Ongoing accurate records are an essential part of ensuring that children's experience of science is progressive and developmental; to assist teachers in keeping records, a master record sheet is printed on the inside back cover of this Teachers' Book. This may be freely copied so that a complete record of progress can be maintained for each pupil and accompany him/her from one class to the next.

Experience of scientific ideas
The science concepts and ideas covered in the activities in *Junior Pupils' Books 1–4* are shown in Table 3 (ii) on pages 124–5. The experiences provided by each of the activities are described briefly in Extension C in each of the Junior Teachers' Books.
Science skills
The science skills developed in the *Longman Scienceworld* series are shown in Tables 2 (i) and 2 (ii) in Extension A in each of the Junior Teachers' Books. The science skills for each level of the scheme are listed in the Teachers' Books at the beginning of the description of the Topics – in this book Level 1 skills are listed on pages 2–3 and Level 2 skills are on pages 55–6.

Using the record sheets
The scientific skills which the children should ideally achieve are listed on the record sheet, accompanied by a series of boxes. The boxes cover a range of comments, from 'not yet able' (for children who are a long way off reaching the described skill) to 'competently' (for those children who can perform in the manner described). In between, the boxes allow for qualified responses (ticking as appropriate), matching the child's ability to the skill description.

It is not possible to suggest with any confidence how an individual child will progress in each of the described skills not only because children vary greatly in ability but also because, by this stage, their experiences of science may be very different. Some children may have done little or no science. Some children may have done 'science' but concentrated largely, for example, on observing and recording. Others will have become quite proficient in a range of skills and their handling of scientific investigations. Nevertheless, most of the children should be able to achieve most of the described skills 'fairly well' by the end of a level, although skills such as classifying, controlling variables and investigating may prove to be more difficult for some children.

Extension I Classroom organisation

Teachers embarking on the teaching of science may regard some aspects of classroom organisation as a major problem. Their concern is justified since it is probably true to say that a well-organised classroom can bring you at least halfway to success. The classroom has to be organised effectively and it has to be right for the individual teacher and for the children. In the following discussion, general points about preparation for teaching the science activities are explored and particular attention is paid to the organisation of time, space and children. Detailed consideration of the organisation of resources will be found in Extension J (page 148).

General considerations

It would have been unrealistic to have produced a science scheme which required teachers to alter radically systems of organisation which have worked well over the years; but some teachers may find it useful to consider modifications which might be made in the long term in response to the particular demands which science makes. Science is a practical subject. Children will be investigating in a practical fashion. That can be messy and it takes up space. Practical investigation needs to be fed with bits and pieces (rather than equipment) and these need organising if work is not to be held up by questions of the sort, 'Please where is . . .?' or 'Have we got . . .?' It is well worth looking at the classroom and the timetable at an early stage so that time can be saved and later disappointment avoided. The old adage, 'Never leave to good luck what can be achieved by good management', was never more appropriate.

Preparation

Before embarking on a topic, it is a good idea to read carefully through the relevant pages in the *Pupils' Book* and to follow the notes in the *Teachers' Book*. Particular note should be made of the equipment and materials which are required. Materials and equipment which are used with some frequency are listed in Extension J and these items should be always to hand. Items which are peculiar to a particular activity or used infrequently will be identified in the 'You need' instruction for the activity. It is well worth collecting together everything you require for the topic before work on that theme starts. You may find it useful to make up boxes for the activities so that everything is in one place. Boxes can contain unique items, common items and a note of any other items which need to be collected from elsewhere to complete the set of equipment.

Another method of organisation is to keep a card index, with a card for each activity. This could list the items required for the activity and say where they are to be found. Coloured cards for special items which need to be located well in advance could be put in 'early warning' positions, so that you have time to prepare.

Finally, you will want to check through the notes in the *Teachers' Book* so that you know at which points in the activities the children may require additional information, materials or equipment.

Organising the work

Group work or class work?

The short answer is, 'Both'. Some activities involve elements which can be tackled profitably by class discussion or by an introductory lesson/investigation which serves to introduce the activity. The rest of the activities are designed for individuals or small groups to tackle. The optimum size for a group depends on several factors: children's previous experience of working in groups, the space available, resources and materials which are available, etc. Ideally a group should not be too large. If two children are working together they are both completely involved. If there are three or more, there are likely to be spectators. In these situations it is likely to be the girls who are the spectators and the boys who are the performers. On the other hand, an exploratory discussion which involves four or five children can be much more productive and enlightening than one which takes the form of a conversation between two children so that there are a variety of factors to consider. Small working groups and larger groups to discuss and explore common experiences is an arrangement which has merit.

You may find it easier to have only a small number of children carrying out investigations at any one time. It is a way of keeping demands on space, resources and teacher time at a reasonable level so that the work does not become a burden and the pleasure of working with the children is not diminished. The problem lies in deciding what work to organise for the rest of the class. A possible solution is to set work which has low teacher participation and a second 'in hand' activity will ensure that if any of the children do get stuck they can get on with something useful. Those who finish the first piece of work are also catered for. Amongst the 'Further activities' which are suggested for each activity there are often ideas which the children who are not engaged in practical activities at that time could follow. Many of the practical activities provide the stimulus for various kinds of writing – reports for specific purposes, letters and so on. There are many more possibilities which could be developed.

Time allocation

If children are to develop their abilities to work scientifically they must have time to do this. It would be frustrating to be told at a crucial point in an investigation that work must stop because time has run out. Obviously timetables exist and there are limits to flexibility, but reasonable latitude is necessary within the limits imposed by the rest of the timetable. In 'Extension D   Language in science' and 'Extension E   Using mathematics in science', the importance of using language and mathematics within the framework of motivating practical experience has been emphasised. If these ideas are put into effect, the blurring of timetable definitions is an inevitable and natural outcome.

Having said that we have attempted to design the activities so that they can either fit into a timetable slot or fit in with a more open time structure, each of the activities should provide a child/group of children with work for about one hour. This means that for a topic with four science activities children will need at least four hours to complete the science work. Whether you choose to let the children spend four hours in one week on the Topic or whether you spread the work over a number of weeks is a matter for personal choice.

It is possible to organise a rotation system for group teaching. The children are divided into groups of ten producing, as appropriate for working purposes, pairs or groups of other sizes. The groups then rotate in this manner.

		Group A	Group B	Group C
Week 1	Lesson 1	Class introduction to the Topic		
	Lesson 2	Activity 1		
	Lesson 3		Activity 1	
	Lesson 4			Activity 1
Week 2	Lesson 5	Activity 2		
	Lesson 6		Activity 2	
	Lesson 7			Activity 2
Week 3	Lesson 8	Activity 3		
	Lesson 9		Activity 3	
	Lesson 10			Activity 3
Week 4	Lesson 11	Activity 4		
	Lesson 12		Activity 4	
	Lesson 13			Activity 4

Each child will spend one hour per week on the science work and take four weeks to complete the science of the Topic. The teacher's time commitment for each Topic is thirteen hours and it should be possible to cover three or four Topics each term. (**Note**   Some Topics have three science activities and some have four.)

Obviously this idea can be modified to fit particular circumstances. For example, you might want to introduce more class discussions or you might want the children to complete the work on a topic in two weeks rather than four. Nevertheless the table is intended to show that it is possible to organise group teaching within the constraints of a structured timetable.

However you arrange the work for the children, you will want to spend some time at the end of the topic drawing out relevant points, comparing results, sharing experiences, discussing conclusions etc. In the grouping system suggested, every child will have experienced all the activities and will be able to experience not only personal achievement but will also be able to share in the class achievement. The grouping system also allows for ability banding, if this is usual or desired. Pairing children within the large groups allows you to put a good reader with a weak one which can be a useful way of overcoming reading difficulties for some children.

It cannot be emphasised too strongly that there is no single correct way of organising a class. The best method for a particular class will be that with which the teacher is most comfortable and which fits best the circumstances in which he or she works.

Whatever organisation is used for the science work, the other two elements of the work associated with the Topic ('Making and doing' and 'People and their jobs and occupations') should not be neglected and an adequate time allowance must be made for this.

Allocating space

The science activities do not require very specialised apparatus and conditions. For many activities the children will be able to work at their own desks or tables if this does not interfere with whatever else is going on in the classroom. However, for other activities more space will be needed – several tables or desks pushed together, a larger table or your own desk! If a part of the room can be assigned to practical activities many problems are overcome immediately. Unfinished work can be left intact, tools can be kept in a handy but safe place, materials and equipment can be stored adjacent to the working area and messy activity is segregated from the rest of the classroom. It is also valuable sometimes to have an area of the room which is a 'no go' area for other members of the class for safety reasons (e.g. when a kettle of water is being boiled or liquids are being heated on an electric hot plate).

Good science teaching depends on good organisation. We hope that the comments in this Extension and the information provided about equipment and resources in Extension J will serve to reassure you and give you confidence.

Extension J   Equipment and techniques

Part 1 Equipment, materials and storage
    a) Equipment and materials
    b) Storage
Part 2 Techniques
    a) Growing plants and seeds
    b) Keeping animals
    c) Simple electrical circuits

Part 1   Equipment, materials and storage

a) Equipment and materials

The science activities described do not require very much specialised equipment or apparatus. All the activities can be carried out in the classroom, in its vicinity or in the playground. For a number of activities, access to water and a power point are required, while for a few others you need a refrigerator or an oven for a short time. Much of what you need will be already in school and most of the rest can be borrowed from home, although you will probably find it more convenient to establish a store of the most commonly used items in school. The problem of storage is discussed in the next section.

    The materials and equipment which will be commonly required for the junior years are listed on the following pages. Any additional items are listed in the description of the activity.

Classroom equipment and materials
The following equipment and supplies which are usually available in school should be included:
Apparatus and equipment
construction sets (particularly Lego, Legotechnic and meccano)
water play apparatus (particularly funnels, bowls and transparent plastic tubing)
toy cars
Consumable materials
a variety of paper (including kitchen, blotting, tissue, crêpe and sugar papers)
drawing and colouring materials (including chalk, wax crayons, drawing charcoal, paints and paint-brushes)
modelling materials (including plasticine and clay)
adhesives (including polyvinyl adhesive)
paper clips (wire and brass)
bulldog clips
drawing pins
pipe cleaners
scissors
string, twine of various kinds
rubber bands
adhesive labels
Blu-Tack
sellotape
wallpaper paste
drinking straws and art straws
coloured transparent plastic sheet or cellophane
balloons

General household equipment and materials
cling film
aluminium foil
polythene bags (small and large rolls)

greaseproof paper
brown wrapping paper
paper towels (kitchen roll)
cotton wool
tissues
thin plastic sheet (dry cleaning covers, shop bags, etc.)
black dustbin liners
parcel tape
cocktail sticks
needles and pins
cotton and threads
safety pins
stapler
matches
candles
washing line
clothes pegs
wire coathangers
florists' wire
wire wool
eye dropper
lollipop sticks
torch
tent pegs
washing-up liquid
washing powder
plaster of Paris (or Polyfilla)

Kitchen equipment and supplies

an electric hot plate
one or two glass pans (coffee making flasks could also be used. Glass laboratory beakers can be substituted but they are more fragile.)
a variety of bowls, jugs, plates, dishes, etc. (of various shapes, sizes, materials, e.g. plastic, pottery, stainless steel, aluminium, heatproof glass; some identical pairs and some sets would be useful. Most of these can be brought from home as required.)
a variety of cups and beakers (various shapes, sizes, materials, e.g. transparent and opaque plastic, pottery, paper, heatproof glass, etc.)
a variety of cutlery (metal and plastic, of different sizes)
a collection of cooking implements (wooden spoons, tin opener, bottle opener, rolling pin, funnel etc.)
a collection of cooking equipment (e.g. mixing bowl, pastry board, kitchen scales)
trays (metal and non-metal)
ice cube tray
washing-up bowl
bucket

Foodstuffs

flour
rice
sugar (granulated, caster, icing, crystal)
salt
cooking oil
food colouring
vinegar

Garden equipment and supplies

potting compost (peat-based for convenience)
garden canes
atomiser
plant pots
seed trays
sand
garden wire

Workshop equipment and supplies
hammers of various sizes
screwdrivers of different sizes
nails and screws of different sizes and made of different metals (e.g. steel, brass)
aluminium
pot hooks
small saws
G clamps
dowel rod
pieces of soft, hard and balsa wood
house bricks

Junk
A major requirement for a class of children who are enthusiastically pursuing scientific and technological activities is a large, varied, motivating and never-ending supply of junk. A stock of junk should include:
newspapers and magazines
plastic sheet and bags (all sizes, all thicknesses)
rigid plastic sheet (transparent)
paper of all kinds (wallpaper particularly)
corrugated cardboard
jars and bottles with and without screw caps (all shapes and sizes, glass and plastic, rigid and squeezy)
soap or hand cream dispensers
egg boxes
cheese boxes
cuboid boxes (large and small; with and without lids; plastic, wood, cardboard, metal)
sweet jars (plastic, preferably)
plastic food trays
plastic cartons (yoghurt, margarine, etc.)
aluminium foil dishes, trays and cartons
pieces of fabric (any shape or size; any fibre type, colour or texture)
pieces of floor coverings (cork, vinyl, tiles of all kinds, carpet)
cardboard tube (toilet rolls, kitchen rolls)
expanded polystyrene (pieces of block, tile, packaging, etc.)
bottle tops
cotton reels
plastic beer glasses (transparent – one pint)
plastic cups and beakers (transparent, opaque, expanded polystyrene, double sided)
pieces of wood (particularly soft wood of small cross-section)
metal
plastic
ball bearings

Collecting junk
Every teacher can use parents, friends, the school kitchen and local shops as a rich supply of containers, boxes and the like. Particularly useful to remember are:
wine shops – the strongest cardboard containers with useful compartments, some packing materials;
furniture shops – large cardboard containers, large sheets of strong plastic, bubble plastic packing sheets;
white goods suppliers – large cardboard cartons, polystyrene packaging;
DIY shops – bits and off-cuts of all sorts of materials;
paint and wallpaper shops – out-of-date pattern books, colour cards, damaged polystyrene tiles, odd rolls of wallpaper, etc;
timber merchants – off-cuts of all kinds of wood cross-sections, lengths of soft wood which children can saw (dowel rod, lathe), different kinds of wood;
monumental mason – bits both rough and polished of a variety of stone, marble and granite.

Less often considered or exploited as a source of junk are local companies, particularly manufacturing companies. They produce all sorts of material which is waste for them but of value to schools. Companies do not want waste material left lying around so it is quickly destroyed if it does not find a better home.

Why not see if you can come to an arrangement with local companies, and put some of their junk to good use? You probably pass companies on your way to school and there may be some in the area surrounding the school. You could write to them or, better still, call in. Most people will be glad to help in some way and you will have found a reason to make contact and establish a link between your school and the company. That can bear fruit in all sorts of ways: inviting the people from the company to visit your school; you and maybe the children visiting the company; more information about people and their jobs; more examples of people using science; and more ideas for topic work.

Science equipment
magnifying glasses (a large, flexible arm, table mounted, magnifying glass is useful. Hand lenses should be readily available, and there is a range of magnifiers for observing specimens – some form the lids of small specimen boxes.)
binocular microscope (invaluable item)
large mirror (to put flat on the table)
small hand mirrors
large and small standard magnets (bar and other shapes)
one or two pairs of strong magnets (Alnico or similar)
specimen jars
filter paper
pooters
Newton meters
spring balances
magnetic compasses
torch bulbs (1.5v–6v)
torch batteries (1.5v) and battery holders (from Philip Harris – see page 158)
plastic covered bell wire
bulb holders
crocodile clips
tape recorder
camera
two thermometers (marked in degrees Celsius)
iron filings

Mathematics apparatus
sorting circles
measuring tapes
30 cm rules (unmarked and marked)
metre sticks (unmarked and marked)
one litre and half litre measuring jars and calibrated capacity measures
balance scales
bucket balance
graduated masses
bathroom scales
stop clocks
compasses
metal washers

b) Storage

Central storage or classroom storage
Various problems arise in planning how to store science equipment and materials. Firstly, a decision has to be taken as to whether to establish a central store or whether to store equipment and materials in each classroom. This will depend on the particular circumstances of your own school but certain requirements and considerations will be common.

Infrequently used specialised equipment is certainly better kept in a central store to which all teachers have access. For more generally used small scale equipment and materials it makes sense to arrange storage in individual classrooms; however, it is most important that someone should make a record of what is where, and that everyone concerned has access to this record. The person who keeps the record should also be responsible for ensuring that equipment is maintained in a serviceable condition and that materials are replaced.

Activity boxes

It may be advantageous to collect together the equipment needed for a particular activity and to put it in its own labelled box so that it is available for anyone wishing to use that activity. The box can contain specific items and a note of anything else that is needed to complete the set of equipment for that activity.

Various boxes, trays and cartons made from card or plastic can be purchased commercially but there is a wide range of useful containers available free from a variety of sources. Shoe shops can provide a variety of smaller boxes while greengrocers have stacking boxes, e.g. tomato boxes, which can be most useful.

Pupil access to materials

The biggest headache is trying to make satisfactory arrangements for the storage of equipment, material and junk to which pupils should have access. It requires considerable thought to devise a system which gives encouraging and necessary freedom of access but at the same time affords reasonable security for equipment.

Junk in particular takes up a lot of room and needs to be neatly stored if it is not to overflow in all directions. Again, commercially produced storage boxes, bins and containers can be attractive but strong cardboard boxes, e.g. wine shop boxes, can be stacked between solid walls or pieces of furniture to form a storage range. They can be placed in the classroom or in a wide corridor – but do check that you are not contravening fire or safety regulations.

A storage range

Small items can be stored in plastic containers which have had a corner cut away. They are free, look tidy and are easy to store side by side on a shelf.

Plastic container used for storage

The important thing is that the materials are to hand and that children are not held up for want of a jam jar of the right size or a yoghurt carton. Children, like teachers, will appreciate a system which is maintained in an orderly fashion so that everyone knows where things should be and finds that they are there. That in itself is good education.

Part 2   Techniques

a) Growing plants and seeds

A number of activities involve growing plants and seeds. These are particularly rewarding activities not only because of the scientific/observational interest but also because they give children the opportunity to take individual responsibility for the care of a living thing. Below are some very basic guidelines which will help to ensure success. If you want more detailed information you should consult a gardening book or a local garden centre.

Compost

Seeds and plants need something to grow in. In the garden, they grow in soil but in the confinement of a pot or box they are likely to flourish better if planted in a specially prepared compost. There are basically two different types of compost: peat-based or loamless (various brands, e.g. Levington's), and loam-based (John Innes composts, which are sold made up under many trade names).

Each type of compost has different grades, depending on whether it is intended for seed-sowing, small plants in small pots or large plants in large pots. There are also general purpose composts. For classroom use, you will find a peat-based general purpose compost most suitable and convenient. The peat-based composts are clean to use and light in weight for their bulk. It should be noted, however, that if plants are to be grown on for more than two or three months, feeding is necessary. Peat itself does not contain plant nutrients and the compost relies on added substances, which need to be replaced as the plant grows.

Growing plants

Pots or boxes for plant growing must have good drainage: yoghurt cartons etc. should have holes punched in their bases, and the pots should not be left to stand in puddles of water. Plastic food trays are useful for standing pots on. Virtually anything can be used as a container provided it has good drainage. Most plants object strongly to having their roots water-logged and more plants probably die of over-watering than under-watering. Generally, if you have any doubt about when to water it is better for the plant actually to look as if it needs water than to give it too much. Some plants, however, do object to being allowed to go dry and plants which are flowering or growing freely usually require much more water than slow growing or dormant plants. Also, plants can cope with more water when they are in a warm place than when they are in a cold one.

Plants which like dry conditions, e.g. cacti and succulents (fleshy leaved plants), are best kept in clay pots (with a specially prepared compost) but most other plants are quite happy in plastic pots and general purpose compost.

Plants should be planted firmly with thumb pressure on the compost, but the compost should not be packed down. They should be fed with a liquid fertiliser (or other pot plant fertiliser) about once a fortnight.

Small plants need small pots and most flowering plants flower best if kept in pots which appear to be full of roots. Eventually, a plant will need repotting when it gets too big for its pot. Likely signs are that it stops growing, its pot seems very full of roots and it looks unhappy. Plants should only be repotted during the growing season and a plant should be transferred to a pot which is only slightly bigger than the old one. Before repotting, the plant should be on the dry side and the new compost should not be too wet since after repotting the plant should be carefully watered. Repotting is a shock process for plants and they need sympathetic treatment.

root mass

root mass

new compost

Repotting

Some plants like bright light and some prefer shade. Very few like strong direct sunlight and most hate draughts. Finding out where plants are happy is often a trial and error matter. Reference books will tell you whether a species of plant is a sun or shade lover and what temperature it requires, but after that it really is a case of trying the plant in different places until you find a spot where it is happy (i.e. grows, keeps its leaves and maintains a good leaf colour). If any plant is not thriving try moving it to various places in the room since even very small differences in the amount of light can affect the plant's well-being considerably.

Growing seeds

Seeds need warmth and moisture for germination. After germination, they also need light and ventilation. Seeds such as peas and beans which can be handled individually should be planted about 4 cm deep, in well moistened compost. Finer seeds should be nearer the surface, and very small seeds should be sprinkled on the surface of the moist compost and covered with a very thin layer of fine compost.

The seed pots or boxes should be covered with cling film and put in a warm place (but not in direct sun) with newspaper over the top. As soon as the seeds germinate, the newspaper and the cling film should be removed but a loose covering of plastic sheet may be useful in conserving moisture. Tiny seedlings need to be watered (sprayed) very gently. They need plenty of light but avoid direct sunlight in the early stages. For growing on instructions, you should consult the seed packet.

Sprouting bean shoots

Various kinds of seeds which can be used to produce bean sprouts can be obtained from health food stores. The following method produces good results.

The ideal container is a square fruit juice bottle but any similar wide-necked jar can be used. The mouth of the jar should be covered with a piece of muslin, surgical gauze or similar, held in place with a rubber band. To start the beans off, the jar is rinsed with water and most of the water drained out. About 1 level dessertspoonful of seed is put in the jar and tossed about, so that the wet seeds stick to the sides of the jar. With the muslin cover in place, the jar is put in a warm, dark cupboard.

glass fruit juice bottle

seeds sticking to sides of jar

muslin cover

The seeds or shoots should be washed with clean water and drained twice a day until the bean shoots are the desired length – about 4 to 6 cm. This will take only a few days, the exact time depending on the variety. You will find more information on the seed packet.

b) Keeping animals

Keeping animals in the classroom is very worthwhile not only as a focus for science activity but also as a source of pleasure and satisfaction for the children. Children can gain a great deal from having an animal to care for at school. The children should be responsible for the care of the animals, and great emphasis should be placed on the idea that these small creatures rely entirely on the children for their well-being.

Study of classroom animals can continue throughout the year and it is important that the animal cages and fish tanks should not become just part of the classroom furniture. For details of housing, feeding and care of animals and fish you should consult one of the many specialised books or pamphlets which are available (see reference list). The following notes may help you in deciding which animals to keep.

Rabbits

They are particularly good for younger children – easy to handle, not easy to lose in a classroom as they are not too quick, they sit still long enough for the children to have a really good look at any particular feature, and they do not bite. However, they need a big hutch and as they are not completely indoor animals they need access to outdoor pens. They smell very little. Arranging for their care at weekends and holidays can be a problem. Rabbit hutches are not easily transportable.

Guinea pigs

As for rabbits, but they can live indoors all the time. They are ideal for younger children. They do not smell, they do not bite and the cage is small enough to transport easily to its 'holiday home'. If the cage is put on a sand tray the guinea pigs can be left to potter in and out and they develop very clean habits. They are nervous animals though, and can suffer from over handling.

Both rabbits and guinea pigs make small puddles if free in the classroom but no more than a floor-cloth is needed.

Hamsters and gerbils

Hamsters and gerbils are small and attractive. There is no smell, and little in the way of puddles although they can have accidents. They move very quickly and are easy to lose behind cupboards etc. They can bite; hamsters are nocturnal animals and can become aggressive if continually disturbed during the daytime. With gerbils, the pregnant females, nursing mothers and very small young can be handled without any ill effects.

Rats
They are intelligent and make good pets. They appreciate spacious wooden housing where they can move easily (they can grow as large as a small rabbit), and explore their surroundings.

Mice
Mice are very appealing but they move very quickly and are easy for small children to lose. Unfortunately, they do smell.

Note
1 Classroom animals can carry bacteria harmful to human beings and children must be taught to wash their hands after handling the animals and particularly before eating.
2 Monkeys, squirrels and other wild animals should not be kept as classroom pets because they constitute a health hazard.

c) Simple electrical circuits

Below are some basic notes about simple electrical circuits of the kind used in torches.

In a torch, a battery and a bulb are joined by conducting material to form a circuit. A switch is incorporated so that the circuit can be closed and the bulb will light.

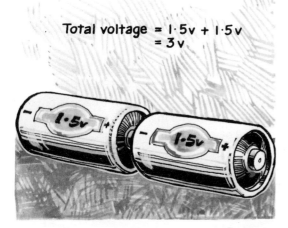

Total voltage = 1·5v + 1·5v
= 3v

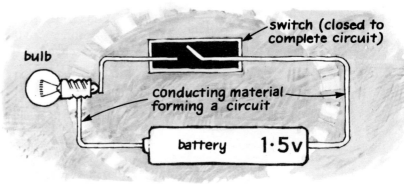

The battery
The battery is the electricity store. When a circuit is formed, the battery pushes the electricity through the circuit. How hard it pushes is measured in volts. The batteries which are used in torches are usually 1.5 volt batteries. If two are arranged inside the torch in line, the push is 3 volts. Holders for 1.5v batteries can be obtained from Philip Harris (see page 158) and these enable batteries to be joined easily to each other and to other circuit components.

The bulb
A bulb looks like the drawing on the left.
The space inside the bulb contains no air and there is a very fine wire which is coiled and the ends fastened to the side and end of the bulb. (It is easier to see the coil in a normal clear light bulb.) When electricity passes through the bulb filament, it becomes extremely hot and glows white hot – and so gives out light. How brightly it glows depends partly on how hard the electricity is being pushed through, i.e. it depends on the voltage of the battery. Torch bulbs are rated according to the battery which will make them light up well, so they are labelled with a voltage; the voltage of the bulb should match the voltage of the battery within narrow limits. If the voltage of the battery is much above the voltage of the bulb, the filament in the bulb will become overheated and break. Always check that bulb and battery match (or nearly).
    e.g. 1.25 volt bulb with 1.5 volt battery (maximum)
          2.5 volt bulb with 3 volt battery (maximum)

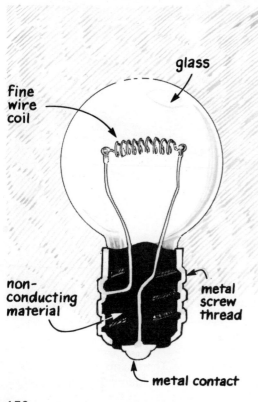

glass

fine
wire
coil

non-
conducting
material

metal
screw
thread

metal contact

The conducting material

The conducting material is always metal – wire, strip or even part of the torch case. The metal contact at the end of the bulb usually touches one terminal of the battery directly.

Note

1 A material which is not a conductor is a non-conductor.
2 Arbitrarily, a very effective non-conductor is called an insulator.

The switch

In a torch, this is merely a mechanical means of making or breaking the circuit. If there is a physical gap in the circuit, the bulb can only be switched on if the gap is bridged by a conducting material.

The circuit

When the switch is closed there is a continuous path of conducting material from one terminal of the battery through the bulb and back to the other terminal of the battery. Only when the circuit is complete can a current flow and the bulb light up.

Setting up a circuit in the classroom

Connections can be made to a 1.5v battery in a holder. The connections to it can be secured either by crocodile clips or paper clips. N.B. The covering at the ends of the wires must be removed so that connections are to bare wire.

It is easier to make good connections to the bulb if the bulb is put into a bulb holder. The bulb holder takes the wire from one screw to one end of the bulb coil and the wire from the other screw goes to the other end of the bulb coil.

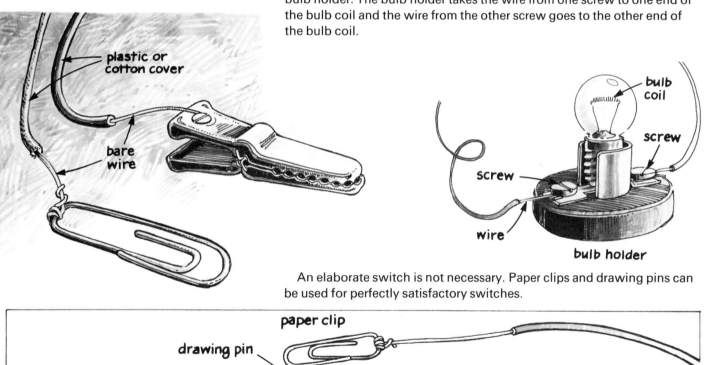

An elaborate switch is not necessary. Paper clips and drawing pins can be used for perfectly satisfactory switches.

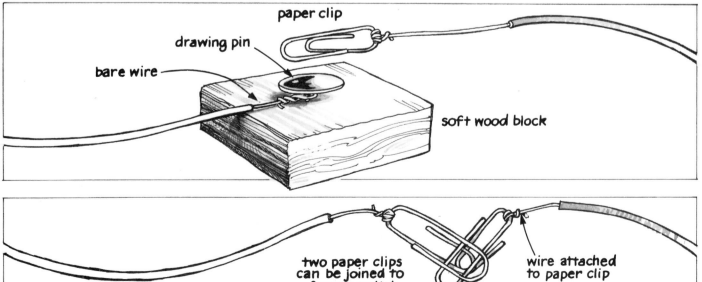

Some useful reference material

Curriculum

The DES Assessment of Performance Unit (APU) has published various reports and documents on science education. These include:
Science in Schools. Age 11: Report No. 3, DES 1984
Science Assessment Framework. Age 11: Report No. 4, HMSO 1984
Copies of these reports and others in the series are available from: The Association for Science Education, College Lane, Hatfield, Hertfordshire, AL10 9AA.

DES, *Science 5–16: A Statement of Policy,* HMSO 1985
Formulating a School Policy: with an Index to Science 5–13, (Learning through Science Project), Macdonald Educational 1980

Scottish Education Dept, *Learning and teaching: the environment and the primary school curriculum,* HMSO Edinburgh 1984
Savelands R N (ed), *Handbook of environmental education,* Wiley 1976
Primary science development project (8 booklets), Moray House College of Education, Edinburgh 1985

General information

Open University course EHP531 *Primary Science: why and how.* The main components of the course are:
Block 1 The study book
Block 2 The science book
Block 3 The planning book
The resource book
The reader: Hodgson B and Scanlon E (eds) (1985) *Approaching Primary Science,* London, Harper and Row/The Open University. There are also three 25-minute television programmes, which are available on an E90 video-cassette as well as by live broadcast.
The Open University, PO Box 76, Milton Keynes, MK7 6AN.

Computer programs

'Animal', 'Factfiles' MEP – from Techmedia Ltd, 5 Granby Street, Loughborough, Leicestershire LE11 3DU
'Seek', Longman
AMS (Advanced Memory Systems) Art Mouse – from AMS, Green Lane, Appleton, Warrington, Cheshire WA4 5NG

The care of living things

Animals in Schools, 2nd edn, RSPCA 1985
Gregory V B A, *Keeping of Animals and Plants in School,* RSPCA 1985

A variety of books, leaflets and posters on the care of animals and plants are available from the RSPCA and from the Schools Natural Science Society.
RSPCA publications from local pet shops or from Royal Society for the Prevention of Cruelty to Animals Education Department, Causeway, Horsham, West Sussex RH12 1HG. Schools Natural Science Society publications from the Association for Science Education (see above for address).

Animals and plants, Nuffield Junior Science Project, Collins 1967
Project pets (bibliography of material available) (1980), Pedigree Petfoods, Stanhope House, Stanhope Place, London W2 2HH
Pets in the eighties (project pack) (1983), Pedigree Petfoods Education Centre, Waltham on the Wolds, Melton Mowbray, Leicestershire LE14 4RT

People and their jobs and occupations

A source of excellent, well-presented information is COIC (Careers and Occupational Information Centre), Moorfoot, Sheffield S1 4PQ. The *Working in . . . .* series in particular provides bright, colourful material giving information for the teacher and attractive pictures for display. Local Education Authority careers service offices will be able to provide examples of this material.

Look at Industry (work pack), Ian Ritchie, Public Relations Dept, C & J Clark, Street, Somerset BA16 0YA (1985)
Althea, *A visit to a factory,* Dinosaur Publications 1979
People at work (*Technology and society* series), BP Educational Service, Brittanic House, Moor Lane, London EC2Y 9BU (1982)

Resource books

Bainbridge J W, Stockdale R W and Wastnedge E R, *Junior Science Source Book,* Collins 1970
Science Resources for Primary and Middle Schools, (Learning through Science Project), Macdonald Educational 1982
Apparatus, Nuffield Junior Science Project, Collins 1967
'Goldmine' (items available from various sources – it lives up to its title) – from 64 Newland Road, Worthing, West Sussex BN11 1JX (1984)
Teaching materials; available from industry and commerce, Information Officer, UBI Resource Centre, Sun Alliance House, New Inn Hall Street, Oxford OX1 2QE (1987, 6th edn £1)
The resource book – part of The Open University course *Primary science: why and how,* 1985

Equipment and apparatus

Note If you can find suitable items on the domestic market they are likely to be cheaper than those obtainable from educational suppliers. (The mass market rules, ok?)
Equipment catalogue, E J Arnold, Butterley Street, Leeds LS10 1AX
Primary mathematics and science equipment catalogue, Philip Harris Ltd, Lynn Lane, Shenstone, Staffordshire WS14 0EE
'Metals, rubber, plastics, fibres' (class pack of materials with teachers' notes), Alan Kilby, Society of Chemical Industries, 14–15 Belgrave Square, London SW1X 8PS (1985)

More ideas for science and technology activities

Finch I, *Nature study and science,* Longman 1971
Kincaid D and Coles P S, *Science in a Topic* series, Hulton Educational 1973
Science 5–13 series, Macdonald Educational 1975
Learning through science series, Macdonald Educational 1980–5
Starting science series (two books and teachers' notes), ATV network, Heinemann 1984
Catherall E, *Young Scientist* series, Wayland 1981
Collins M, *Urban ecology: Teachers' Resource Book,* Cambridge Educational 1984
Problem solving: science and technology in primary schools, SCSST, 1 Birdcage Walk, London SW1H 9JJ
Jinks D and William P, *Design technology 5–13,* Falmer Press 1985
Insight into Industry, CRAC, Bateman Street, Cambridge CB2 1LZ (1985)

Books to support the Topic activities

Junior Pupils' Book 4

(P – Pupils' Book; some of the others may also be suitable)

TOPIC 4.1   FAIR TESTS
Science from Toys, Stages 1 and 2 (*Science 5–13* series), Macdonald 1980
Science from toys – background information (*Science 5–13* series), Macdonald 1980
Science, Models and Toys, Stage 3 (*Science 5–13* series), Macdonald 1980
P   Lines C, *Looking at Cars,* Wayland 1984
P   Kerrod R, *Cars* (Granada Guide series), Granada 1986
P   Dixon M, *Young Engineer On the Road,* Wayland 1982
P   Raitt G, *Building a Road* (*Young Engineer* series), Macdonald 1983

...ORNE

...*Teaching Primary Science* series), Macdonald

...*dels and Toys,* Stage 3 (*Science 5–13* series),
...d 1980

...*s and Forces,* Stages 1 and 2 (*Science 5–13* series),
...nald 1980

...on G, *Young Engineer in the Air,* Wayland 1983

...aid D and Coles P S, *In the air* (*Science in a topic* series),
...lton 1981

...*arting Science,* Book 1, Heinemann 1984

...IC 4.3   PAUL'S PARTY

Change, Stages 1 and 2 (*Science 5–13* series), Macdonald
1980

Change – background information (*Science 5–13* series),
Macdonald 1980

Vegetable Oils and Fats (Ordinary series), Unilever plc,
Educational Service, Unilever House, Blackfriars, London EC4

Fox B A and Cameron A G, *Food Science – A Chemical
Approach,* London University Press (2nd ed) 1970

P   Badelt M and Nizkerk I, *Cookbook for Children,* Invader 1985

P   Sedgwick U, *My Fun to Cook Book,* Hamlyn 1969

P   Beveridge M and Pugh T, *What's for Breakfast?; What's for
Lunch?; What's for Dinner?* (*Food Around the World* series),
Wayland 1984

P   Ridgway J, *101 Fun Foods to Make,* Hamlyn

McGee H, *On Food and Cooking: the science and love of the
kitchen,* Allen & Unwin 1986

Hanssen, *E for Additives: The Complete E Number Guide,*
Thorsons 1984

Experimenting with Industry No. 4 Sugar Challenge, ASE
Experiments with Milk, National Dairy Council, 1–7 John
Princes Street, London W1M 0AP

TOPIC 4.4   BUILT TO LAST

Structures and Forces, Stages 1 and 2 (*Science 5–13* series),
Macdonald 1980

P   Haigh B, *Bridges* (*Topic Books* series), Macdonald 1985

P   Kingston J, *Bridges* (*How it is made* series), Faber 1985

P   Fyson N and Greenhill S, *Carpenter* (*Bears* series), A & C Black
1980

P   Langley A, *Working on a Building Site* (*People at Work* series),
Wayland 1983

P   Raitt G, *Building a House* (*Young Engineer* series), Macdonald
1983

P   Kurth H, *Concrete,* World's Work 1972

This is Concrete, Cement and Concrete Association, Wrexham
Spring, Fulmer, Slough SL2 4OS

P   Dixon A, *Bridges* (*Science Explorers* series), A & C Black 1981

P   Jennings T, *Structures* (*The Young Scientist Investigates*
series), Oxford 1984

P   Unstead R J, *Houses,* A & C Black 1972

P   Kurth H, *Houses and Homes,* World's Work 1980

P   *Houses and Homes,* Usborne 1978

P   Karavasil, *Houses and Homes around the World,* Macmillan
1983

TOPIC 4.5   HOSPITAL

Ourselves, Stages 1 and 2 (*Science 5–13* series), Macdonald
1980

Paul A A and Southgate D A T, The Composition of Foods,
HMSO London (4th ed) 1978

P   Eldin P, *Body Magic,* Beaver 1984

P   Langley A, *Doctor* (*People* series), Franklin Watts 1985

P   Clarke B, *Nurse* (*People* series), Franklin Watts 1984

P   Gallant R, *Me and My Bones,* World's Work 1973

P   Ward B, *Health* (*Just Look At* series), Macdonald 1984

P   Jessel C, *Paul in Hospital,* Methuen 1972

P   Wade B, *Linda Goes to Hospital,* A & C Black 1981

P   Pepper S, *Hospital* (*Behind the Scenes* series), Franklin Watts
1984

P   Jackson G, *Medicine* (*Science World* series), Franklin Watts
1984

P   Baldwin D and Lister C, *Your Body Fuel* (*You and Your Body*
series), Wayland 1983

P   Baldwin D and Lister C, *The Structure of Your Body* (*You and
Your Body* series), Wayland 1983

P   Ward B, *The Skeleton and Movement* (*The Human Body*
series), Franklin Watts 1981

P   Ward B, *Food and Digestion* (*The Human Body* series),
Franklin Watts 1981

P   Gaskin J, *Eating* (*Your Body* series), Franklin Watts 1984

TOPIC 4.6   SEASIDE

The following are all in the *Science 5–13* series – published by
Macdonald in 1980: *Changes,* Stages 1 and 2; *Change –
background information; Metals,* Stages 1 and 2; *Metals –
background information; Children and Plastics,* Stages 1 and 2;
*Children and Plastics – background information; Working with
Wood,* Stages 1 and 2; *Working with Wood – background
information; Like and Unlike,* Stages 1, 2 and 3.

TOPIC 4.7   POND LIFE

Angel and Wolseley, *The Family Water Naturalist,* Michael
Joseph 1982

Water Animal Identification, SNSS leaflet no. 8, ASE 1968

Clegg J, *The Observer's Book of Pond Life,* Warne 1956

Minibeasts (*Science 5–13* series), Macdonald 1980

Using the environment 'Ways and Means' (*Science 5–13 Using
the environment* series), Macdonald 1980

Engelhart W, *The Young Specialist Looks at Pond Life,* Burke
1964

P   Catherall E, *Life in Freshwater* (*Young Scientist* series),
Wayland 1984

TOPIC 4.8   PROPAGATING

Thrower P, *Percy Thrower's Encyclopaedia of Gardening,*
Hamlyn 1983

Titchmarsh A, *The Allotment Gardener's Handbook,* Severn
House 1982

P   Stonehouse B, *A Closer Look at Plant Life,* Hamish Hamilton
1977

P   Hunt P F, *Discovering Botany,* Longman 1979

*Successful Gardening by Schoolchildren; House Plants;
Hydroponics* – leaflets, Phostrogen Ltd, Corwen, Clwyd
LL21 0EE

Hessayon Dr D G, *The Lawn Expert,* PBI publications 1982

TOPIC 4.9   SPORTS DAY

Ourselves, Stages 1 and 2 (*Science 5–13* series), Macdonald
1980

P   Eldin P, *Body Magic,* Beaver 1984

P   Ardley N, *The Science of Energy,* Macmillan 1985

P   Parker S, *Your Body,* Kingfisher 1985

P   Gaskin J, *The Heart; Breathing; Moving* (*Your Body* series),
Franklin Watts 1984

P   Baldwin D and Lister C, *Your Heart and Lungs* (*You and Your
Body* series), Wayland 1983

P   Ward B, *The Heart and Blood; The Lungs and Breathing* (*The
Human Body* series), Franklin Watts 1982

P   Jackson G, *Medicine* (*Science World* series), Franklin Watts
1984

P   Greenberg S, *The Guinness Book of Olympic Facts and Feats,*
Guinness Superlatives 1983

TOPIC 4.10   MOVING ON

Science, Models and Toys, Stage 3; *Holes, Gaps and Cavities,*
Stages 1 and 2 (*Science 5–13* series), Macdonald 1980

Using the environment 'Ways and Means' (*Science
5–13   Using the environment* series), Macdonald 1980

Mirrors and Magnifiers (*Teaching Primary Science* series),
Macdonald 1976

P   Catherall E, *Sight* (*Young Scientist* series), Wayland 1981

Anno M, *Anno's Magical ABC,* Bodley Head 1981

Index

Note: Table 3(ii) (pages 124–5) in Extension B lists the basic scientific ideas to which the children are exposed in Longman Scienceworld Pupils' Book 4. The specific activities in which the ideas are explored are identified in